For my friends,
CLAIRE and PETER CLAY
once of the hospitable "George II,"
Luton, Bedfordshire, and now
of the "Coach and Horses," Rickmansworth,
Hertfordshire, England.

Man, have pity on man.
Rain from the outraged sky
drowned the innocent earth
yet the seed did not die.
Flowering from that rebirth,
man, have pity on man
as you hold the fire in your hand
that can destroy mankind
and desolate every land.
If the power and the glory is this,
a flame that burns to the bone,
what shall be left to grow
when you and your fires have gone?
What maimed and desolate few
shall recover life's full span
from among the ashes of time?
Man, have pity on man.

                    Ursula Vaughan Williams

AIRWAR: VOLUME II

TRAGIC VICTORIES

EDWARD JABLONSKI

DOUBLEDAY & COMPANY, INC., GARDEN CITY, NEW YORK

ISBN: 0-385-04125-X
Library of Congress Catalog Card Number 72–134086
Copyright © 1971 by Edward Jablonski
All Rights Reserved. Printed in the United States of America
9   8   7   6

Preface

THE previous volume closed with the coming of the inconclusive, but destructive, blitz upon the cities and towns of England after it was realized in Nazi Germany that the Battle of Britain had not been what they had hoped for; nor would an invasion of England be attempted. This was the major outcome of the Battle of Britain.

When Japan attacked Pearl Harbor on December 7, 1941, legend has it that Hitler was unhappy, that he liked to call the grand strategic shots. But this is unlikely. When the Japanese struck, the Germans were not doing too well. The Russians had begun a counteroffensive and the British were about to stop Rommel's Afrika Korps to relieve Tobruk. There were later temporary victories, but Moscow and Tobruk did not look well on the record of the invincible Wehrmacht and Luftwaffe.

The Japanese assault upon Pearl Harbor, one in which aircraft played the major role, is generally regarded as a magnificent victory—and, in a way, it was. But in another it failed, for its major function in time proved to be to draw the United States into the war. It was carried out with remarkable tactical precision, destroyed ships, killed men, but did not eliminate the United States from the war. It was a great victory, but it decided nothing in the victor's favor. In time, it would cost him everything.

In the early, confused months of the war it might have appeared as if Japan had, indeed, achieved a decisive master stroke. Americans became desperate for a triumph of their own. For a time only a small band of flyers of fortune, known popularly as the Flying Tigers and based in China, appeared to provide any ray of hope. But their quasivictories, magnified in the press, were bought at great cost to them in misery, privation, frustration, and for some, at the cost of their lives. They did prove that the mysterious Zero fighter was not invincible and that the Japanese was not some form of superpilot. But they were also the victims of corruption, waste, neglect, and cynical masters: the Chinese leaders for whom they fought. When it was possible to get away, most did and then served in the U. S. Air Force.

The most exciting non-victory of the early months of the war was Doolittle's daring raid on Tokyo. Militarily it accomplished nothing, cost a number of lives, and lost all the aircraft involved in the attack. Still, it was a victory of courage, imagination, and sheer flying skill; but these do not really win wars.

The Battle of Midway, a concatenation of tragedies and loss, was a true turning point. But its details, those details which lie way below grand strategies and tactics, could—and should—make strong men weep. The sacrifice and pain on both warring sides, if viewed in retrospect, make one wonder why it was not decided to stop it all then and there. Instead, each became more grimly determined to press on "at all costs," to the rhythm of recurring tragic victories.

In Europe, until the Allies could cross the English Channel, the only way of reaching the industrial heart of Germany was by air, by bomber. While individual combats afforded glamour and excitement for the magazines and newspapers, the daily and nightly (in the case of RAF's Bomber Command) grind was a monotony of dread. Otherwise it was waiting, briefings, waiting, bombing-up, waiting, taking off, forming (another form of waiting), and flying to the target—the deadliest wait of all. The key to impact lay in concentration. The bigger the bomber formations, the greater the destruction to the target—and environs (inevitably hit by spillage and inevitably inhabited by the "innocent," women, children, and the old).

The early history of the heavy bombing campaigns against Germany is a recitation of great deeds and small accomplishment. Great plans were devised, carried out with incredible valor, and then it was discovered that it hadn't quite worked out as planned. What were the right targets to hit? How hard? And how often—at what cost in men and planes? These were the somber questions that could only be answered after the dismal fact.

The great Thousand Bomber Raid on Cologne, the raid of Gibson's Dam Busters, the American forces that fought in the affrighted skies over Ploesti and Schweinfurt are such tales of human performance that they should never be forgotten; nor should the men who participated. Their perseverance, sacrifice, gallantry, and the terror and pain they had to suffer are beyond imagination.

Nor should it be forgotten that despite their effort, and loss, the outcome too soon after was almost as if the effort and the loss had never occurred. Such deeds must be justified—not rationalized long, and safely, after that event, but understood within the context of the war and the limitations of the men who fought it. When the Ruhr dams burst it was expected that the ravages of their waters would cripple Germany's arms industries—and for a time they did. But for a disappointingly short time. The oil fields of Ploesti were not knocked out long enough to have justified the loss of the crews of sixty aircraft. But no one (except the enemy) expected, or hoped for, the loss of those men and planes. And it was the same with Schweinfurt.

These were all great victories for the human spirit if not for the military "art." But the human spirit might be better devoted to more creative pursuits. Besides, inside each victory is a hard core of tragedy for both the vanquished and conqueror. It is one of the fortunes—and facts—of war.

EDWARD JABLONSKI

Contents

TRAGIC
VICTORIES

BOOK I
Greater East Asia Co-Prosperity Sphere

If it is necessary to fight, in the first six months to a year of war against the United States and England I will run wild. I will show you an uninterrupted succession of victories. But I must also tell you that if the war be prolonged for two or three years I have no confidence in our ultimate victory.

—ADMIRAL ISOROKU YAMAMOTO

I

"HARK! THE VOICE OF THE MOMENT OF DEATH"

THE huge aircraft carrier pitched in the dark, heavy sea and great lashing waves saturated the small groups of men struggling on the vast, perilous deck. Ropes had been strung between open spaces to give them something to which to cling. Alongside, dangerously close, a fuel tanker bobbed and tossed, threatening to snap the hoses coupling it to the carrier. The howling wind drowned out all communication, even shouting, so that refueling the carrier was dependent upon hand signals. Their previous training for such a contingency had not prepared the men for this. Even the massive carrier seemed an insignificant cork in the turbulent seas.

The two ships pitched eccentrically, a hose ripped apart, whiplashing across the carrier deck. Seamen were swept overboard screaming into the icy Pacific. Their shipmates stared in helpless stupefaction, but only for a moment, for their officers, prodding and gesticulating, made it clear that the refueling must continue. No attempt was made to recover the men from the water. There was too little time and time was more precious than life in their grand enterprise. Certainly it was more precious than the lives of a few nameless seamen, perhaps even more precious than the life of the admiral himself. He stood on the upper bridge, a squat, heavy old man,

his face a wet, impassive mask. He had been opposed to this operation from the beginning.

The date was November 28, 1941; and he was Vice-Admiral Chuichi Nagumo. Aristocratic, conservative, a samurai, he was, with misgivings, leading a massive Japanese task force upon the "Hawaii Operation." Nagumo's flagship, the *Akagi,* originally designed as a cruiser, had been converted into a heavy carrier to subvert the restrictions upon battleships as result of the Washington Conference (1921–22). Under Nagumo's command were no less than six carriers: besides the *Akagi* there were the other heavy carriers *Kaga, Soryu,* and *Hiryu* and two light carriers, *Zuikaku* and *Shokaku.* To these had been added two battleships and two heavy cruisers in the support force (under Vice-Admiral Gunichi Mikawa); the scouting force, under Rear Admiral Sentaro Omori, consisted of a light cruiser and nine destroyers. Three submarines patrolled in advance and along the flanks of the armada. A supply force of eight tankers would attend to the necessary, and hazardous, chore of refueling the task force in its three-thousand-mile passage from Tankan Bay in the Kurile Islands to a point in the Pacific Ocean about two hundred miles north of Oahu, Hawaiian Islands.

Vice-Admiral Chuichi Nagumo, Japanese Imperial Navy, who commanded the Japanese Task Force in the Hawaii Operation. A traditionalist, Nagumo had little faith in aircraft in a sea war. (U. S. NAVY)

Hideki Tojo, a general in the Japanese Army, whose rise to political power culminated in his appointment as premier of Japan in October 1941, and led to war with the United States and Great Britain.

(NATIONAL ARCHIVES)

Despite the imposing forces at his command, Nagumo was tormented by doubts. He was, after all, a traditionalist, a torpedo expert, and the heavy reliance upon aircraft for the success of the operation impressed him very little. Sea battles were decided by the great battleships trading volleys, not by a few flimsy aircraft.

The Hawaii Operation had been the brain child of Admiral Isoroku Yamamoto, Commander in Chief of the Combined Japanese Fleet. Called "the father of Japanese naval aviation," the fifty-six-year-old Yamamoto possessed the sharpest mind in the Japanese Navy. Harvard-educated, he had served in Washington in the Japanese embassy during 1925–27. Yamamoto liked Americans and their ways and had become a devoted baseball fan, an excellent bridge player, and quite deadly at poker. It was during his stay at Harvard, where he majored in the study of the oil industry, that Yamamoto became interested in aviation. This was around the close of the First World War. Japan, allied in that war with Great Britain, France, and the United States, though not very active, was rewarded after the war with the German possessions in the Pacific north of the equator: the Marshall and Caroline islands and the Marianas (excepting Guam, which was a possession of the United States). These islands, little known to Americans in the twenties, would become household terms in the forties.

Yamamoto, like most of the leaders of the Imperial Japanese Navy, did not want to go to war with the United States. However, the United States had traditionally been the major, if hypothetical, adversary of the Japanese Navy in the Pacific. The Japanese Army regarded Russia as its foe, although China was its earliest real victim. For his stand against war with the United States Yamamoto had risked assassination by the zealots promulgating the "Greater East Asia Co-Prosperity Sphere." Among these were General Hideki Tojo, who in October 1941 became Premier of Japan—a triumph for the Japanese war party.

Tojo, a veteran of Japanese aggression in China, in progress since 1931, was head of the Kodo (Army) party. He had served as commander of police security forces in Manchuria (established as the puppet state Manchukuo in 1932). Tough, aggressive, authoritarian, Tojo was an admirer of Hitler and his methods. The concept of the Greater East Asia Co-Prosperity Sphere was an Army inspiration that originated with General Hachiro Arita while he served as Minister of Foreign Affairs. He had also engineered a pact with the Axis powers against Russia.

Arita's Greater East Asia Co-Prosperity Sphere called for recognition of the economic and political interdependence of the Japanese Empire and the so-called Southern Regions—the raw-material-laden East Indies, Malaya, the Philippines, Java, Sumatra, Thailand, and Burma. On the surface, the scheme appeared to be a plea of "Asia for Asians" (the Chinese, apparently, excepted), but its ultimate and true aim was the acquisition of oil, primarily, for the Army and Navy of Japan. Tojo and his followers in the cabinet realized that such a course would inevitably lead to dealing with Russia on land and with Britain, the Dutch, and the United States on the sea.

However, with both Russia and Britain embroiled with Germany and with Holland under domination, only the United States remained as the major obstacle to the dream of a Japanese Empire in the East. By September 1940 Japan had signed a Tripartite Pact with Italy and Germany, stipulating that the signatories would assist each other should any one of them be attacked by a nation not then at war when the pact was signed. Obviously this could have been only the United States. A year later, at an Imperial Conference, Japan resolved to go to war with the United States "when necessary."

Yamamoto opposed the pact with the Axis; so did Premier Prince Fumimaro Konoye. But the war party was gaining power rapidly and Japanese expansion in the Pacific had begun to arouse the British, Dutch, and Americans. Steps were taken to curb Japanese designs. President Franklin D. Roosevelt placed an embargo on scrap iron and steel "to all nations outside the Western Hemisphere except Britain." On October 8, 1940, the Japanese Ambassador to the United States, Admiral Kichisaburo Nomura, referred to the embargo as "an unfriendly act."

In Tokyo the Army party was less euphemistic and Premier Konoye, fearing a collision course in international relations leading to war with the United States, summoned Yamamoto. The Prince anxiously inquired about the chances of victory in the event of war. Yamamoto's reply was characteristically outspoken and terse. "I can raise havoc with them," he said, referring to the United States, "for one year or at most eighteen months. After that I can give no one any guarantees."

Yamamoto, as usual, spoke from facts with which he was completely familiar. He knew the status of the Japanese fleet and the naval air forces; he realized at the same time how long the limited supply of oil would hold out in the event of war, "when necessary."

Prince Konoye, weak, vacillating, but hoping for peace, tried to curb Tojo, then serving as Minister of War. The Army and the industrial trusts, the *Zaibatsu* controlling factories, mines, trading firms, banks, and newspapers, had too firm a grip on the government. Even the exalted Emperor could not restrain the jingoistic surge to war.

The Konoye cabinet fell on October 18, 1941; Tojo then became Premier and formed a new cabinet around his war party. War was now inevitable. The implement would be the plan, conceived by Yamamoto in May 1940, called "the Hawaii Operation." If war they must, Yamamoto contended, then the United States fleet must be eliminated from that war at the outset. While the stunned Americans picked up the pieces from this single, sharp blow, the Japanese would be free to swoop down upon

Target of the Hawaii Operation: Pearl Harbor; Ford Island lies inside the harbor, most of its area devoted to airstrips. Pearl City is to the right; above left: *U. S. Navy Yard. This photograph was taken some weeks before the attack; the ships are not situated as they were on December 7, 1941.*

(NAVY DEPT., NATIONAL ARCHIVES)

the rich islands to the south. A defense perimeter running from Japan through the Pacific around the Marshalls and Gilberts, New Guinea, and the East Indies up into Burma would be established. The military forces, it was assumed, of Britain and the United States would then be battered against the strong perimeter until they cried for a negotiated peace.

But all depended upon the Hawaii Operation, Yamamoto said. For all its audacity and now admired brilliance, it was not an original idea. As early as 1909 the American Homer Lea, who had served as a general in the Chinese Army, had

warned of such an attack. This he put forward in his book *Valor of Ignorance*. But this was theory. In 1938, however, it was proved in practice by Admiral H. E. Yarnell, U. S. Navy. This occurred during a naval practice maneuver, Fleet Problem XIX, in which Yarnell led what he called a "task force" (a new term at the time) from the carrier *Saratoga*. Yarnell staged a successful surprise attack upon Pearl Harbor by launching aircraft just before dawn on a Sunday. No aircraft rose to meet the "attackers," which executed mock bombings upon the Ford Island Naval Air Station, the Army's Hickam and Wheeler fields, and the Wailupe radio station. All "enemy" aircraft returned to the *Saratoga* after theoretically sinking the ships in Pearl Harbor. The portent of Fleet Problem XIX was lost neither upon Admiral Yarnell, who failed to get a sympathetic ear, nor upon Admiral Yamamoto, who did not lack for bellicose ears in Tokyo.

All minds, however, were not attuned to Yamamoto's. When it became obvious that there would be war with the United States, Yamamoto set in motion studies predicated upon an attack on the U. S. Pacific Fleet, then based as a deterrent to Japanese expansion, at Pearl Harbor. It had been there since April 1940; Yamamoto began considering his Hawaii Operation the following month. By the beginning of the next year the secret explorations for Hawaii Operation had begun in earnest.

Yamamoto's chief of staff, Admiral Shigeru Fukudome, first learned of the plan when he was ordered to find an air officer "whose past career has not influenced him in favor of conventional operations." Fukudome was expected to accomplish this quietly, without admitting even other members of the Naval High Command into the planning.

His choice was Rear Admiral Takijuro Ohnishi, then serving as chief of staff to the commander of the Imperial Navy's land-based air force. One of Ohnishi's major problems was to devise a means of launching aerial torpedoes into the shallow waters of Pearl Harbor. This was critical, for either the torpedoes, as now used, would bury themselves into the mud in the harbor bottom, or else they would bounce over the decks of ships without result. To assist him, Ohnishi called in another naval aviator, Commander Minoru Genda. Only recently returned from London, Genda was quite excited over a recent feat of Britain's Fleet Air Arm. His own intelligence reports had revealed how in November 1940 torpedo-laden Fairey Swordfish bombers took off from the carrier *Illustrious* on a nighttime mission against the Italian fleet based at Taranto and succeeded in sinking three of Italy's six battleships. A mere eleven torpedoes launched from the obsolescent Swordfish had, in a single attack, completely transformed the naval situation in the central Mediterranean. Italy's battleship strength had been cut in half, leaving the remaining half at the mercy of the Royal Navy. Both Genda and Yamamoto had noted this exploit with considerable interest, especially since the depth of the Taranto harbor was about eighty feet (Pearl Harbor was just a bit more than half that). The torpedoes had been specially prepared by the British with the simple addition of wooden fins. If the British had succeeded, why not the Japanese? It was a matter of devising a torpedo which could work in a depth of about forty feet.

But Genda and Yamamoto were not alone in recognizing the fuller significance of the Taranto attack. American Secretary of the Navy Frank Knox informed Secretary of War Henry L. Stimson in a memorandum that the "success of the British aerial torpedo attack against ships at anchor suggests that precautionary measures be taken immediately to protect Pearl Harbor against a surprise attack in the event of war between the United States and Japan. The greatest danger will come from the aerial torpedo. . . ."

Stimson agreed and so informed the Hawaiian Command. But Admiral Husband E. Kimmel, Commander in Chief, Pacific Fleet, objected to the placement of torpedo nets in the harbor because of the resulting interference with the movement of ships in so confined an area. He was, of course, right in his judgment, but it would prove to be an exorbitant rectitude. It was all but unthinkable that Japan, though launched on a campaign of conquest, would venture so far from home waters. Then too there was the problem of the torpedoes. True, the British had cut the required depth for launching in half; nothing pointed to the possibility of Japanese technicians cutting it in half again. Besides, it was widely known that the Japanese had inferior aircraft and that their equally inferior pilots would never master the technique of dive-bombing. It was an audacious conceit indeed.

After completing preliminary studies Ohnishi estimated a 60 per cent chance of success for the Hawaii Operation, provided absolute secrecy was maintained—and along with it complete surprise. His superior, Fukudome, was less optimistic; he gave the plan about a 40 per cent possibility. Yamamoto, however, upon analyzing Ohnishi's conclusions, was more than ever convinced that the plan could succeed. Though still opposed to war with the United States, Yamamoto firmly believed that if his government wanted war his Hawaii Operation was the only assurance of short-range success.

The General Staff of the Imperial Japanese Navy, which was responsible for operations, did not con-

Frank Knox (center), although opposed to Roosevelt's New Deal, was appointed by him as Secretary of the Navy (1940–44). Roosevelt hoped that this appointment would contribute to national unity in a time of crisis. It did and Knox would, before his death, become secretary of one of the world's largest navies. To his right is William Halsey; on his left is Chester Nimitz. Both of these men were to play important roles in the rebuilding of American naval power in the Pacific following the Pearl Harbor disaster.

(NAVY DEPT., NATIONAL ARCHIVES)

Husband E. Kimmel, commander of the U. S. Pacific Fleet at the time of the attack on Pearl Harbor. Relieved of his command subsequently for "errors of judgment," Kimmel believed to the end of his life that Roosevelt was responsible for Pearl Harbor.

(NAVY DEPT., NATIONAL ARCHIVES)

Roosevelt's Secretary of War Henry L. Stimson (left) in conversation with Major General James Doolittle (this photograph was taken somewhat later in the war, after Doolittle's famous raid on Tokyo).

(NATIONAL ARCHIVES)

cur. The consensus was that it was too risky. When war games were held in Tokyo during August the General Staff was further convinced of the risks when, on paper, two carriers were lost when the plan was tried out. While they argued, the Imperial Conference on September 6, 1941, decided that, "when necessary," Japan would go to war with the United States.

This did not settle the arguments between the General Staff and Yamamoto, but it did precipitate the need for definite planning. Some members of the Naval General Staff believed that Japan should strike to the south and attack America only in self-defense should the American fleet venture out of Pearl Harbor—which, of course, it would do as soon as Japan attempted to move into the Philippines.

In the face of opposition Yamamoto stood adamantly. Upon receiving a detailed paper from the General Staff in which five major objections to the Hawaii Operation were enumerated (the major one being that any loss of surprise would prove costly in casualties), Yamamoto sent a blunt message to the Staff. Unless his plan was accepted Yamamoto "must resign from his position and retire into civilian life." The date was now November 3, 1941—and this was quite a blow. The crisis was resolved quickly. Rather than lose their respected commander in chief, all argument over the feasibility of his plan ended. The Hawaii Operation was on.

Within two days Yamamoto issued Operation Order Number 1, of which the critical sentences were: "In the East the American fleet will be destroyed. The American lines of operation and supply lines to the Orient will be cut. Enemy forces will be intercepted and annihilated. Victories will be exploited to break the enemy's will to fight." This was followed shortly by Yamamoto's setting "X-Day" for Sunday, December 7, 1941. This day was selected because of the well-known American propensity for relaxing on weekends; it was likely, too, that a good proportion of the fleet would be in Pearl Harbor, in keeping with that propensity.

The fervid Army war party was anxious to open the war on December 1, but Yamamoto held out for the additional week in order to have a little more time for preparations. The Army Command, which was to lead a simultaneous attack southward into the Philippines and Malaya, acceded. On this same date, exactly one month before X-Day, Yamamoto appointed Admiral Nagumo, head of the First Air Fleet, commander of the Pearl Harbor striking force.

Surreptitiously, in twos and threes and singly, the carriers and ships of the striking force slipped out of their various ports and made for the assembly area, Tankan Bay in the cold and fog-enshrouded Kurile Islands to the north of Japan. By November 22 the thirty-one-ship armada, including the three screening submarines, had anchored in Tankan Bay for refueling and final orders. Only then did the pilots of the six carriers learn the reason for the many weeks they had spent in practicing shallow-water torpedo bombardment. The news that they were to attack the United States fleet was received with exultant acclamation. Healthy young men excitedly screeched out their banzais ("Ten thousand years!") to the Emperor and to Japan. Their joy was tinctured by their realization of the great risk of their mission and of the possibility that they would all die in such a venture. To die for the Emperor in glorious battle was the dearest wish of every pilot in the striking force.

They were to be led by Commander Mitsuo Fuchida, an experienced naval aviator of some twenty-five years' service, who had trained them for their "divine mission." Fuchida had, aboard the 6 carriers, 423 aircraft, of which 353 were to be used in the attack; the rest of the planes were held in reserve or patrolled over the ships of the striking force. Fuchida's planes were the Nakajima B5N (later named "Kate" by the Americans), the Aichi D3A ("Val"), and the Mitsubishi A6M ("Zero"). The Kates had a dual function: some would operate as high-altitude level bombers and others as low-level torpedo bombers. The Val, with its fixed landing gear, obviously German-inspired, was to function as a dive bomber. The Zero was a fighter aircraft, completely unknown in the West, and would serve as escort for the bombardment aircraft. The Zero was superior to any fighter planes the Americans then had in the Pacific.

While Nagumo contemplated the wretchedness of his lot and Fuchida's young pilots glorified theirs, hundreds of miles to the south of the main task force the advance force of twenty-seven submarines refueled at Kwajalein in the Marshalls and bore down upon Hawaii. Five of the submarines were

Zero fighters on a carrier deck ready to take off for Pearl Harbor. (NAVY DEPT., NATIONAL ARCHIVES)

assigned to the "Special Attack Unit" and carried midget, two-man submarines on their decks in a large tube. The conventional submarines were to encircle Oahu to sink any American warships that might escape Nagumo's planes and cut off any reinforcements and supplies that might be sent to Hawaii from the American mainland. The midget submarines were expected to penetrate into Pearl Harbor itself, after the aerial attack had begun, to contribute to the havoc. The air leaders, and Yamamoto himself, did not approve of the submarines' participation in the attack, but were overruled. The submarine service wished to take part in the divine mission also. The men in the midget submarines, certain they were going to death, gloried in the sentimentality of such lovely doom. Most, as it eventuated, found that very destiny.

That not one of Nagumo's thirty-odd ships was

Map of Pearl Harbor carried by Japanese pilot indicating positions of ships (not always accurate) and depth markings. (NAVY DEPT., NATIONAL ARCHIVES)

spotted during the eleven-day voyage from Tankan Bay to the point about two hundred miles north of Oahu where the planes were to be launched, must be one of history's most curious accidents. Nor were the submarines discovered until early in the morning of December 7, about five hours before the actual air attack had begun. Absolute radio silence was maintained by all ships. To cover up this blackout, ships remaining in the home waters supplied the missing signals of the absent ships.

The course of Nagumo's armada lay pretty much out of the usual shipping lanes, which is one good reason he was not discovered. If he had been discovered before December 5 the whole operation would have been canceled. The weather, too, proved an ally, although costing the lives of a few crewman. As the striking force veered southward on December 4, it approached improved if not ideal weather conditions. No word had come, as Nagumo hoped, to call off the attack. Instead, on December 2 Yamamoto radioed from his flagship *Nagato*, anchored in Hiroshima Bay, *Niitaka Yama nabore* ("Climb Mount Niitaka"), which philosophically meant "Climb the highest mountain." Niitaka is the highest peak in Formosa. This was the order to carry out the Hawaii Operation.

The ships with the beautiful names, "Flying Crane," "Haze," "Summer Cloud," "Wind on the River," "Blue Dragon," proceeded as planned. On December 6 the course shaped due south. In an emotion-packed ceremony the tattered, history-imbued flag flown by the immortal Admiral Heihachiro Togo at the Battle of Tsushima Strait (where he wiped out the Russian fleet in 1905) was run up the mast of the *Akagi.* All hands who could be spared were permitted on deck, where they joined in singing the national anthem. Impassioned cries of banzai pierced the night air and ascended to a cloud-dimmed moon. The ships in Nagumo's task force surged ahead at twenty-four knots, leaving the tankers behind.

There was one frustrating note that night. Reporting from Honolulu, Ensign Takeo Yoshikawa, posing as "Vice-Consul Morimura" in the Japanese embassy while keeping an expert eye on the American fleet in Pearl Harbor since August (1941), reported that as of 1800 (6 P.M.), December 7 (actually December 6 in Hawaii), Pearl Harbor, although a paradise of targets (more than ninety ships), harbored not one American carrier.

This was bitter news for Yamamoto, who hoped to cripple the American's chances of retaliation from the air. To Nagumo the absence of the carriers made little difference. Yoshikawa had reported nine battleships in the harbor (actually there were eight); this was target enough. Still Nagumo was made additionally uneasy when he considered that the American carrier planes could wreak havoc with the carefully laid plans of the Hawaii Operation if they caught the task force at the launching point.

Unknown to the Japanese only two of the expected four carriers were in the Pacific. The *Hornet* and the *Yorktown* had been transferred to the Atlantic; the *Saratoga,* it was known, had left long before for the West Coast for general overhaul. That left the *Enterprise* and the *Lexington.* Where were they? Yamamoto, aboard the *Nagato* three thousand miles away, was concerned. Aboard the *Akagi,* Admiral Nagumo did not sleep.

The elusive American carriers had, in fact, slipped out of Pearl Harbor days before. On November 28, just two days after the Nagumo task force left Tankan Bay—in fact, on the day that Nagumo had lost seamen during the first refueling—the *Enterprise,* under Rear Admiral William F. Halsey, had set out for Wake Island accompanied by three cruisers and nine destroyers. Aboard the *Enterprise* were the men and planes of Marine Fighter Squadron 211 (VMF-211), led by Major Paul A. Putnam. The squadron took off from the flight deck of the *Enterprise* in their dozen Grumman F4F-3s (Wildcats) on December 4 to bolster the garrison at Wake. On December 7 Halsey was well on his way back to Oahu—about two hundred miles to the west—when the attack came.

As for the *Lexington,* it too had left Pearl Harbor, under Rear Admiral J. H. Newton, in the company of three heavy cruisers and five destroyers. The *Lexington* was bound for Midway Island to deliver there Major C. J. Chappell, Jr.'s VMSB-231 (a scout-bomber squadron) and eighteen Vought SB2U-3s (Vindicators). Newton had not arrived at Midway on December 7, and when he learned of the attack, he turned around and returned, with the Vindicators, on December 10.

On Sunday morning, December 7 (December 8 in Tokyo, across the International Date Line), at six o'clock, Nagumo reached latitude 26° north, longitude 158° west—about 275 miles due north of Pearl Harbor. This was the launching point. Already two float planes, one each from the heavy cruisers *Tone* and *Chikuma,* had been catapulted into the dawn's darkness to scout ahead and for one final look at Pearl Harbor for signs of unusual activity.

The flight decks of the Japanese carriers erupted into feverish preparation. Planes were manhandled and pushed around, engines snarled, figures darted here and there. In the pilots' briefing room Fuchida reviewed the plan of attack. He would lead the first wave in one of the high-altitude Kates. If certain that surprise had been achieved, he would fire a single flare, in which case the attack was to open with the torpedo attacks upon the ships in the harbor by the Kates. This would be followed by the other Kates with conventional bombing after which the dive-bombing Vals would swoop down. The Zeros would contend with any American attempt at defense and could strafe the installations also.

Pearl Harbor bound: December 7, 1941. The Americans are about to be introduced to the Mitsubishi "Zero," an aircraft superior to any then in the Pacific.
(NAVY DEPT., NATIONAL ARCHIVES)

The spearhead of the Japanese attack on Pearl Harbor: the Nakajima "Kate" (Type 97) attack bomber/torpedo bomber. These Kates are armed with torpedoes.
(NAVY DEPT., NATIONAL ARCHIVES)

If surprise had been lost, Fuchida would fire two flares. The attack then would begin with the Vals, dive-bombing to create confusion to enable the Kates above to concentrate on their bomb runs, particularly on the harbor defenses. Then the torpedo bombers could deal with the ships.

As he spoke Fuchida referred to a blackboard on which the disposition of the American fleet in Pearl Harbor was chalked. Pilots made last-minute notations. Fuchida then left the briefing room and hurried up to the bridge, saluted, and told Nagumo, "I am ready to carry out my mission."

The old man replied, "I have confidence in you." It was a solemn moment, grim, simple, and gloriously infused with ineffable *amor patriae*. Neither man realized, in the exhilaration of the moment, the fuller implications of what they were about to do. Only Yamamoto, tense though impassive in

Hiroshima Bay, understood—for he had grasped the significance of the absence of the American carriers. Neither Yamamoto nor Nagumo was to live to see the devastation the Hawaii Operation would bring upon their beloved Japan. The seed of tragedy, as Yamamoto knew, was implanted in the blossom of victory.

Aircraft engines throbbed, then roared, on the pitching carriers whipped with salt spray. The early morning darkness was alleviated only by two parallel lines of soft blue lights along the flight deck, designating the runway. The carriers almost in unison turned into the wind—northward, opposite to the direction in which they had been moving—so that the planes could take off into the wind. In the uneasy seas the aircraft would need all the lift possible.

Fuchida sprinted to his waiting Kate. He wore a

white silk *hashimaki* (the traditional warrior's head-band, symbol of his willingness to die), a gift from the maintenance crews. The ends of the band fluttered in the slipstream as Fuchida clambered into the cockpit. At the opposite end of the flight deck a faint green light described a circle in the murky darkness; the pilot throttled the engine into full power. The Kate bounded along the wet deck, which lurched in the swelling sea. Blue lights winked past each wingtip as the Kate thundered down the flight deck. When it had almost reached the end, the carrier itself seemed to heave the Kate into the air. Cries of banzai celebrated the airmanship of the take-off.

While Fuchida circled above, the other planes of the first attack wave rose from the carriers to join him—183 aircraft in all, and all were air-borne without an accident. Fuchida had taken off the *Akagi* at 6 A.M. By six-fifteen all planes were ready to form up for the flight south. Cloud layers had formed from about three thousand feet to ten thousand. Leading his formation, Fuchida climbed into the clear air above the clouds. From that height he could not see the ocean, and no one on the ocean could see him. Fuchida's Kate was followed by forty-eight others—the level bombers. To his right, and slightly below, Lieutenant Commander Shigeharu Murata, of the *Akagi,* led forty torpedo-bearing Kates; to Fuchida's left, and above, Lieutenant Commander Kakuichi Takahashi of the *Shokaku* spearheaded the Vals, fifty-one in all, to serve as dive bombers. Lieutenant Commander Shigeru Itaya's forty-three Zeros appeared to dart nervously over the bomber formations, ready to pounce at the first sign of enemy activity.

But there was no activity. An Army radar station on the northern tip of Oahu, manned by two privates, George Elliot and Joseph Lockard, had earlier picked up the blip of one of the float planes scouting ahead of the attack force. They noted it, but because it was a Sunday they could assume that it was a private pilot out for an early morning flight. It was a fine morning for it. If the weather just north of Hawaii was a bit murky, it was fine over the islands: the clouds had begun to break, a dazzling sun came through. It promised to be a glorious day.

When Elliot and Lockard reported their plot, nothing was made of it. One officer, perhaps not

An Aichi "Val" dive bomber, its dive brakes down, plunges on "Battleship Row," Pearl Harbor.
(NAVY DEPT., NATIONAL ARCHIVES)

quite recovered from Saturday night's festivities, cracked, "Hell, it's probably just a pigeon with a metal band around its leg."

A couple of minutes after seven o'clock the two men were startled to see one of the most massive blips they had ever seen on the radar screen. Had the green Elliot caused the set to go haywire? Lockard checked it over and it seemed all right; sure enough, there was a big plot about 140 miles to the north and just about 3 degrees east. They immediately reported this—for they had never seen such a plot before—to the plotting center at Fort Shafter near Honolulu. They failed to arouse any official reaction. The duty officer, Lieutenant Kermit Tyler, was quite certain that they had spotted the Boeing B-17s due in that morning from California; or else the *Enterprise,* returning from Wake, had launched some planes.

The Japanese planes had been air-borne for an hour and a half; the sun had begun to break through the cloud which had hidden the formations from observation from below. Fuchida "strained [his] eyes for the first sight of land. Suddenly a long white line of breaking surf appeared directly beneath [his] plane. It was the northern shore of Oahu."

The Kate banked to the left, swinging toward the western shore of Oahu as the great formation followed. The sky over Pearl Harbor appeared to be clear—of cloud as well as aircraft. "I peered through my binoculars at the ships riding peacefully at anchor. One by one I counted them. Yes, the battleships were there all right, eight of them! But our last lingering hope of finding any carriers present was now gone. Not one was to be seen." But "below me lay the whole U. S. Pacific Fleet in a formation I would not have dared to dream of in my most optimistic dreams."

As his radio operator sent the signal to attack, "To . . . to . . . to . . . ," Fuchida fired the flare. In the Sunday-sleepy harbor below it was obvious that they had carried off the surprise. The dive bombers climbed out of harm's way to fifteen thousand feet as the level bombers swooped down to about three thousand and the torpedo bombers knifed down to sea level. They would initiate the attack. But something was obviously wrong. The Zeros had not taken their "Surprise Achieved" positions. Fuchida, realizing that the fighters may not have seen the signal, fired another flare. As far as

the bombers were concerned, surprise had been lost, and the plan became confused. The dive bombers, along with the now alerted Zeros, plunged into action. Worse, the torpedo planes too were screaming in upon Pearl Harbor from the sea. Fuchida looked at his watch: seven forty-nine, Pearl Harbor time.

Despite the last-minute blunder with the two signal flares, Fuchida was certain that they had caught the Americans completely off guard. More off guard than he imagined, for the delivery of the official ultimatum in Washington, delayed while the lengthy message was being decoded in the Japanese embassy, was delivered an hour and twenty minutes after the attack had begun. Instead of giving the Americans a half hour advance notice, as Yamamoto had anticipated, the other blunders of the day had plunged Japan into a Pacific war with a "sneak attack."

"*Tora . . . tora . . . tora . . .*" ("Tiger, tiger, tiger"), Fuchida's radio operator signaled to the anxious Nagumo on the *Akagi,* informing him that the surprise attack was successful. Because of some freakishness in the atmospheric conditions, the message was distinctly picked up in distant Tokyo and by Yamamoto's flagship in Hiroshima Bay.

The Army's Wheeler Field, a fighter base, was the first objective. Neat rows of Curtiss P-40s were lined, wingtip to wingtip—as a precaution against sabotage—on the field. Twenty-five Vals, led by Lieutenant Akira Sakamoto, proceeded to erase all fighter opposition they might have expected from Wheeler Field. At the same time Lieutenant Commander Takahashi, who led the dive bomber units, pounced with twenty-six Vals upon Hickam Field, the Army bomber base, just south of Pearl Harbor. The formation diverged as some of the Vals broke off to attack the various installations on Ford Island, in the center of Pearl Harbor. It was around the island that most of the important ships, singly and in pairs, were berthed.

The languid Sunday tranquillity was shattered by the scream of diving aircraft, the whine of falling bombs, explosions—followed by the characteristic blossom of thick, black smoke of flaming metal. This same smoke, as he feared, complicated the mission of Lieutenant Commander Murata's Kates, which were to torpedo the ships grouped around Ford Island.

A Japanese photograph records the first strikes around Ford Island. Outer row of ships are (left to right): Vestal, West Virginia, and Oklahoma; inner row: Nevada, Tennessee, and Maryland. Of these the Oklahoma *was sunk, the* West Virginia *sunk but later repaired, the repair ship* Vestal *and battleships* Nevada, Tennessee, *and* Maryland *damaged and later repaired.*

(NAVY DEPT., NATIONAL ARCHIVES)

A Val has just dropped a bomb near the Oklahoma and Maryland *on the far side of Ford Island. On the near side, the* Utah *(a target ship the Japanese thought was the carrier* Saratoga)—*the third ship from the* left—lists to port. In the upper right of the photograph another Val sweeps over the Navy Yard.

(NAVY DEPT., NATIONAL ARCHIVES)

One of Murata's pilots, his second-in-command, Lieutenant Inichi Goto, was infuriated when, just as he was leveling off for the run on the battleships at anchor, the Vals flashed by him. Goto was then flying in the vanguard of one column of Kates, while Murata led the other. Not realizing that Fuchida had fired the second flare which precipitated the attack by the Vals, Goto was angrily certain that the dive bombers had jumped the gun to steal the glory of making the first attack on the Americans.

There was nothing else to do but proceed, despite the confusion and now the smoke. Goto concentrated on his run: speed, height, and then the correct release point. The battleship—the *Arizona*—grew larger in his sight; there seemed to be no one on the decks of any of the ships. Oblivious to everything else, Goto timed the moment of release, and the torpedo, with its odd wooden fins, dropped from the Kate's belly. The weight gone, the Kate vaulted as Goto pulled back on the stick and kicked the rudder bar to get up and away. For a fleet moment he twisted his head to see over the tail: a foaming white wake churned the water, leaving a momentary track which terminated at the side of the *Arizona*.

Antiaircraft fire from American ships, once the impact of the surprise attack had worn off, begins to seek out Japanese Vals. (NAVY DEPT., NATIONAL ARCHIVES)

Panorama of Pearl Harbor minutes after the opening of the attack: ships burn in the harbor and the sky fills with antiaircraft bursts.

(NAVY DEPT., NATIONAL ARCHIVES)

Struck by the heavy concentration of fire from the American ships, a Val begins a fiery plunge into Pearl Harbor. (NAVY DEPT., NATIONAL ARCHIVES)

A broiling geyser of flame, smoke, and water shot high into the air.

"We hit her!" Goto shouted and circled round to view the damage.

But the "Americans were better prepared and reacted much faster after the shock than I would ever have thought possible." Machine-gun tracers were fanning and curving up at the Kate; Goto decided to pull away from the heated air over Ford Island. It was true, within minutes after the first bombs fell some of the men on some of the ships had begun firing at the Japanese planes. But the sudden impact of the realization that there were real aircraft, with orange-red circles on their wings, dropping real bombs and shooting real bullets created uncertainty and confusion on the ships as well as ashore. Army personnel were sure that some crazy Navy pilots were having sport with them—and vice versa. That this could be real war took time to penetrate. Men who once regarded themselves as professionally military wandered about not quite knowing what to do.

Those who might have gone into immediate action were handicapped for other reasons: many guns were simply not ready to be fired, or there was no ammunition available—and if it was, perhaps it was

locked away and no one seemed to have the key. For many there were simply no weapons at all. One sailor, in impotent despair, threw wrenches and other handy objects at the low-flying Japanese planes. Adult males burst into blubbering tears of helpless frustration. The abrupt reality of what was happening was difficult to grasp: one minute it had been a typical, peaceful Sunday; the next it had become an incredible concatenation of hundreds of swirling, flashing airplanes, explosions, acrid smoke, shouting, the sound of bugles, alarms, waterspouts, and little, moving, parallel scallopings of water caused by the twinkling guns in the planes strafing them. Suddenly someone you had known for years was inexplicably dead. Or the ship on which you had served for a decade had become a shattered, smoking hulk sinking into the mud of Pearl Harbor.

The battleships clustered around Ford Island were sumptuous objectives. The Kates hammered them from the side in torpedo attacks and from above with level attacks. Within minutes, so-called Battleship Row and American naval power in the Pacific were a shambles. Simultaneously the same destiny was allotted to the Naval Air Station at Kaneohe, on the eastern side of Oahu, where twenty-seven of thirty-six Consolidated PBYs (Catalinas) were destroyed. The Marine Corps Air Base at Ewa, ten miles west of Pearl Harbor, lost almost all of its fighter planes (forty-seven out of forty-eight), belonging to Marine Aircraft Group 21 (MAG-21), to strafing Zeros.

At Hickam Field, just south of Pearl, gouts of oily smoke ascended from mangled old Douglas B-18s, as well as from the more recent Douglas A-20s (Havocs) and Boeing B-17s. Several of the factory-fresh, unarmed B-17s, just flown in from California, were caught up in the attack as they came in to land. Many of them were shot up by Zeros as they attempted to land and if they landed, were strafed along with their hapless crews. As at Wheeler, the Army fighters at Bellows Field, almost directly east of Honolulu, were rent and flared where they rested on the ground. Very few American fighters, in fact, got off the ground.

Several pilots of the 47th Pursuit Squadron succeeded in reaching Haleiwa, a small, relatively insignificant training field in northwestern Oahu, by automobile. The field had not been as diligently worked over by the Zeros as the major airfields and

U. S. Naval Air Station, Pearl Harbor. The Chance Vought OS2U "Kingfisher" has been hit by a bomb. *It is one of eighty U. S. Navy aircraft destroyed in the attack.* (U. S. NAVY)

A rescue party searches for survivors from the burning West Virginia. One seaman is being assisted out of the *water; two more may be seen on the bridge.* (NAVY DEPT., NATIONAL ARCHIVES)

Hickam Field, the Army Air Force bomber base near Pearl Harbor; more than twenty bombers were destroyed at Hickam. (U. S. AIR FORCE)

As the Pearl Harbor attack opened, twelve new B-17s were approaching Hickam Field after a flight from the United States. Early radar detection of the Japanese attack were mistaken for the approaching B-17s, many of which arrived over Pearl Harbor during the attack. This was one of the new B-17s. Piloted by Captain Raymond Swenson, it was attacked by Zeros. A bullet ignited flares in the radio compartment and upon landing the burning plane broke in half. All of the occupants escaped except Flight Surgeon William Schick, who was killed by a strafing Zero as he ran from the wreck. (NAVY DEPT., NATIONAL ARCHIVES)

a few of its planes were still flyable. Taking off, without orders, by the way, a fact which would have later consequences, in P-40s as well as obsolescent P-36s, they attempted to intercept the attackers. Neither of the American planes was any match for the Zero. Even so, Lieutenant George S. Welch claimed four enemy planes before the Japanese finished with Pearl Harbor; although Welch received the Distinguished Flying Cross for his actions that day, a request that he be awarded the Congressional Medal of Honor was turned down because he had taken off without orders. Other pilots who managed to take off were Lieutenants John J. Webster, Harry M. Brown, Kenneth A. Taylor, and John L. Dains. On his third time up the last-named was shot down over the Army's Schofield Barracks by antiaircraft fire. Other pilots of the 44th and 46th Pursuit Squadrons attempting to get into the battle were shot down by the fast, amazingly adroit Zeros; many American pilots were killed on the ground as they ran for their planes.

Ten thousand feet above the writhing shambles, Fuchida prepared for the run by the level bombers upon the battleships moored around Ford Island. A few, berthed inland and adjacent to another ship, were difficult for the torpedoes to hit. Antiaircraft bursts from both the ships and the land batteries burst around the Kate formation. Fuchida's Kate recoiled as the firing became uncomfortably accurate. The plane bounced from a close one which punctured the fuselage and damaged a rudder control wire. But the plane remained in flight so Fuchida, with his eye on the lead plane, continued on the bomb run. Just then they flew into cloud, missing the release point—they would have to do it again. The air around the Kates was pocked with the gray-black puffs of shellbursts.

Fuchida's pilot banked the Kate, circled around Honolulu, and returned to Battleship Row. Other planes, meanwhile, had succeeded in dropping their bombs. Just as he was about to make a second attempt, Fuchida witnessed a "colossal explosion in Battleship Row," the violence of which tossed the Kate about seven miles away from Ford Island. The battleship Arizona, anchored at the northeastern tip of the island, adjacent to the repair ship Vestal, had gone up in one massive explosion. Bomb hits from above (for the ship was moored inland from the Vestal and was barely hit by torpe-

does) on the powder magazines and boilers tore the old battleship apart. A fireball shot five hundred feet into the air, a shock wave flared out, blowing men off the decks of nearby ships into the oily waters of Pearl Harbor. A complete loss, the Arizona sank into the offshore mud, taking 1103 lives with it of the total of 1400 men aboard. Among those lost were Captain Franklin Van Falkenburgh and Rear Admiral Isaac C. Kidd, who died instantly as they stood on the bridge of the Arizona.

Antiaircraft smudges continued to harass Fuchida but he proceeded with the bomb run. This time the lead plane dropped its bombs and the other Kates dropped in unison. Fuchida then fell to the floor where he lay, eye to peephole, to observe the results. The size of the bombs diminished as they plunged downward. He saw concentric ripples in the water where some missed, but as he watched two of them fell directly to the left of two ships moored side by side. The Maryland and Oklahoma shuddered under the detonations.

Upon completing their runs, the bombers fled to the north and the safety of the carriers. No attempt was made to screen the direction—there wasn't enough fuel left for that. By 8:30 A.M. almost all aircraft of the first attack wave, excepting Fuchida's Kate and a few strays, had left for the carriers. An unreal quiet suffused the air over Pearl Harbor, seemingly clear of Japanese aircraft. But the harbor itself and the area around it were choked with the effluvium of flaming ships, aircraft, harbor installations, and men. The living, now wrathful, made preparations for what might come next. Makeshift gun installations of wreckage and debris were erected; guns were ripped off ruined planes and set up in odd places. Guns were even issued to the weaponless (some, it is true, without firing pins and many without ammunition). Rescue operations were under way immediately in Pearl Harbor itself.

The second wave came in around 8:54 A.M. Lieutenant Commander Shegekazu Shimazaki of the Zuikaku led the formation of 170 planes. Shimazaki personally led the 54 Kates assigned the level bombing; Lieutenant Commander Takashige Egusa (Soryu) led the 80 Val dive bombers and Lieutenant Saburo Shindo (Akagi) commanded the 36 Zero fighter covers.

Fuchida, as over-all commander of the aerial attack, had remained behind to observe and direct

One of the spectacular explosions witnessed by Mitsuo
Fuchida as he lay in the belly of a Kate: the Shaw
blowing up in a dry dock in the Navy Yard.

(NAVY DEPT., NATIONAL ARCHIVES)

the second wave. As he watched, the Zeros darted
in to strafe Battleship Row and the airfields. The
Vals hurtled in from the east to maul further the
ships at and around Ford Island. Most of the level
bombers concentrated on Hickam Field as others
bombed Ford Island and the Kaneohe Naval Air
Station. Smoke and flame of the early attack interfered with bombing accuracy—and antiaircraft was
fiercely thick. Despite this not one bomber of the
second wave was lost, although several were holed
by gunfire. Six Zeros and fourteen Vals of the second wave did not return to the carriers. The first
wave had lost only three Zeroes, one Val, and five
Kates. The total losses of both waves were twenty-
nine aircraft and their crews (fifty-five men).

In terms of "the values of war" it was a small
price to pay. In roughly two hours at a "reasonable"
expenditure of a handful of men and a few planes
(plus one submarine and all five of the midget

submarines), the Japanese had achieved precisely
that which Yamamoto had promised them with the
Hawaii Operation. The nearly total crippling of the
American Pacific Fleet at Pearl Harbor cleared the
way for the conquest of the Philippines, Malaya
—and for the other objectives of the Southern Operation.

American losses were appalling: 2403 killed,
1178 wounded. Of the 68 civilian dead, many died
in or near military installations. Those killed in
Honolulu were undoubtedly the victims of American shells incorrectly fused in the chaos of activity.
At Pearl Harbor, of the battleships, the *Arizona*
and *Oklahoma* were destroyed beyond recovery; the
California and *West Virginia*, also sunk, were

Seamen salvage a Kate from the waters of Pearl Harbor; only five were lost in the attack.

eventually put back into service; the *Maryland, Tennessee, Pennsylvania,* and *Nevada* had all suffered damage but could—given time—be salvaged. Of the cruisers, the *Helena, Raleigh,* and *Honolulu* were damaged but repairable. Destroyers *Cassin* and *Downs* were lost; the *Shaw,* though hit and spectacularly exploded, was later restored to service. Both the *Utah,* a radio-controlled target ship, and the *Oglala,* a minelayer, were completely out of action. The repair ship *Vestal,* which had been next to the *Arizona,* was restored to service. So was the seaplane tender *Curtiss,* which lay smoldering under the wreckage of Lieutenant Mimori Suzuki's Zero, which had crashed into the deck during the attack.

Not a single battleship which lay in Pearl Harbor that day escaped the attack, which had been most thoroughly planned and efficiently executed. Although the damage was not absolute, it would be a long time before the salvageable ships would be ready for action.

Almost half of all the aircraft—Army, Navy, Marine—on Oahu were destroyed, a total of 188 of the pre-attack strength of 394, not all of which were truly operational. But the carriers had been spared and so had the repair shops at Pearl Harbor. And so had the fuel depots, rich with oil. Instead, the Japanese had bombed a baseball diamond in the belief that it was a cleverly camouflaged fuel tank farm.

Upon reporting to Nagumo aboard the *Akagi,* Fuchida—as well as other air commanders—suggested an additional strike at Pearl to deal with targets that might have been obscured by smoke

The first Zero to go down under American guns: it is the aircraft of pilot Takeshi Hirano of the Akagi's *first wave.* (U. S. NAVY)

or simply overlooked in the excitement of the moment. Besides, he hoped it might give them the opportunity to deal with the still untouched carriers, wherever they might be. But Nagumo, with his chief of staff, Rear Admiral Ryunosuke Kusaka, concurring, maintained that the attack had accomplished its strategic objective—excepting those hauntingly missing carriers. The task force, therefore, before the Americans completely recovered, would set course north-northwest and withdraw. No amount of respectful debate could force Nagumo to change his mind. At one-thirty that vivid Sunday afternoon the *Akagi* raised a signal flag: all ships were to head for home waters. Swiftly and silently the ships slipped into the heavy mist.

Back at Pearl Harbor frenetic preparations were under way for the invasion which seemed the inevitable next phase in Japanese operations. Wild rumors swept Oahu; nervous sentries became a greater menace than the new enemy. The least unexpected noise or light ignited a chain of frenzied shooting.

Everything that flew was fair game. The planes of the *Enterprise* suffered from friend and foe alike. Early in the morning Commander Howard L. Young with Lieutenant Commander Bromfield B. Nichol as his passenger took off from the carrier and headed for Pearl Harbor. Nichol was a member of

Admiral Halsey's staff and was being sent ahead to report the delivery of the men and planes to Wake Island; the information was considered highly secret and therefore could not be sent by radio, even in code. The two men were accompanied by another plane, also a Douglas SBD (the Dauntless). Other SBDs were launched later to scout the seas. The *Enterprise*'s crew was envious, for the planes would be in Oahu within two hours—the carrier would require an additional six.

But by the time Young arrived over Ford Island, conditions of the island prompted him to think that all safety precautions were being violated by the Army. Then one of the "Army" planes pulled away from the island and hurtled at them. Nichol was rather surprised to note that "a lot of burning cigarette butts" came flashing by. Some, flicking against the wing, ripped pieces of aluminum into the slipstream. Then the plane turned and the red-orange circles became visible.

Young and his wingman dived their Dauntlesses for Ford Island, escaping the Japanese planes but running into shattering fire from "friendly" guns on the ground. As Young braked the Dauntless, a sailor stood up with a machine gun; he hated all aircraft. He was prevented from firing at Young's Dauntless by a pilot who recognized the plane—but this only by threatening the sailor with a tremendous rock.

The other planes from the *Enterprise* were not so fortunate, especially those of Scouting Squadron 6. Swarms of Zeros pounced on them as they came in for landings. The death of one young pilot was heard at the *Enterprise,* which then learned that Pearl Harbor was under attack. Ensign Manuel Gonzales was heard over the radio, "Do not attack me! This is 6-Baker-3, an American plane!"

Then Gonzales' voice again, "We're on fire. Bail out!"

Soon after, flags were run up the yardarm of the *Enterprise.* There was something unreal about their message: *Prepare for battle.* Scout planes, torpedo planes, and fighters were launched to search for the attackers. Grumman Wildcats hovered overhead on combat air patrol (CAP). The Wildcats also escorted the torpedo-carrying Devastators, but although there were many alarums, there were no enemy carriers or planes about. That night the Devastators returned to the *Enterprise,* but the Wildcats because of less fuel capacity were ordered to

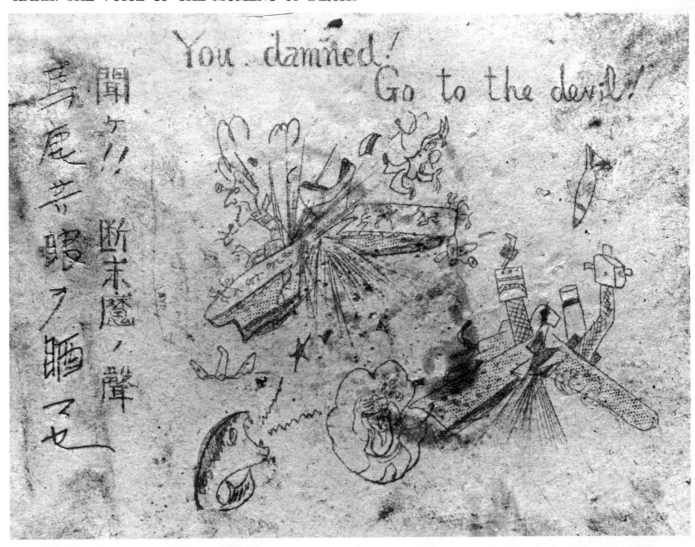

A homemade propaganda leaflet dropped by a Japanese pilot over Pearl Harbor. Japanese inscription on left reads: "Hark! The Voice of the Moment of Death. Wake up, you fools." Japanese wishful thinking is evident in the bursting aircraft carrier, not one of which was in Pearl Harbor the Sunday of the attack. That the carriers escaped would have its later effect in the Pacific war; but "the fools" had been rudely awakened that morning. (NAVY DEPT., NATIONAL ARCHIVES)

return to Pearl Harbor. The six planes with landing lights full on and with wheels down wheeled in over Ford Island after clearing with the tower. A single machine gun opened up on them across the channel from Ford Island, another joined in, then others, and all of Ford Island flashed as tracers converged on the Wildcats. One merely continued its glide across the channel into Pearl City, where it crashed and burned, killing pilot Herbert Menge. Two others were shot down, one crashing and burning in a cane field. Three of the pilots flicked off their lights and jammed their throttles and headed out to sea until things quieted down. Two managed to land, but pilot David Flynn's engine gave out and he was forced to parachute. It had proved a costly and fruitless search for the Japanese carriers.

But they had vanished into the spacious Pacific. Yamamoto had proved that the airplane was more than a match for the immobile battleship, but it was an infamous victory.

2

AMERICAN RENEGADES

Mei-ling Soong, exquisite, formal, and hard as nails, best known to the world as Madame Chiang Kai-shek of China, referred to a small band of American youngsters as her "angels—with or without wings." It was a neatly turned phrase, much used during the early months of the Pacific war, even if few could explain its precise meaning. Another winsome phrase, also widely quoted, was "the Lady and the Tigers," with all its curious ambiguity Not to the "angels," however. If the genteel Madame had to make the choice, for all her endearing phrases, they would be angels indeed. There was no sacrifice too great, in terms of the lives of others, for her beloved China.

Within weeks after Japan went to war in the Pacific, Madame Chiang's "angels" were renowned as the "Flying Tigers"; no one knows the derivation of the name. The Japanese preferred calling them "American renegades," partly because they had become, as the American Volunteer Group, members of the Chinese Air Force and partly because of their unorthodox fighting style. In fact, during those grim

early months of the Pacific war, only the Flying Tigers spoiled the succession of Japanese aerial victories—and this while flying inferior aircraft.

Credit for the Flying Tigers' tactics and for their ability to meet the Japanese in battle with a type of aircraft which, in other areas, the Japanese destroyed readily, must go to the man who led them, an ex-U. S. Army Air Corps captain, Claire Lee Chennault. Hard-bitten, tough, and self-sufficient, Chennault had been in China since 1937, when he was retired from the Air Corps because of chronic bronchitis and partial deafness. He had been hired by Generalissimo Chiang Kai-shek to serve as his adviser in military aviation; Madame Chiang, it might be noted, was the National Secretary of Aviation. Chennault, then forty-seven, was given the rank of colonel in the Chinese Air Force.

He found, however, that he had little effective air force to command. The Japanese were well established in Manchuria and bombing Chinese cities at will. The Chinese armies, those under Chiang's command, fell back before the better-equipped and disciplined Japanese. The Generalissimo abandoned Nanking, then Hankow, until the seat of his Kuomintang government was temporarily established inland at Chungking. The Japanese, however, were not Chiang's only foes. He was either at odds or made deals with various provincial governors, war lords and the Communists under Mao Tse-tung. Consequently during the war in China there were in fact several wars as these factions fought together and then fought each other.

Into this typical oriental political situation descended Claire Chennault, who was fated to an extraordinary education in duplicity, graft, cupidity, nepotism, equivocation, and the old-fashioned double cross. While these themes are not directly germane to the development of the air weapon, they were to vex Chennault considerably during his service in China. The cost in goods, time, money, and lives would not be trivial.

Chennault's was not the first attempt at patterning the Chinese Air Force along foreign lines. As

early as 1932 an "unofficial" air mission led by Colonel John H. Jouett gave it a try. Bringing nine American pilots—including one Harvey Greenlaw, who would in time become Chennault's chief of staff—Jouett found the Chinese Air Force ineffectually graft-ridden. With Chiang Kai-shek's blessing Jouett generally shook up the organization, set up a proper training school, and arranged for the purchase of modern foreign planes. But diplomatic pressures from Japan, as well as differences with Chiang, forced Jouett out of China in 1934. In desperation Chiang turned to other nations for assistance in building a modern air force; he found the Russians and the Italians most willing. However, the occidental soldier-of-fortune *laissez faire* outlook (this was especially true of the Italians) did little to improve the efficiency of Chiang's air force. Very soon the planes Jouett had purchased piled up around the Chinese countryside.

Madame Chiang attempted to remedy the woeful situation by hiring a couple of ex-U. S. Army Air Corps stunt fliers, William C. McDonald and John H. Williamson, to organize a flying school in 1936. The two men had been members of a trio known as "Three Men on a Flying Trapeze," which had thrilled the crowds at air shows and races. Their most celebrated stunt was flying through complex aerobatics while their planes were attached, wing to wing, by a twenty-foot length of rope. The leader and third member of the group was Claire Lee Chennault. McDonald and Williamson suggested that Madame Chiang approach Chennault to do something about the hapless Chinese Air Force. Chennault, by then retired, was known for his textbook *The Role of Defensive Pursuit,* the doctrine of which had made a deeper impression upon the younger pilots than Chennault's superiors.

Chennault's first exposure to the internationally manned air force was disheartening. Many an aircraft was wiped out merely in the process of landing; half of his small force of American and British fighters (eleven out of twenty-two) was destroyed in this way; likewise four out of five Martin bombers. The last bomber was lost during a surprise Japanese air raid. The polyglot air force took off in every possible direction, crashing into the bomber on the ground and further erasing fifteen fighters from the operational inventory.

One of Chennault's first moves was to institute

Madame and Generalissimo Chiang Kai-shek and Chinese dignitaries at the inauguration of Chiang as president of China, October 1943.
(U. S. OFFICE OF WAR INFORMATION)

Claire Lee Chennault, master tactician and pilot who created the "Flying Tigers." This photograph was taken *after the Flying Tiger phase—when Chennault commanded the Fourteenth Air Force later in the war.*
(U. S. AIR FORCE)

Back door to China: the Burma Road, more than seven hundred miles of hazardous driving—and corrupt Chinese officials. (U. S. OFFICE OF WAR INFORMATION)

was an almost insuperable effort. The Russians, who had been supplying the Chinese with money, planes, guns, and even aircrews, had, by the summer of 1941, a Nazi invasion to contend with—which closed that avenue of aid. The Japanese controlled the eastern seaports of China, as well as Indo-China (thanks to Vichy France), leaving the one major life line into China via the port of Rangoon, Burma. Materials delivered to Rangoon were sent by rail to Lashio, in the north; this was the western terminus of the Burma Road, a curling ribbon of more than seven hundred miles, a tortuous drive by truck, which had been all but clawed out of the mountains by hand during 1937–38. At the eastern end of the road lay Kunming, China.

By March of 1941 the United States, awakening to the Japanese threat in the Pacific, was committed to full lend-lease aid to China. The Burma Road thus became more crucial than ever. Only two obstacles intervened in the full exploitation of the Burma Road: the Japanese bombers based at Hanoi and the Chinese officials responsible for the Burma Road. Graft, featherbedding, and sheer inefficiency prevented the delivery to China of much of the materials that arrived in Rangoon. Even despite the official commitment to China and the widespread sympathy in the United States for the Chinese, there was no overwhelming aid on the way, in fact. Both military and government officials in the United

an early warning system with lookout stations, linked by radio, strewn across China. Whenever the Japanese bombers left their base at Hanoi, Indo-China (after the fall of France), it took but a few minutes before Chennault knew about it in Kunming. In the beginning (before the Flying Tiger era) the main job was to get the few surviving Chinese aircraft dispersed or evacuated to escape bomb damage. Later, of course, the early warning system could be employed for interception. Proof of Chennault's capabilities as a teacher was demonstrated late in the summer of 1937. Chinese pilots, taught by Chennault, intercepted Japanese bombers over the battered city of Nanking and shot them out of the skies.

But the teaching of tactical potency was Chennault's minor problem. He required more men and more aircraft. Merely getting materials into China

Curtiss P-40 "Tomahawk" with Flying Tiger shark's mouth, Rangoon. (U. S. AIR FORCE)

States, with wary eyes upon Europe and recent developments in north Africa, viewed Hitler and not Tojo as the major threat.

Prompted by the seriousness of the China situation, Chennault returned to the United States in the spring of 1941 accompanied by General P. T. Mow of the Chinese Air Force. Chennault by this time was a brigadier general. With the co-operation of T. V. Soong, Chinese Foreign Minister and brother of Madame Chiang, Chennault eventually reached the sympathetic ear of President Roosevelt. Basing his plea for aid to China on the importance of keeping the Burma Road open, Chennault asked for aircraft—and a voluntary force of experienced American pilots to fly them. This was a delicate proposition politically, for such open aid would be in violation of American-Japanese neutrality, such as that was. Besides, Hitler continued to engage American attention.

The aircraft were forthcoming, thanks to the intervention of Secretary of the Treasury Henry Morgenthau, Jr., who had Roosevelt's backing. Although all first-class aircraft were high-priority items for the burgeoning U.S. national defense program, or for shipment to Britain and Russia, Chennault was able to obtain the release of a hundred Curtiss Wright P-40Bs ("Tomahawk"), originally allocated to Sweden—and which had already been rejected by the RAF as obsolescent. Despite this rejection, the P-40s were better planes than those Chennault already had. And the RAF continued to use them until the later D and E models ("Kittyhawk") appeared.

Assured of his aircraft, Chennault broached the subject of trained pilots. Predicting a general outbreak of war in the Pacific, he succeeded in arousing the sentiments of Roosevelt as well as officials in the War and State departments. So it was that from May through July of 1941, various Army and Navy air bases were visited by Chennault or by Captain Harry C. Claiborne, C. B. Adair (both ex-U. S. Army Air Corps men), and Richard T. Aldworth, a former World War I pilot and a vice-president in an organization known as CAMCO, Central Aircraft Manufacturing Corporation.

This was an interesting firm. It was, in fact, the contracting agent between the American volunteers and the Chinese government. According to the contract signed by the pilots and ground crew volun-

teers, they were to serve for one year in China "to manufacture, service and operate aircraft" as members of the American Volunteer Group. There was no mention, not even in fine print, of fighting the Japanese. Minimum salary for flying personnel was $600 per month in American money (lend-lease, of course). Flight leaders received $675 and squadron commanders $750. A bonus of $500 was promised for every confirmed Japanese plane destroyed— this point was verbal and also not included in the CAMCO contract. Ground crew salaries ranged from $150 to $350 a month; for this time—the summer of 1941—these could be regarded as very good salaries.

The attractive fiscal promises were not the sole reasons for volunteering. Some pilots, in training for years, longed for a little action. Others sensed that, in time, the United States would have to go to war and hoped to gain combat experience (this was especially true of the Navy pilots). Some volunteers were driven by the simple spirit of adventure and others by a dedication to the cause of China. This was before they learned that the cause of China and the cause of the Chiang Kaisheks were not necessarily identical. Others admitted that they were out for the money—so there was a complexity of reasons for the forming of the American Volunteer Group. Some may even have succumbed to the rather exaggerated blandishments of the recruiting staff—who were rewarded for their efforts in bounty, so much per head. As Gregory Boyington, an ex-Marine pilot who had volunteered to escape serious financial problems, observed, "The two ingredients necessary to accomplish this human sale were greedy pilots and a few idealists."

Whatever their motivations, 90 pilots (over half of whom came from the ranks of the Navy and Marines) and 150 non-flying personnel assembled in July in San Francisco. Among the ground people were radio operators, mechanics—even a flight surgeon and two nurses. Supplies, too, had been purchased with lend-lease funds by Soong and Chennault, who had gone on ahead to arrange for a training base in Burma. The first contingent of the American Volunteer Group slipped out of San Francisco aboard a Dutch ship on July 11, 1941, more or less secretly. The furtiveness encompassed some quite blatant passport falsification. When he left on a subsequent ship, Boyington was, according to his passport, "a member of the clergy." It could hardly be considered inventive typecasting.

It was September, after a meandering voyage of many stops, before the first of the American Volunteer Group arrived at Rangoon, some twenty miles up the Rangoon River from the Gulf of Martaban. A subsequent trip by rail took them deeper into the jungle to an RAF base at Toungoo, where they were to receive their schooling from Chennault. Burma, it turned out, was not quite the tropical paradise painted by the recruitment staff. Getting off the toy train at Toungoo, many a young pilot felt foolishly country-clubbish as he carried tennis rackets and a set of golf clubs. There were no golf courses or tennis courts at the Kyedaw airdrome, about ten miles out of Toungoo. There were only moldering troop barracks, oppressive heat, an incredible proliferation of insect life, giant rats, poor food.

Some of the P-40s, however, had arrived at Rangoon, and were assembled and flown up to Toungoo. "The runway," Chennault wrote in describing the place, "was surrounded by quagmire and pestilential jungle. Matted masses of rotting vegetation carpeted the jungle and filled the air with a sour, sickening smell." Even before training got under way, Chennault was handed the resignations of five pilots who "were eager to return to the United States and air-line jobs."

Chennault drew upon his past experiences with the Japanese and as a teacher, "ranging from the one-room schools of rural Louisiana to director of one of the largest Air Corps schools," to prepare the new pilots for what would come. He stressed the excellent flying qualities of the Japanese pilots, although emphasizing their tendency to fly mechanically and employ a set tactical routine. Chennault also introduced the Americans to the Zero fighter, indicating its strong points as compared with the P-40: higher ceiling, superior maneuverability, and better climbing ability. But, Chennault also pointed out, the P-40 was a more rugged aircraft, could take more punishment, and, thanks to the self-sealing fuel tank, was not so readily combustible. The P-40 was also equipped with armor plate, which the Zero lacked, thanks to the Japanese pilots' insistence on high maneuverability. Also, the heavier P-40 could outdive (that is to say, outrun) the Zero. "Use your speed and diving power to make a pass, shoot and break away," Chennault told them.

Another dictum: "Fight in pairs." These tactics were quite unorthodox to pilots who had been trained along the romantic dogfight concepts of the First World War. The "hit and run" principle was particularly upsetting (but exceptionally wise, as they would learn). When this idea filtered around, the RAF issued an order that any British pilot seen diving away from a combat would be subject to court-martial. The Chinese Air Force had a more direct solution: a firing squad.

But Chennault prevailed, although his lecture on the Zero seems to have led to a few more pilot resignations. Those who remained then had to contend with the P-40, for which few had little regard. Many longed to use the Brewster Buffalo, which the RAF had, instead. Chennault, no admirer of the P-40 himself and particularly not of its liquid-cooled Allison engine, realized that for all its imperfections, the P-40 could be used to beat the Japanese, if properly handled.

The transition to the P-40 by pilots who had been trained in other aircraft (some had even piloted B-17s) was not simple. The narrow-tread landing gear of the P-40 made landing upon hard, earthen runways a hazard. Even experienced pilots washed out precious planes. And there were other accidents. Former Navy pilot John D. Armstrong (Hutchinson, Kansas) collided in a mock dogfight in mid-air with Fighter Leader John G. Bright. The latter managed to take to his chute, but Armstrong did not and died in the crash. A few days later Maax Hammer (Cairo, Illinois), caught in a sudden monsoon, crashed while attempting to land and was killed. On another training flight, Peter W. Atkinson (Martinsburg, West Virginia) suffered a malfunction of his propeller governor; the propeller ran wild and the P-40 all but fell apart in a screaming power dive, taking Atkinson with it.

There being no spare parts for the P-40s, the wrecks were salvaged for replacement parts. There were no replacements for the men. As training progressed, both men and aircraft, especially the latter, were consumed. The military grapevine began to transmit the libelous rumor that Chennault's volunteers would not, as worded in a wire from T. V. Soong, "be ready before February 1942 and will not last two weeks in combat. Your comment requested."

Chennault's printable comment was that the group

would be ready by November 1941. He was correct, although by this time he had only forty-three operational P-40s and eighty-four pilots. Of these "survivors," Erikson E. Shilling (who doubled also as Group Photo Officer) conceived the idea of decorating the remaining P-40s with a blood-red mouth, shark teeth, and an evil eye in the radiator area. The Japanese, Shilling was certain, would be superstitious about the shark and the evil eye. This was not original with Shilling, of course, for the British had so decorated their P-40s and the Germans had used similar designs on their Ju-87 Stuka and the Me-110. At the same time someone with Hollywood connections had approached the Walt Disney studios for an idea of an identifying insignia. A Disney artist came up with a cunning leaping tiger, with tiny wings, jumping through a V, the V for Victory sign popularized by Churchill. It was from this insignia that the popular name Flying Tiger came into currency, although the group was already called that before the design had been drawn, possibly because of the tiger shark connotation.

Chennault divided the remaining men and planes into three squadrons. The first, called "Adam and Eve," was commanded by Robert J. Sandell, an ex-Army pilot from San Antonio, Texas; the second, "Panda Bear," was led by John Van Kuren Newkirk, formerly of the Navy and Scarsdale, New York; "Hell's Angels" was the popular name of the third squadron, which was under the leadership of Arvid Olson, a Californian and onetime Army pilot.

Despite this paper readiness, the Flying Tigers had not yet tangled with the Japanese in November, as Chennault had predicted; nor, for that matter, did they join in battle immediately after the Pearl Harbor attack. Wisely, Chennault did not wish to send his pilots into combat until they had the fullest possible preparation. There were other considerations: a promised delivery of supplies had not materialized in November and there was an acute shortage of aircraft, ammunition, and parts.

II

Curiously, the popular belief continues that the Flying Tigers fought against the Japanese before the Pearl Harbor debacle. In fact, nearly two weeks passed—during which the Americans who fought back, especially in the Philippines, suffered badly—before the Flying Tigers encountered Japanese planes for the first time.

On December 10 Chennault initiated the evacuation of the Kyedaw airdrome. Arvid Olson led the Hell's Angels (i.e., the 3rd Squadron), consisting of twenty-four pilots and twenty-one Tomahawks, south to Mingaladon, near Rangoon, to co-operate with the RAF in protecting the port from Japanese aerial attacks. This handful of men and planes were added to another handful in No. 67 Squadron, a British fighter squadron equipped mainly with the Brewster Buffalo (later they were to receive Hurricanes). The remaining two AVG squadrons left for the main base at Kunming, China, on December 18, some flying their operational aircraft and others, mainly ground personnel, taking to the Burma Road in trucks and other vehicles. "The departing travelers," observed Russell Whelan in his story of the group, "shed no tears as they looked their last on Toungoo, that suburb of Gehenna."

Kunming was no Garden of Eden either, although the AVG base had been rather sumptuously appointed with fine living quarters, a library, a good hospital, tennis courts, and a baseball diamond (Chennault was an ardent proponent of physical conditioning). But Kunming, capital of the Yunnan province, had been bombed by the Japanese just prior to the arrival of the Americans. With a population of more than 500,000, Kunming was an enticing target for Japanese Army air units based in French Indo-China. From former French air bases formations of Kates, escorted either by Claudes or Zeros, came over to bomb Kunming, and like most oriental cities, it burned with a lovely light, or so it appeared to those flying safely above the shambles. It was this destruction, rather than a quaint Chinese city, that the Flying Tigers first saw when they came to the Yunnan province.

The following day, December 19, 1941, was uneventful while the 1st Squadron waited impatiently in the ready shack. The next morning the Adam and Eves took the morning patrol—five P-40s and Squadron Leader Robert Sandell in his plane. But the sky remained clear of the enemy. The six men, tense, almost disgusted by the inaction, landed to refuel. It was then that the radio crackled and word came through that a formation of Mitsubishis (Sallys) appeared to be headed for Kunming and were then about sixty miles away. Chennault immediately ordered Newkirk and three others of his Panda Bear squadron up to protect the field. As soon as Newkirk sighted the enemy formation, he radioed Chennault, who then dispatched Sandell and thirteen others to intercept.

Within moments the Flying Tigers and the Japanese met in battle for the first time. The bombers, confident after so many uncontested months, had no fighter escort. The Tigers approached the Sallys from above—the Japanese planes unconcernedly flying in a beautiful flat-V formation. Sandell had spotted "ten enemy two-engined bombers, single tail, aluminum construction—and that red sun on the wing tips." The Tigers, as per Chennault's teaching, attacked in pairs, leaving a "weaver" above to look out for the unexpected appearance of fighters.

At Sandell's signal the dozen P-40s pounced upon the neat Japanese formation. Fritz E. Wolf (Shawano, Wisconsin) "attacked the outside bomber of the V. Diving down below him, I came up underneath, guns ready for the minute I could get in range. At 500 yards I let go with a quick burst from all my guns [four .30 caliber in the wings and two .50s in the upper nose]. I could see my bullets rip into the rear gunner. My plane bore in closer. At 100 yards I let go with a burst into the bomber's gas tanks and engine. A wing folded and a motor tore loose. Then the bomber exploded. I yanked back on the stick to get out of the way and went upstairs. . . ."

Selecting another bomber, Wolf dived down again. Pulling up behind he watched the Japanese rear gunner frantically firing, but felt no hits. He closed in to within fifty yards before letting loose with his full battery of guns, concentrating on one of the Mitsubishi's engines. Flame and smoke wisped into the slipstream, followed by a blossom of fire, and the Japanese bomber was ripped to pieces in a violent orange-red explosion. Wolf kicked rudder and dived away from the massive zone of flame and debris.

The Tigers swooped into the bomber formation from all directions, confusing the gunners but not disrupting the symmetry of the formation itself. Chennault had been right, the Japanese flew almost mechanically. When a bomber fell burning, another plane gracefully moved in to tighten the formation.

In an attack on the formation Edward Rector

Edward Rector of Marshall, North Carolina (in a post-Flying Tiger portrait), flight leader of the 2nd ("Panda Bears") Pursuit Squadron. Rector remained with the Flying Tigers even after it was officially disbanded in 1942.

(U. S. OFFICE OF WAR INFORMATION)

(Marshall, North Carolina) sliced under the Mitsubishis, got one, and took a burst of fire himself. His smoking Tomahawk was last seen by other Tigers under control; obviously Rector was seeking an emergency landing place. There were few of these in the thick jungle below.

Finally, after perhaps twenty minutes or so, with ammunition gone, or guns jammed, the Tigers, excepting Rector, returned to the Kunming base. They had lost one, but the Japanese had lost six, and even some of the remaining four Mitsubishis limped back toward Hanoi trailing smoke. It was a very good score, but Chennault's laconic comment was, "It was a good job . . . next time get them all."

A search party went out to look for Rector but had to return empty-handed when darkness enveloped the jungle. The next morning Rector himself phoned from a nearby town. He had crash-landed the P-40 in the jungle, had somehow managed to

Arvid E. Olson, Jr., Los Angeles, California, squadron leader of the 3rd ("Hell's Angels") Pursuit Squadron, AVG. (U. S. OFFICE OF WAR INFORMATION)

find his way to the town, and was on his way back to Kunming with only minor injuries. The first Tiger encounter with the Japanese had proved an almost total victory. But Chennault cautioned them; the next time there would be fighter escort. But they had learned, too, of the Japanese aircraft's susceptibility to fire because of the lack of self-sealing fuel tanks.

Meanwhile, a thousand miles away in Rangoon, the men of the Hell's Angels fretted, anxious about the presence of the Japanese. Certainly Burma lay in the path of the conquering juggernaut of Japan. The victories at Kunming only galled them more. Finally, on the morning of December 23, 1941, the not very efficient air raid sirens of Rangoon sounded, but after the exciting scramble no bombers appeared in the sky. Before noon the sirens wailed again. Antiaircraft fire was seen bursting irregularly in the sky over Rangoon, and the distant *chunk* of bombs bursting on the ground signaled that the Japanese planes had truly arrived.

At Mingaladon airdrome the Tigers and the RAF roared into action: about twenty-seven Allied aircraft, P-40s and Buffalos, swept up to meet the bombers. The first wave consisted of eighteen bombers and the second of about thirty. The latter was escorted by a large swarm of twenty Zeros.

The Tigers leaped upon the second formation, concentrating upon the bombers, hoping to disrupt their formations before they could release their bomb loads. The British pilots, in their Buffalos, gallantly went for the Zeros. First blood of the bomber formation went to Kenneth Jernstedt (Yamhill, Oregon), who destroyed one of the bombers in his first diving attack. His wingman was Henry Gilbert (Lovell, Wyoming), at twenty-one the youngest of the Flying Tigers. As he dived Gilbert shot out bursts at a couple of bombers, striking them but without hitting vital spots. In the attack, his P-40 was hit by a cannon shell and screamed out of the battle to crash into the jungle below. There had been no parachute and Henry Gilbert was the first Flying Tiger to die in combat.

The second fatality came soon after. Charles Older (Los Angeles) had flared one of the bombers, which burst into an inferno of detonating ammunition and bombs. Neil Martin's (Texarkana, Arkansas) P-40 flew into the spewing mass and followed the wreckage of the bomber to the ground.

Older by then had whirled about to shoot another bomber out of the air, which had become turbulent, fiery, and confused as fighter attacked bomber and fighter attacked fighter. The Zeros joined in the tumbling and soon Tiger Paul Greene (Glendale, California) found himself beset by Zeros. The nimble craft danced around him, firing into the P-40 until the plane took fire. Greene swooped the P-40 onto its back and dropped out of the cockpit. But once his chute had opened, one of the Zeros had flipped around to deal with Greene, dangling helplessly in the chute. Frantically grabbing at the chute risers, Greene managed to avoid the bullets, but the chute itself was holed. As a result Greene landed so forcefully that he injured his spine.

Greene's plane, of course, was lost, as were those of Gilbert and Martin. Another, piloted by George McMillan, was wiped out when he came in for a landing, although he escaped injury. The Tigers, therefore, had lost two men and four aircraft in their first air battle over Rangoon. Five RAF Buffalos, with pilots, had fallen to Japanese guns. The Japanese lost six bombers (probably with five-man crews) and four fighters. It was, then, a victory for the Tigers and the RAF. But Rangoon had been heavily bombed by the first wave of bombers. Fires raged and the toll was high—at least two thousand killed. The looting of corpses and sacking of dwellings in the bombed-out sections of the city somehow seemed more horrifying than the merciless bombing itself. The Burmese harbored little fidelity to the English and loved the Indians and Chinese only a little more.

Two days later, Christmas Day 1941, the Japanese returned. There was scant advance warning, for the single radar unit then operating in Burma was hardly sufficient (to say the least) and was further burdened by out-of-date equipment and an inefficient telephone service.

To circumvent this handicap, Squadron Leader Arvid Olson had put up a trio of P-40s for aerial reconnaissance. George McMillan, who had lost a plane in the battle two days before, sighted a large bomber force approaching Rangoon. About sixty miles from the city, there were about eighty bombers and twenty fighters. McMillan immediately radioed the base; at about the same moment the RAF received its report.

Thirteen P-40s and fifteen Buffalos were rushed aloft in an attempt to gain altitude before the bombers reached the city. About ten miles from Rangoon, the Japanese force divided—about half proceeding on to Rangoon and the rest heading for Mingaladon airdrome. The Tigers dived at the stream heading for the city, leaving the RAF's Buffalos the thirty or so bombers aiming for Mingaladon.

The Tigers, employing Chennault's hit-and-run technique, knifed through the bomber formation at top speed, snapping bursts into the Japanese aircraft and avoiding entanglement with the Zeros as much as possible. Within minutes of their first assault, five Japanese bombers blazed into the rice paddies below. But almost immediately another formation hove into view, this time twenty bombers with eight fighters. There was no lack of targets: a total of 28 Allied planes opposed 108 Japanese bombers and fighters.

Robert Smith (Los Angeles), having dived through the initial formation, had no time to gain altitude, so he attacked the new wave from below. The Nakajima practically blew up in Smith's face, pockmarking his P-40 with bits of engine. The Tomahawk staggered momentarily but Smith got it under control and dived into the battle again. Edmund Overend (Coronado, California) was not as fortunate. Although he had succeeded in ripping the

wing off one of the bombers, he had run into gunfire which jammed his controls and interfered with his maneuverability. A Zero darted onto his tail and Overend had good reason to be grateful for the armor plating which lined the back of the cockpit. Exploiting this safety factor, plus the P-40's diving speed, he left his attacker behind. But then he realized he did not have enough fuel for the return flight to Mingaladon. Rather than abandon the plane, Overend set the P-40, wheels up, into a swamp. Within hours he was back at the airdrome to learn of the battle's outcome.

Of the thirteen Tomahawks which had taken off, eleven had returned to Mingaladon, including one piloted by Parker Dupouy (Farmingdale, New York) with four feet of wing gone. When his guns jammed, Dupouy had a Zero on his tail. Kicking the P-40 around abruptly, Dupouy rid himself of the harassing fighter by colliding with it. The Zero collapsed and fell, but Dupouy made it back to the base.

Like Overend, George McMillan had been knocked out of the battle but had crashed into the jungle and returned on the following day, nursing an injured ankle, in an oxcart. In exchange for the two P-40s, the Tigers were officially credited with destroying thirteen bombers and ten fighters. Other Japanese aircraft had also been destroyed but fell into the Gulf of Martaban and could not be confirmed. The RAF pilots were credited with six bombers and the thwarting of serious damage to the base. The cost to No. 67 Squadron was five pilots and their Buffalos. The total Japanese loss was at least twenty-nine aircraft, most of them bombers, or about a third of the attacking force. It was a most disproportionate exchange.

However, the Christmas Day bombing of Rangoon proved even more vicious than that of December 23, the casualty toll reaching as high as five thousand dead. But Japanese losses impressed the enemy and large bomber formations stayed away from Rangoon for a while. During this uneasy period thousands fled the city, causing near paralysis of its functions and vital services—including the movement of supplies up to the Burma Road. But in time a local paper could announce a return to near normality with: "Daylight robberies have started again."

During the lull Olson's 3rd Squadron was relieved

Pilots race for their P-40s. (These are not, of course, Flying Tigers, but the base is in China and re-creates the action of a Tiger interception.) (U. S. AIR FORCE)

by Newkirk's 2nd (Panda Bear) Squadron, which arrived at Mingaladon by December 29, 1941. The Japanese bombers and fighters came back in force on the same day. Again a handful of Tigers in their P-40s and the British in their lumbering Buffalos rose to meet the formations, which as on Christmas Day split in two to strike at both Rangoon and Mingaladon. The bombers this trip, however, succeeded in getting to the air base in addition to contributing to the panic and waste in Rangoon. But again the losses for the Japanese were off balance, the Tigers claiming eighteen and the British seven. One P-40 flown by Allen Christman (Fort Collins, Colorado) was lost in the encounter, but Christman parachuted to safety. The RAF lost six pilots with their planes. By this time the Americans had begun to appreciate the ruggedness of the P-40s and no longer envied the British in their Buffalos.

Burma had become an aerial thorn in the side to the Japanese. All other aerial battlefields—over the Philippines, Malaya, Hong Kong—were dominated by Japanese bombers and the superb Zero fighters. Only the "American renegades" and a squadron of the RAF Buffalos (rapidly depleting) seemed capable of spoiling the succession of Japanese victories.

The Japanese closed the year with a change in tactics. First a small formation came over to lure off the Tigers and the RAF, and then a larger formation would follow at about the time the defenders would have to return to the ground to refuel and rearm. There was more concentration also on Mingaladon. On the first attempt seventeen Allied planes were dispatched to fend off about sixty Japanese attackers. Fifteen of these, officially, did not return to their base at Hanoi.

By January 1, 1942, the Flying Tigers had sixty confirmed victories to their credit. It prompted a tribute to them, and to Chennault, via Radio Tokyo: "We warn the American aviators at Rangoon that they must cease their unorthodox tactics immediately, or they will be treated like guerrillas and shown no mercy whatsoever." Radio Tokyo also inflated the forces of the AVG—man and planes; the victory claims over them, if true, would have wiped out Chennault's small band three or four times over.

But they were not supermen. At besieged Rangoon hunger was added to their other discomforts, among which were fatigue and illness. And they contributed further to their fame as "no angels" in the bars of Rangoon, which seemed more impervious to the ill fortunes of war than most other businesses. It became a tiresome war, almost without purpose and without hope of victory. To the men in Burma it seemed obvious that their fate was but a secondary consideration in the larger strategies. Supplies, tools, materials of all kinds only trickled in. Their P-40s before long had become a patchwork of scraps. Engines, rejects to begin with, wheezed and smoked and maintenance became a heroic epic in itself.

The truth was that the China-Burma-India theater of operations did rank low on the priorities lists. Churchill and Roosevelt had met and resolved that the major enemy was Nazi Germany and that first considerations in terms of strategic thinking, men, and supplies would be devoted to that philosophy. The Pacific, meanwhile, was subsidiary, with the beleaguered China-Burma-India area at the bottom of the list. Even those supplies that were eked out for delivery on the Burma Road often were intercepted en route and "requisitioned" by other services and areas.

It was then with a feeling of being neglected stepchildren that the Flying Tigers took to the air day after day to fight overwhelming numbers of Japanese. Though they fought remarkably, miraculously well, the end, so far as Burma was concerned, was inevitable. Unknown to the Tigers, the political situation would affect them. Churchill had hoped to reinforce the British garrisons in Burma but to his

David L. "Tex" Hill of Hunt, Texas, squadron leader of the "Panda Bears" (2nd). Hill's score was more than a dozen Japanese aircraft.
(U. S. OFFICE OF WAR INFORMATION)

bitterness he was refused an Australian division which he had wanted to send to Burma. This left a Burmese army to confront the surging Japanese.

Late in December, Chiang Kai-shek, realizing what a Japanese invasion of Burma would mean to the Burma Road, offered to send Chinese troops to help in its defense. But Sir Archibald Wavell, the commander in Burma, demurred. He had no love for Chiang and little confidence in Chinese troops. He had other complexities, for the Burmese resented and detested the British as well as the Chinese, believing that such allies were a greater threat than the bringers of the Greater East Asia Co-Prosperity Sphere.

The Tigers, too, with the New Year, changed their tactics: they went over to the offensive. On January 3, 1942, John Newkirk led Noel Bacon (Randalia, Iowa) and David Hill (Hunt, Texas; Hill was, naturally, called "Tex") on a strafing mission. Leaving Mingaladon while it was still dark, the three Tigers swept in upon the Japanese base at Tak, Thailand (about two hundred miles east and slightly north of Rangoon). But as Newkirk gunned the Japanese planes parked along the runways, about a half-dozen enemy fighters, already air-borne, tumbled out of the clouds upon the attacking Tigers. One of the Japanese fighters attached itself to Newkirk's tail as he, unaware of it, hammered at the grounded aircraft. Bacon came to his leader's aid and began shooting at the plane shooting at Newkirk. In turn, Bacon was attacked and Tex Hill swooped in to his aid. Another Japanese fighter joined the train as Newkirk, leading a formation of shooting aircraft, gave his full attention to strafing the men and planes on the ground. So intent was he on his "work" that he was still unconscious of the drama unfolding in his wake. Bacon shot the fighter off Newkirk's tail and Hill cleared Bacon's tail and whipped around to destroy another Japanese fighter. Hill, however, had his share of problems, for a fuel tank had been punctured in such a manner that it did not seal and he was losing gas; in addition he was out of ammunition. Hill had to streak for home while Newkirk and Bacon continued strafing Tak. Soon they too pulled away and flew westward.

Upon landing at Mingaladon, they were greeted by Hill, who congratulated Newkirk upon his flying skill, which had so frustrated the Japanese fighter

James H. Howard, St. Louis, Missouri, squadron leader at one time of the "Panda Bears"; Howard later transferred to the Ninth Air Force in Europe (when this photograph was taken). (U. S. AIR FORCE)

on his tail over Tak. Newkirk found this unbelievable until he checked the tail section of the Tomahawk and found more than twenty bullet punctures in it.

While the three Tigers had been strafing Tak, others had intercepted a large formation of Japanese fighters near Rangoon. Two had gone down in an early attack, but five of them concentrated on Allen Christman's P-40. The deadly cross fire shredded the plane's rudder and ripped out an aileron. The plane lurched out of control so that Christman was for the second time forced to jump. But the Japanese, who so heartily condemned the "unorthodox tactics of the American renegades," were not finished with Christman. They bore down on him as he floated under his chute, gunning him as they flashed by. Seeing this, George Paxton (Abilene, Texas) rushed in to aid the helpless Christman. Although he succeeded in driving off the Japanese fighter, in the encounter Paxton was wounded in the arms and legs and had to leave for the base.

The other Tigers, infuriated by the attack upon Christman, attacked the remaining Japanese so ferociously that they drove them off. But this was only a temporary reprieve for Christman. Twenty days later—January 23, 1942—he was once again forced to leave his seriously damaged Tomahawk during an air battle and was later discovered dead in a rice paddy. He and his parachute were riddled.

Early in January, probably because of the mauling their formations took, the Japanese introduced another innovation: night bombing. None of the aircraft at Mingaladon were equipped for night flying, so the Japanese bombers came over, took careful aim, enjoyed a fine bomb run, and generally ranged over Rangoon unmolested. The only antiaircraft fire of any consequence came from the warships in the river—and these guns were of little use above three thousand feet. On January 8 an attempt was made to intercept the bombers, but it was a vain attempt. Also, in trying to land in the dark, Peter Wright, blinded by gushing hydraulic fluid from a damaged landing gear, lost control of the Tomahawk. The plane veered off the runway and skidded into a parked car. Wright was not seriously injured but Kenneth Merritt, who had been asleep in the vehicle, died in the flaming wreckage.

It was the day's second loss, for during a strafing attack upon Meshot airdrome, Charles Mott's Tomahawk, evidently hit by ground fire, streaked flame. Mott parachuted to safety—and imprisonment for the duration.

The next day's strafe proved more successful. Newkirk and four other Tigers, accompanied by six RAF Buffalos, paid a return visit to Tak. When all planes pulled away safely they left behind at least two dozen burned Japanese aircraft, three burned-out trucks, and a pocked, windowless administration building.

In mid-January Chennault sent reinforcements from Kunming. Robert Sandell flew down with five others of the 1st Squadron; among these was Gregory Boyington. Shortly after, an additional eight men flew in to bring relief to the exhausted men of 2nd Squadron.

Boyington was happy to be away from Kunming, where he had not endeared himself to Chennault's second-in-command, Harvey Greenlaw. Greenlaw's experiences in China, begun in 1932 with the arrival of the unofficial Jouett air mission, no doubt

*P-40s over the unfriendly, mountainous terrain of China,
the "theater of operations" of the Flying Tigers.*
(U. S. AIR FORCE)

made him useful to Chennault. Greenlaw's wife, Olga, was listed on the AVG roster as "War Diary Statistician." According to Boyington, her husband was not very popular with the pilots. He had acquired the rank of lieutenant colonel, in the Chinese Air Force, and had a penchant for threatening one and all with immediate court-martial for minor as well as major breaches in discipline. The Flying Tigers found discipline, except in the air, a most unimportant commodity in their forgotten theater of operations. Boyington could not bring himself to take Greenlaw and his threats seriously either. From time to time he found himself snarling at Greenlaw, "Get lost, Greenlaw, or I'll bend your teeth."

That there were personality problems among the Flying Tigers was of course normal, if not in keeping with the legend of dedication and self-sacrifice to the Cause as propounded in the semifictional newspaper accounts of the time. Considering their living and fighting conditions, it is surprising that they managed to fight at all—let alone not clash from time to time with one another. The Flying Tigers, they themselves would have conceded, had more than

their fair share of mavericks—it was the very nature of the unit. They even, though rarely, had a coward or two. Boyington must be included among the more colorful mavericks.

In his first encounter with the enemy, however, Boyington came away profoundly disappointed with himself. He had taken off as part of a ten-plane formation. Two of the planes, led by veteran Louis Hoffman (San Diego, California), at forty-three the oldest member of the Flying Tigers, served as top cover. The other eight, presumably led by another veteran, were to deal with any Japanese planes. It was too late when Boyington realized they were being led into combat for the first time by one of their own inexperienced number. They then stumbled upon a large formation, perhaps forty or fifty Japanese fighters with fixed landing gears (either Nates or Claudes), within minutes after taking off.

Their formation "leader" blindly led them directly beneath the Japanese planes flying about two thousand feet above them. Between the misled Tigers and the Japanese flew Hoffman and the other pilot, both oblivious to the danger overhead, assuming that the "leader" knew what he was doing.

Boyington, twisting his head, looked up in time to see the Japanese planes begin to peel off to dive

A helping hand: Chinese warn American pilots of the presence of Japanese aircraft in the vicinity. An elaborate if primitive but most effective warning system was devised by Chennault. If he received desultory co-operation from Chinese officials, Chennault was graciously treated by the Chinese people.

(U. S. AIR FORCE)

upon the P-40s. Hoffman's plane took a heavy pounding and fell straight down. The remaining Tigers scattered in all directions, like startled minnows. Suddenly Boyington found himself all alone in a wide, empty sky—except for Japanese fighter planes determined to shoot him out of it. Smarting under the ignominy of it, Boyington put the P-40's diving ability to full use: he ran for his life. Then he relearned something he forgot in the confusion of the moment: never try to outturn a lighter aircraft, or attempt to dogfight with a more maneuverable aircraft. Also, that day Boyington learned something they were not telling the folks back home. The Japanese were very skilled pilots who obviously did not suffer from myopia and could shoot.

Boyington fired at the darting little planes, but did not succeed in knocking one down. The rattle of return fire sounded ominously funereal. The P-40

tossed under the strike of an incendiary shell which came into the cockpit, pinking Boyington's arm—although he was not aware of it at the time. When he landed the shell stuck into his sleeve and had burned his arm slightly. Boyington was so upset by his performance that he hardly found the wound worth mentioning.

Hoffman had crashed near the field and was buried the next day; he had left a wife and two children. The day after that, January 28, 1942, Boyington, having been introduced to the facts of war, went into battle again. He was a member of the same formation, excepting Hoffman of course, that had been in the earlier battle. But this time he came in from above. Still terribly affected by the death of Hoffman, the Tigers fought savagely. Boyington destroyed two planes himself. During the battle he heard a voice over his radio shouting, "This is for

Cokey [Hoffman], you son of a bitch!" Sixteen Japanese aircraft never left the vicinity of Rangoon on that day.

To the residents of Rangoon, particularly the English colony, it was, as Boyington put it bitterly, "a bloody good show." But they lived in a vacuum and on borrowed time. Certain that the Empire would win the last round as it had always, according to tradition, they merely waited for that final day. They were unaware, or seemed to be, that the only battle being won was the small one in the air over Rangoon. On the ground the invading Japanese approached inexorably.

The last bastion of the Burra Sahib was the Mingaladon Golf Club, but even that fell to the invasion of boisterous young pilots, British and American. This was most disturbing, for the youngsters laughed loudly, shouted vulgarly, drank the whisky, and bought up the cigarettes. The managing member was approached by a delegation ordering him to see that the sale of cold beer and cigarettes to "the young roughnecks" be stopped. After all, he was reminded, "the members' needs must be considered first. If we sell our stocks to all these young fellows there'll be nothing left for the members."

The members were in fact running out of everything, including time.

On January 20, 1942, two divisions of the Japanese Fifteenth Army had crossed the Thai frontier at Moulmein; within ten days they had flanked the Indian division defending the area and had taken the city. The Japanese now had a firm foothold in Burma. The handwriting was on the clubhouse wall and the roof about to fall in.

Not until mid-February was it deemed crucial enough to accept Generalissimo Chiang Kai-shek's offer of aid, which took the form of two crack units, the Chinese Fifth and Sixth Armies. But it was already too late, even as they moved southward toward Rangoon. Also arriving too late was Lieutenant General Joseph W. Stilwell, who had been appointed chief of staff to Chiang Kai-shek. The outspoken, fifty-nine-year-old, gruff Stilwell, an expert in Chinese affairs (he spoke and wrote the language), was descending into a political-military miasma. There was little love lost between Chiang Kai-shek (and of course the Madame) and the British, who were, in fact, doing most of the fighting in the theater.

High-level decisions also spelled trouble for Chennault. Plans had already been made to establish a Tenth U. S. Air Force in the China-Burma-India theater with Brigadier General Clayton Bissell in command. The Flying Tigers would, it was proposed, be absorbed into this command as the 23rd Fighter Group. Chennault would then be subordinate to Bissell. Neither Chennault nor Chiang found this ideal. Quickly a feud between Bissell and Chennault developed. Stilwell, soon enough, found himself entangled in it besides developing an antipathy to Chiang and feuding, in turn, with Chennault also.

On February 14, 1942, Stilwell left the United States for this prickly assignment. There being yet no efficient Air Transport Command, his long voyage was confused, miserable, and meandering. On the day his plane took off from Miami for Africa, Singapore, the impregnable, fell to the Japanese. In his diary Stilwell had written, "Events are forcing all concerned to see the vital importance of Burma." By the time Stilwell landed in India, on February 25, the fall of Rangoon—and of Burma—was only days away. Perhaps Burma was of vital importance, but Stilwell had neglected to consider other elements besides Japanese terrorism—namely a crumbling colonialism, feudalism, and the infinite capacity for pettiness among the great.

The state of the tattered Flying Tigers at Rangoon was low too. "Where, oh where is the U. S. Army?" one Tiger noted in his diary. "Where, oh where is General Wavell? Does the First Squadron of the A.V.G. and a few R.A.F. kids have to handle the whole Japanese invasion?" Men as well as machines had begun to wear dangerously. Robert J. Sandell, commander of the 1st Squadron, was killed testing his newly repaired Tomahawk. Robert H. Neale (Seattle, Washington) succeeded Sandell as leader of the Adam and Eves, and now commanded the AVG effort in Burma. His command, in late February, consisted of ten weary pilots, nine overworked ground crew men, and seven wearier P-40s. The British had three Buffalos, four P-40s, and twenty Hurricanes.

The evacuation of Rangoon began in earnest around February 20, 1942, although it had initiated with the first bombings. Now the road to the north and the river were choked with refugees and every description of vehicle. The dacoits (professional thieves) preyed upon the refugees, Burmese as well as British, killing them for their few possessions and money. Rangoon itself was shambles.

O. D. Gallagher described the final blistering days: "With few exceptions the normal civilian population had gone, including the fire-brigade and all municipal employees. The empty streets were patrolled by troops carrying tommy-guns and rifles. The only other inhabitants were criminals, criminal lunatics and lepers."

One civil service officer, having misread his instructions pertaining to the evacuation of Rangoon, had inadvertently released five thousand convicts upon the already afflicted city. "At night," Gallagher recalled, "they made Rangoon a city of the damned. They prowled the deserted streets in search of loot. When they were seen looting they were shot by the soldiers." As for the diseased— "Lepers and lunatics wandered about aimlessly in search of food some sharing pickings of the refuse-heaps with the many mongrel dogs." Fires, set by looters or by the owners of property themselves who did not want the Japanese to take over their homes, raged through the city. Military demolition contributed to the holocaust. Ammunition, fuel, and other supplies which might be put to use by the Japanese went up in smoke. Looters destroyed medical supplies on the docks. It seemed to them there was no possible use for the small bottles except to throw them against walls of buildings. The more volatile liquids exploded and burned wastefully, chokingly, to the gleeful laughter of the now maddened Burmese.

This was the final deranged scene that the few remaining Tigers, the last defenders of Rangoon— for the British had pulled out three days before —witnessed before they scrambled away to a new base at Magwe, farther north. Neale led a formation of the few operational Tomahawks; the rest, pilots and ground crew under crew chief Harry Fox, piled themselves and their equipment into whatever trucks they could commandeer and took to the north road. In one of the last air battles over Rangoon Edward J. Liebolt's plane had been shot up so that he had to take to his parachute. He floated down into captivity, for by then Japanese troops had all but encircled Rangoon.

Rangoon fell on March 7, 1942; at Magwe the Tigers and the RAF dug in. The remnants of the Burma Army escaped up the Irrawaddy River toward Prome. The Chinese armies coming south were still of no help. Chiang and Stilwell had an early disagreement over the disposition of these troops: Chiang believed they should attempt to hold Mandalay; Stilwell thought it would be better to reinforce the British farther south and to keep, if possible, the Japanese from ever getting to Mandalay.

By March 20 reconnaissance planes reported that Japanese planes were already based at Mingaladon. The British quickly dispatched ten old Hurricanes and nine Blenheims to bomb their former base. Arriving unexpectedly the small force succeeded in destroying sixteen planes on the ground and, in the ensuing air battle, a further eleven in the air. Of these, two were knocked down by the Blenheims. It was a blow in the face to the conquering Japanese.

Retaliation came the following day and continued into the next. On the morning of March 21, with but little advance warning, the first wave of ten Japanese bombers, with an escort of twenty fighters, came over Magwe. Five planes rose to meet them, three Tigers (William Reed, Kenneth Jernstedt, and Parker Dupouy) and two Hurricanes. Even as their engines labored to get the five aircraft high enough to meet the attackers, more enemy bombers and fighters came in from the northeast. Bomb bursts erupted on the airdrome as the Tigers dived into the Japanese formations.

Dupouy, on his first pass, slashed a Zero out of a seven-plane formation, only to find himself besieged by the remaining six. These whirred and darted about his P-40 until Dupouy himself was struck. He dived for Magwe. Reed had already suffered the same fate and had returned to the field also. Jernstedt careened into a formation of ten bombers, the guns of which focused on his plane and rapidly sieved it, wounding the pilot. Jernstedt too was forced to return to the doubtful "safety" of besieged Magwe.

Soon, also, one of the Hurricanes came scurrying in, attempted to set down on the bomb-pocked runway, struck a hole, overturned, and came to a grinding crash near a slit trench occupied by some of the Tigers. Frank N. Swartz (Dunmore, Pennsylvania), John Fauth (Red Lion, Pennsylvania), and a ground crew man, William Seiple, scrambled from the trench to pull the British pilot out of the Hurricane. As they ran a bomb explosion caught them and all three went down. Dr. Lewis Richards, surgeon of the Tigers, left the trench to administer to Swartz, who appeared to be injured most seriously. Richards then had Fauth and Seiple pulled into the trench and he, despite the bursting bombs and strafing Zeros, placed Swartz into a jeep and raced to the base hospital. Fauth died the next morning and Swartz and Seiple were evacuated to Calcutta, but Swartz later died of his wounds. Magwe itself was a ruin—besides damage to the buildings and runways, six P-40s, eight Hurricanes and three Blenheims had gone up in smoke.

The next day brought more of the same; remaining at Magwe was pointless. Some of the Tigers flew their flyable aircraft farther north to Loiwing. The RAF remained longer in a vain attempt to hold off the Japanese but they too were quickly overwhelmed. More planes were damaged and five of the surviving P-40s had to be evacuated to Loiwing by truck. The British fled to the west, to Akyab on the Bay of Bengal and eventually to India, out of harm's way, to attempt a recovery. Except for the few impoverished Tigers at Loiwing, it was the end of air power in Burma.

Driven out of Burma, the RAF flew to India and the Tigers returned to Kunming. Chennault then planned a surprise raid on the major Japanese air base at Chiengmai in central Thailand. To accomplish this, Chennault mustered a handful of men and aircraft of the 1st Squadron, led by Robert Neale, and the 2nd Squadron, led by John Van Kuren Newkirk: a total of ten P-40s.

Chiengmai lay beyond the range of the P-40 so the Tigers flew to a nearly deserted advance field at Nam Sang on March 23, and slept that night under the wings of their planes. They had gassed up for a long flight and took off in two sections before daybreak of the twenty-fourth. The plan was to rendezvous near Chiengmai (rather than approach it en masse, which would alert the Japanese) and then swoop down upon the base while it was still dark. The ground would be discernible from the air, though the Tigers' P-40s would be difficult to see from the ground.

For some reason the two groups missed the rendezvous. Neale's small unit of six planes arrived first, but there was no sign of Newkirk and his men. They were unable to wait: both the covering dark-

ness and surprise would be lost. Neale ordered William D. McGarry and Edward Rector up to twenty thousand feet to provide high cover and then, leading Boyington, William Bartling, and Charles Bond, dived on a fine concentration of Japanese aircraft below.

At twelve thousand feet they were met with vicious antiaircraft fire. Plunging through, luckily unhit, the four P-40s, their engines howling and guns chattering, spread fire among the planes and running figures. Flames shot up in their wake as they pulled up, banked, and came in for another pass. Now the field was alight with the fire of burning planes and they could better see their targets. But with more light also came more intense ground fire. Rifle and machine-gun slugs nicked and ripped at the Tomahawks.

To McGarry and Rector, observing the inferno from above, the excitement was too much to ignore. When the original quartet dived in for a third pass, the top-cover men plummeted down to contribute also. With all six guns hammering, the two extra Tomahawks intensified the flaming havoc as they ran the gamut of heavy ground fire. At least twenty fires were burning on the field and Neale knew it was time to get away. As they did the sky puffed with random bursts of antiaircraft.

McGarry obviously was in trouble, for his P-40 trailed smoke as they left Chiengmai. Though he tried desperately to keep the plane in flight, McGarry realized that with rapidly failing oil pressure he had no chance. But they were still fifty miles from the Salween River, inside Thailand. On the other side of the river lay the safety of the Chinese troops, but the oil pressure went completely and McGarry inverted the plane and parachuted into the jungle. (He was captured by the Siamese and turned over to the Japanese and remained a prisoner until the war ended.)

Meanwhile Newkirk, realizing that he and the Panda Bears had missed the rendezvous with the Adam and Eves, decided that they could attack another, nearby field while the 1st Squadron attended to Chiengmai. But they found no aircraft on the satellite airdrome so Newkirk pulled away and headed for Chiengmai also. On the way they strafed a railroad station, setting some warehouses afire. Newkirk then spotted two armored cars on a road. They were tempting targets and so, followed by Henry Geselbracht and Frank Lawlor, Newkirk dived upon the cars with all guns shuddering the P-40. As he shot over the cars, Newkirk's plane suddenly gushed flame. The stricken Tomahawk hurtled into the ground at full speed, trailing fire and molten metal, scorching a trail through the jungle before it came to rest, a blazing mass of crumpled metal. His wingmen found it hard to accept the death of "Scarsdale Jack" Newkirk, who had led the 2nd Squadron from the inception of the Flying Tigers. For miles, as they returned to China, they could see his black funeral pyre curling out of the green jungle of Thailand.

Newkirk's successor as commander of the 2nd

Kweilin, China, the last—and best—major base of the Flying Tigers. It had a mile-long runway, revetments for the protection of parked aircraft, and caves in the hills for men and machines. (U. S. AIR FORCE)

Somewhere in China: Lieutenant General Henry H. Arnold, Brigadier General Claire Chennault, his antagonist Lieutenant General Joseph Stilwell, British Field Marshal Sir John Dill, and Brigadier General Clayton L. Bissell. The latter's position in the China-Burma-India theater was a delicate one since he was placed in com- *mand over the veteran, and favorite of Chiang Kai-shek, Chennault. Bissell's careful attention to details in his planning earned him the nickname of "Old Woman" among the Chinese, accustomed to Chennault's more hell-for-leather approach. (U. S. AIR FORCE)*

Squadron was James H. Howard (St. Louis, Missouri), an ex-Navy pilot of remarkable courage. Soft-spoken, undemonstrative, Howard had made an early impression upon the RAF pilots one day when he singlehandedly plowed into a large formation of Japanese fighters. Howard took his service in the Flying Tigers seriously; he had been born in China.

But they were locked obviously in a losing battle and, despite the Tiger victories, still remarkably disproportionate, the battle had come to seem so aimless. For every Japanese plane destroyed, another ten appeared to take its place. But there were no replacements for the Tigers—and new planes were hard to come by. A few P-40Es (Kittyhawks) had trickled in, but that was all. Exhausted, ill, or depressed, or just simply sickened by conditions, pilots and ground crew men resigned or were "dismissed."

Boyington was one of those who had his fill of fighting for Madame Chiang's China. A six-victory ace, he decided to get out and to have his commission in the Marine Corps reinstated—as had been secretly agreed upon when he signed up for the AVG. Chennault did not take an enlightened view of Boyington's wish to return to his old branch of the service. Boyington left, nonetheless, and worked his way homeward. He found, upon arriving at Karachi, India, requesting transportation by air, that Chennault, instead of authorizing air travel to the United States for Boyington, suggested that the black sheep be drafted into the Tenth Air Force as a second lieutenant. Boyington, steaming, booked passage on a ship bound for New York. His subsequent career in the Marine Corps speaks for itself, though he may have gone on the rolls of the Flying Tigers as a "deserter."

Chennault had other, more serious burdens as

well. The Burma Road was closed (necessitating the flying of supplies over "the Hump" of the Himalaya Mountains between India and China); Chiang Kai-shek and Stilwell detested each other; Madame Chiang demanded more help from the United States, broadly hinting from time to time of making a separate peace with Japan; and then there was Bissell, who would command the Tenth Air Force and Chennault along with it.

Bissell had appeared at Kunming to give a recruiting lecture which proved ill-timed and badly worded. Resentful, morale at low ebb, some of the Tigers trained a young Chinese boy to greet the ever growing number of Air Corps planes carrying brass with the phrase "Piss on Bissell, piss on Bissell." It did not impress Very Important Persons on the arriving aircraft with the state of American military discipline in China.

Chennault and Stilwell too had their disagreements, partly a question of rank (Stilwell being Chennault's superior), as well as the traditional hostility between the ground-oriented soldier and the air expert. Chennault had certainly proved himself, but Stilwell had little faith in the piecemeal air force at his disposal in Burma and China. Crusty and stubborn, he even refused to be evacuated by air from Burma with the Japanese hard on his trail. "The Air Force didn't bring me here," he declared, "and it doesn't have to fly me out. I'll walk." And he did.

"It's the ground soldier," he snapped at Chennault one day, "slogging through the mud and fighting in the trenches who will win the war!"

"But God damn it, Stilwell," Chennault rasped in cogent reply, "there aren't any men in the trenches!"

The men of the Flying Tigers, also, found conditions more and more difficult to take. Dispirited, wearied, repelled by Chinese corruption and indifference to loss of life, they became more disgruntled and found their sacrifices difficult to reconcile with their achievements.

Their relationship with Chennault even deteriorated and at one point, in a disagreement with an order from Chennault (to make a flight over Chinese troops to improve their morale), twenty-eight out of thirty-four Tigers resigned. Whereupon Chennault threatened to have anyone who attempted to leave Loiwing shot. Chennault later reconsidered and the

U. S. Air Force General Henry Arnold visits Chennault in China, shortly after the Flying Tigers had been disbanded. (U. S. AIR FORCE)

resignations were withdrawn, but the mood of the Tigers remained dismal.

It was the irascible Stilwell who summed up the Burma experience: "I claim we got a hell of a beating. We got run out of Burma and it was humiliating as hell. I think we ought to find out what caused it, go back and retake it."

The Tigers, withdrawn to Kunming, existed in military limbo. Their planes were barely operational and some pilots refused to fly them. They speculated upon their future—if any, in the Tenth Air Force. Many only wanted to return to their homes for a while before considering their military future. By May 1942 it seemed that they could contribute so little, with their few planes and exhausted men, to the war in China.

Meanwhile, U. S. Army Air Force brass had also invaded China. Some, men newly from civilian ranks, assumed that the "famous" Flying Tigers were bound to be a "bunch of prima donnas." As the day of contract expirations approached pressure was applied on both pilots and ground crews to transfer over to the U.S. air forces. One particularly arrogant recruitment speech, the gist of which was roughly: "join up now or be drafted a private as soon as your contracts expire," caused a small incident. Many Tigers simply got up and walked out on the high ranker with his mouth open. Such men, fresh from the States, eager to avenge Pearl Harbor, anxious to get on with the war, and undoubtedly a bit envious of the reputation and the actual achievements of the Flying Tigers, could not comprehend the weariness of the Tigers, or their anxiety to get home just once again before "getting on with the war," to recover from nagging illnesses caused by overwork, various tropical diseases, and malnutrition. When disbandment time came they simply wanted to go home for a while.

Radio Tokyo jubilated over the approaching end of the Tigers. A quick dispatch of their replacements in the green Tenth Air Force was joyously predicted by Tokyo Rose. But a transition had been in progress for a long time and the interim would not prove to be as vulnerable a period as Tokyo believed. Chennault was to remain in command of what would be called the China Air Task Force (under Bissell's Tenth Air Force), which would consist of the 23rd Fighter Group and the 11th Bombardment Squadron (M). Chennault had already selected his commander for the 23rd Fighter Group: Colonel Robert Scott. Scott, a Transport Command pilot who had been stranded in China and who had attached himself to the Tigers. Although at thirty-four he was considered overaged for a fighter pilot, Scott had proved himself in fact a "one-man air force" while on missions with the Tigers and on solo hunts.

The bomber squadron was equipped with North American B-25s, the famed Mitchells of the Doolittle Tokyo raid. (Eventually, in March 1943, though not without acrimony and torment, the China Air Task Force evolved into the Fourteenth Air Force, Major General Claire Lee Chennault commanding; the Tenth Air Force then confined its responsibilities to Burma and India.)

The official day of deactivation of the American Volunteer Group was July 4, 1942. By this time it was known that very few of the original Tigers had decided to remain in the China Air Task Force —just five pilots, David Hill, Edward Rector, Charles Sawyer, John G. Bright, and Frank Schiel, Jr., plus a few of the ground crew—that was all. Several pilots, rather than transfer into the U. S. Army, found jobs in China with China National Airways and with aviation industries. Others returned to their homes to rest and then, if they passed their physicals—which many did not—returned to their old branch of service.

Twenty pilots, to confute Radio Tokyo, offered to remain on duty with the 23rd Fighter Group under Scott during the transitional period. During this time one of the veteran pilots, John E. Petach (Perth Amboy, New Jersey), was killed in a dive-bombing attack upon gunboats in a lake near Nanchang. Petach had married Emma Jane Foster (State College, Pennsylvania), who had served, along with Josephine Stewart (Dallas, Texas), as a nurse in the American Volunteer Group.

The 23rd Fighter Group, known also as the Flying Tigers, continued in the tradition of their predecessors in defense of the air route over the Hump (as once the original Tigers had defended the Burma

Robert Scott, ex-transport pilot turned Flying Tiger. During the final days of the AVG Scott roamed the skies with the Tigers or alone and left a pile of Japanese planes in his wake. Scott remained with Chennault to command the 23rd Fighter Group.

(U. S. AIR FORCE)

Men of the 23rd Fighter Group, heirs to the traditions of the Flying Tigers: Colonel C. D. Vincent, Major Albert J. Baumler, Colonel H. E. Strickland, and

Brigadier General Claire L. Chennault, commander of the China Air Task Force (later to form the nucleus of the Fourteenth Air Force). (U. S. AIR FORCE)

Road) and chopped away at Japanese air strength in the China-Burma-India theater. After Scott left for other duties other commanders took over, among them Colonel David Hill, and later, Colonel Edward Rector, of the original AVG.

In the brief span of its operational existence, officially from December 18, 1941, to July 4, 1942, the Flying Tigers had destroyed 286 (confirmed) Japanese aircraft. The true toll would probably be closer to double that number, for many "kills" were not officially accepted when enemy aircraft plunged into thick jungle or water and could not be found. But even the officially accepted figure represents a great loss in terms of planes and men—for most were bombers with multiple crews. The cost to the

AVG was nine pilots (not counting Petach, who was lost after the dissolution of the AVG) and less than fifty P-40s. An additional nine pilots were killed in flying accidents and four were listed as missing in action.

The major contribution of the Flying Tigers, besides proving Chennault's tactical genius, was in the revelation that Japanese aerial invincibility was an illusion. During the early months of the Pacific war, while British and American defenses crumbled, the Flying Tigers, outnumbered, ill equipped, even ill used, but resilient, fought the Japanese and won. That they had done this may have been, in time, even more important than their accredited 286 Japanese aircraft at $500 per head.

3

FIRST SPECIAL AVIATION PROJECT

Man's capacity for "the bold undertaking" is infinite; the romanticism, not the risk, is all. The challenge of unfavorable odds merely increases incentive and, once initiated, the venture is confronted as if success must be the only possible outcome. Risk, motivation, questioning uncertainty—all are submerged in what appears to be the logic of preparation.

So it was with the unique Doolittle raid on Tokyo and other Japanese cities in the spring of 1942, a dismal spring in the wake of a series of Japanese victories in the Pacific. As an expression of human ingenuity, courage, audacity, and daring the Doolittle mission was an immortal feat; as military strategy it was evanescent—but of extensive impact.

Lieutenant Colonel James H. Doolittle, however, on the day after the raid sat dejectedly in the wreckage of the plane that he had had to abandon, certain he would be tried by a military court. All sixteen aircraft which had participated in the attack had been lost; of the eighty men he had led, Doolittle could account for only five. And one of them was himself.

II

To strike back at Japan was all but an obsession in high governmental and military circles in the weeks and months following the Pearl Harbor attack. President Franklin D. Roosevelt rarely missed an opportunity to bring it up during his sessions with the Chiefs of Staff. It was, however, simpler to dwell upon than to execute. There were no land-based bombers near enough to Japan to bomb it. Carriers could not venture near enough to the Japanese home islands to launch their fighters and scout bombers without risking the loss of carriers—as well as the aircraft. However alluring the conception, it appeared to remain impracticable until bases could be established in China, or even Russia. Obviously the Philippines were already lost.

But with all the talk of vengeance in the air, someone was bound to offer some kind of suggestion. This came from the U. S. Navy's Captain Francis S. Low, an operations officer on the staff of Admiral Ernest J. King, Chief of Naval Operations. Low's

Architect of the "First Special Aviation Project," Captain Francis S. Low, operations officer on the staff of Admiral Ernest J. King. Low was the first to offer practical suggestions for activating an idea which a nation shared after the attack on Pearl Harbor: a bombing raid on Tokyo.

(NAVY DEPT., NATIONAL ARCHIVES)

Implementer of the Low concept: Captain Donald W. Duncan, Admiral King's air officer. Duncan proved, on paper and within certain limitations, it was possible to send bombers to bomb Japan.

(NAVY DEPT., NATIONAL ARCHIVES)

idea hinged upon the possibility of finding a long-range medium Army bomber which could take off from the deck of a carrier. Thus could a striking force be launched beyond the danger zone around Japan, keeping the vulnerable carrier out of the reach of bombers. This was an impetuous, perhaps quixotic, but appealing conception—even to the hardheaded King. He sent Low to see his air officer, Captain Donald W. Duncan, on the following day, a Sunday, to explore the probabilities further. King also cautioned Low to speak to no one else of the idea.

The two men met on January 11, 1942. Duncan immediately rejected one aspect of the idea. No bomber, not even a medium, could possibly land on a carrier deck. They required a long runway

and did not come equipped with arrester hooks for carrier landings. But it was possible that such a bomber, fueled and bombed-up, could take off from a carrier, complete its mission, and (thanks to its range) continue on to bases on land.

The plane Duncan had in mind was the North American B-25 (Mitchell), and the carrier, the recently commissioned *Hornet*. He would, however, need to work out the details before offering any real suggestions. Five days later Duncan emerged with thirty handwritten pages (the subject matter being too sensitive to entrust to a secretary for typing) of closely reasoned computations. Weather, winds, range, bomb loads, fuel, number of aircraft, minimum take-off run, and a dozen other complexities had been carefully worked out by Duncan.

Admiral King, who was not easily impressed, *was* impressed with Duncan's work. He then ordered Low and Duncan to approach Lieutenant General Henry H. Arnold, Commanding General of the Army Air Forces, with the idea. He saw them on the next day, January 17, and the subject of their visit must have proved a bit startling to Arnold. On January 4, 1942, for example, he had composed a memorandum upon returning from a White House meeting, part of which read: "We will have to try bomber take-offs from carriers. It has never been done before but we must try out and check on how long it takes." (This was relative to the coming invasion of north Africa and not to an attack upon Japan, however.) The memo went to the War Plans Division of the Army Air Forces for study, but before Arnold had heard from his staff, here were two Navy men confronting him with the idea and assuring him it could be done.

Arnold was most enthusiastic over the idea and promptly called King to settle the division of responsibility and to get things under way. King selected Captain Duncan as the Navy co-ordinator and Arnold agreed to provide a man to undertake the Air Force's end of the project. This was not difficult —the one man who had the flying skill, the technical background, and a love of derring-do was James H. Doolittle of Arnold's staff. One of the great aviation pioneers, Doolittle combined aerial swashbuckling with scholarship. He had received several trophies for breaking records in speed flights, for aerobatics, and for more scientific contributions such as taking off, flying, and landing a plane without ever seeing out of the plane's cockpit. He had served in the Army Air Corps and had a Doctor of Science degree from the Massachusetts Institute of Technology. Resigning from the Air Corps in 1930 (he had enlisted in 1917), Doolittle became manager of the aviation department of the Shell Oil Company. He was recalled to active duty, with the commission of major, in July 1940. Doolittle's job was to work with the auto industries then converting to defense industries. Early in 1942 he was called to Washington to serve on Arnold's staff as a special trouble shooter. One of his first problems was the myth of the "Widow Maker," the pilot's name for the Martin B-26 (Marauder). Doolittle proved that this fast, effective medium bomber was no killer and that pilots properly trained could handle it. He had just about

completed this assignment when Arnold called him into his office to ask an odd question.

"Just what airplane," he began, "have we got that will get off in five hundred feet with a two thousand bomb load and fly two thousand miles?"

No maker of snap judgments, Doolittle informed his chief he would have to give the problem some consideration. Upon returning the following day he told Arnold that either one of two planes just might do it. The Douglas B-23 or the North American B-25 with modifications seemed the most likely.

Arnold offered one more condition. "The plane must take off from a narrow area not more than seventy-five feet wide."

"Well," Doolittle told him, "then the only answer is the B-25. It has a sixty-seven-foot wing span."

The man selected by General Arnold to lead the raid on Tokyo: James H. Doolittle, here standing beneath the nose of a Martin "Marauder," which he had proved was an outstanding aircraft. (U. S. AIR FORCE)

The span of the B-23 spread to ninety-three feet, much too wide for a carrier deck.

Only then did Arnold tell Doolittle what it was all about. He and King had agreed that a Navy task force would move out with the bombers around the first of April. Doolittle was to train the crews and supervise whatever modifications might be required which could enable the B-25s to take off a carrier deck, say within four or five hundred miles off Japan, bomb various military targets, and continue on to land bases in China or Russia.

Doolittle, characteristically, went into immediate action. He flew to Wright Field, near Dayton, Ohio, to confer with Brigadier General George C. Kenney, commander of the Air Corps Experimental Division and Engineering School. Kenney and his staff were given the task of preparing the B-25B aircraft for a mission about which they knew absolutely nothing. However, they too attacked the problem of designing new fuel tanks, bomb shackles, and other innovations for the planes. Soon after Doolittle wrote a memo to Arnold: "The work of installing the required additional tankage is being done by Mid-Continent Airlines in Minneapolis. All production and installation is progressing according to schedule and the 24 airplanes (6 spares) should be completely converted by March 15th."

At the same time other work progressed. By the end of January Brigadier General Carl Spaatz, then serving as Arnold's deputy for intelligence, had furnished a list of ten likely target cities, among which were Tokyo, Yokohama, Kobe, and Nagoya. As for the Navy's role Captain Duncan had arranged for the *Hornet* to be in San Francisco by April 1. Near Norfolk, on February 2, Duncan had stood with Captain Marc A. Mitscher, commander of the *Hornet,* to observe an experiment. The day before, two Army B-25s were hoisted aboard and after being taken out to sea the two Mitchells, piloted by Lieutenants John E. Fitzgerald and James F. McCarthy, proved that a two-engined medium bomber could indeed be flown off the deck of an aircraft carrier.

Admiral Chester A. Nimitz, Commander in Chief, Pacific Fleet (left), who approved of the Special Avia-tion Project and assigned Vice-Admiral William Halsey (right) and the carrier Enterprise *to the mission.* (NATIONAL ARCHIVES)

Upon accomplishing this epochal feat, the two young pilots, mystified, returned to their landlocked base wondering why they had done what they had done.

Duncan later flew out to Hawaii to meet with Admiral Chester W. Nimitz, Commander in Chief, Pacific Fleet, and to arrange for more hands. Nimitz, who approved of the project, assigned Vice-Admiral William Halsey to it, thus adding a second carrier, the *Enterprise,* to the armada. Before he left for San Francisco to confer with Mitscher (and finally to tell him what it was all about), Duncan wired Arnold: *Tell Jimmy to Get on His Horse.* It was the signal for Doolittle and his crews to head for California.

Doolittle had begun assembling his crews immediately after initiating the modification program on the B-25s. All crews came from the three squadrons of the 17th Bombardment Group and its cognate, the 89th Reconnaissance Squadron. These units were not special, hand-picked combat veterans (although some had had experience with dealing with submarine patrols); they were simply the most experienced with the relatively new Mitchell bomber. In other words, they were not an elite unit, but a typical Air Force assemblage of men. However, upon being informed that volunteers were needed for a very hazardous but most important mission, the response was overwhelming. From these volunteers twenty-four crews were mustered and, under Major John A. Hilger (who was C.O. of the 89th Squadron and selected by Doolittle as his second-in-command), reported in at Eglin Field, Florida, by the first of March.

The B-25s to which these crews were assigned were not the planes they had known before. The fuselage interior looked like a Rube Goldberg invention and was crowded with extra fuel tanks in the bomb bay, in the crawlway between sections of the plane, and later even in the position where a belly turret had been originally installed. This lower turret gave so much trouble that Doolittle remarked, "A man could learn to play the violin good enough for Carnegie Hall before he could learn to fire that thing." The malfunctioning, jamming lower turret was pulled out to make room for a sixty-gallon collapsible rubber fuel tank. The one remaining turret, however, would plague the mission with its vagaries, and the added fuel tanks and fittings with theirs.

To save weight the large radios were removed; with radio silence essential the heavy radios would be of no use. For protective firepower the B-25 now had only the twin .50 machine guns in the upper turret and a single .30 in the nose. There had been no tail guns, an oversight attended to by Captain Charles Ross Greening, the mission's gunnery and bombing officer, who fashioned fake twin .50s from broomsticks, painted black and protruding menacingly from the tail. It was hoped these would be enough to discourage attack from the vulnerable rear.

Greening also contrived an ingenious bombsight. The famed Norden sight would not be of any use at the low altitude at which the attack was to be carried out; besides, the Air Force had little desire to risk so valuable an instrument upon so risky a mission. One at least would have been bound to have fallen into enemy hands. Therefore Greening devised a simple gadget, which he called the "Mark Twain," from about twenty cents worth (in 1942) of metal, which proved to be more accurate at the proposed fifteen-hundred-foot bombing altitude than the Norden.

On March 3 Doolittle arrived at Eglin and to an assembly of puzzled airmen said, "My name is Doolittle. I've been put in charge of the project you men have volunteered for. It's a tough one and it will be the most dangerous thing any of you have ever been on. Any man can drop out and nothing will ever be said about it."

Stressing the need for complete secrecy, Doolittle would not reveal to them the nature of their mission or their targets. They would have to follow him blindly and hope for the best—or drop out, as he had offered.

Then their special training began. This was characterized by another rather curious touch, the crews thought. Lieutenant Henry L. Miller, USN, an instructor from the Pensacola Naval Air Station, had come to teach them how to lift a heavily loaded B-25 off the ground within an impossibly short distance. This would require pulling the B-25 up in a dangerously near-stall attitude after a take-off run of about five hundred feet, about one tenth the distance they had been originally trained to use. But with few exceptions, under Miller's tutelage, they learned. Soon twenty-four pilots could yank the B-25 into the air, its tail wheel all but scraping the

Henry L. Miller, an instructor at Pensacola Naval Air Station who was given the job of teaching U. S. Army Air Force pilots how to take off from a carrier deck with a heavily laden bomber. (U. S. NAVY)

ground, some within less than four hundred feet.

While the pilots learned short-run take-offs, other crew members practiced their specialties. It became appallingly obvious that most gunners had never fired a weapon before, nor had any ever operated a power turret. The turrets proved to be consistently troublesome and required so much repair and adjustment that the crews had very little time for actual gunnery practice in flight. Another source of trouble was the auxiliary fuel tanks, which developed leaks. Engines and carburetors were finely adjusted for the most economic fuel consumption— this could mean the difference between landing in the sea or on land.

Simulated bomb runs were practiced over the Florida coast. The B-25s came in from the ocean at low level, skimming housetops, dodging trees, and sweeping under telephone wires. In dropping prac-

tice bombs, they found that Greening's "Mark Twain" sight worked very well.

About mid-March Doolittle became concerned with his part in the mission. Would Arnold pull him out once he had completed the modifications and the crew training? Having come so far, Doolittle wished to go all the way. He flew to Washington hoping to get Arnold's permission to lead the attack. This might not prove to be easy. Doolittle was forty-five, twice the age of most of the pilots on the mission, and he was an irreplaceable member of Arnold's staff. Still Doolittle, applying what he later called "my sales pitch," gave it a vigorous try. He produced every possible reason for leading the mission, all but swamping Arnold with words. In self-defense, Arnold simply passed the buck.

"OK, Jimmy," he managed to wedge in a word, "it's all right with me provided it is all right with Miff Harmon" (Major General Millard F. Harmon, Arnold's Chief of Staff).

Whereupon Doolittle shot into Harmon's office, where he pulled off an ancient ploy in the repertory of every boy whoever talked his parents into giving him something neither really wanted him to have.

"Miff," Doolittle began as soon as his foot was in the door, "I've just been to see Hap and gave him my report on this project I've been working on. I told him I wanted to lead the mission and he said it was OK with him if it's OK with you." Arnold had, of course, counted upon Harmon to say no. But "Miff was caught flat-footed, which is what I intended," Doolittle recalls. Harmon could only answer, "Sure, Jimmy, whatever is all right with Hap is all right with me. Go ahead."

Doolittle went, pausing only long enough outside Harmon's door to hear him explaining to Arnold why *he* had given Doolittle permission to lead the Tokyo raid. Before Arnold caught him to countermand the consent, Doolittle hurried back to Eglin. Not until the *Hornet* had put out to sea was Doolittle absolutely certain that he would lead the mission.

Shortly after Duncan's suggestion that he get on his horse came through, on March 23 twenty-two B-25s took off the landing strip at Eglin for the last time; two others, training casualties, remained behind. Three days later all aircraft arrived safely at McClellan Field, near Sacramento. It was here that the final inspections and adjustments were to be made before the final fifteen planes would put out to sea aboard the *Hornet*.

Doolittle ran the gamut of annoyances at McClellan. The Sacramento Air Depot employed a number of civilians, along with the Army men, as maintenance personnel. None were aware of the pressures upon Doolittle—nor were the civilians particularly impressed with military demands. Suddenly, literally out of the clear blue sky, they had received twenty-two tampered-with B-25s with a little man in charge demanding immediate attention. The crews made a point of sticking together and remaining aloof from the people on the base (a security measure, though mistaken as snobbishness by base personnel). When it became apparent that things were moving too slowly despite his admonitions, Doolittle called Arnold, who managed to stir up some action from Washington. It did not add to Doolittle's popularity.

New propellers, painted black for protection from salt air and water, were to be installed. The crazy tubing of the auxiliary fuel tanks was to be checked. But, Doolittle cautioned, nothing was to be removed

Marc A. Mitscher, captain of the Hornet *and host to Doolittle's Tokyo raiders.*

from the planes, nor were any mechanical settings to be changed. In spite of this there was still margin for well-intended error. One day Doolittle caught a mechanic revving up an engine and backfiring it. That was bad enough, but then the mechanic explained that the carburetors had been "checked, found way out of adjustment and fixed up." Some, as those on the plane he was revving up, had even been changed. The hairline adjustments on the engines made at Eglin now amounted to nothing.

Doolittle stormed and raged, but it was too late to begin a new series of adjustments at McClellan. Doolittle had his own crews try to put the engines back into shape. By this time the men of the "First Special Aviation Project" were quite unpopular around McClellan Field, with Doolittle, otherwise a most genial and friendly type, leading the list. The consensus was that they were all a bunch of "jokers," had odd ideas on how a B-25 should be maintained, and were not quite right in the head.

On April 1 Doolittle was ordered to fly the planes to the Alameda Air Station, not far from McClellan Field. As he was about to climb into his plane he was given a form to sign, a typical Army paper necessary to the clearance of his aircraft. The form invited comment upon the work done at McClellan.

Doolittle took the form and wrote a single word across the face of it: "Lousy."

"Just a minute, sir," the base operations officer stammered. "You must fill in a detailed report. This won't do."

"I haven't got time," Doolittle answered, jumped into the plane, and took off.

John Hilger, his executive officer, stood nearby grinning. The disgruntled base officer came over to him saying, "He has no clearance to leave this base and I won't sign it. . . . Who does he think he is? . . . I'll tell you one thing: your colonel is heading for a lot of trouble."

"He sure is," Hilger concurred. Doolittle invariably found trouble.

III

At Alameda the Navy took over the B-25s, attached them to "donkeys," and towed them to the pier to be hoisted by crane to the flight deck of the *Hornet*. Their crews, all of them graduates—including Doolittle himself—of Captain Henry Miller's special training course, had been selected as the top of their class of the twenty-two flight teams. Doolittle took over the plane of Captain Vernon L. Stinzi, who had become sick. Ultimate selection of the crews was left by Doolittle to his staff and to Miller.

All fifteen Mitchells, as had been originally planned, were aboard when Doolittle scanned the deck and thought perhaps there was room for one more. He suggested to Mitscher that an extra bomber be brought aboard. Once they were out to sea it could be flown off and sent back. It seemed a good idea, even if only to demonstrate to the crews that it could be done. None of them, including Doolittle, had actually done it. "It would give them a lot of confidence," Doolittle offered. Mitscher ordered a sixteenth B-25 lifted aboard. Their Navy instructor, Lieutenant Henry Miller, was then all but kidnapped in order to serve as copilot for the extra Mitchell. Besides Miller, there were also seventy officers and sixty-four enlisted men of the Army Air Forces as guests of the Navy. The *Hornet* pulled out of the harbor at ten-eighteen in the morning (in broad daylight) on Thursday, April 2, 1942. Still no one aboard, except Doolittle, Mitscher, and Miller, knew where they were heading.

There was no little uneasiness among the espionage-conscious aircrews as Task Group 16.2 steamed under the Golden Gate and Oakland bridges in full view of motorists above. It would take little military intelligence to gather that something was afoot: a carrier, three cruisers, four destroyers, and a tanker. The carrier was the oddest sight, with a number of large planes (not carrier planes obviously) lashed to the aft end of the flight deck.

Later that afternoon Mitscher announced over the ship's loudspeaker: "This force is bound for Tokyo." At the same instant the word was flashed to the other ships in the group. Great cheers resounded over the waters as the ships plowed ahead. Morale could not have been better, nor could the relationship—co-operative and considerate—which developed between airmen and seamen. To avenge Pearl Harbor, whatever the risks, was exhilarating and above all the most desirable objective of the war at that moment.

Soon after, the deadly business of preparation got under way. Target folders were distributed and vari-

The flight deck of the Hornet *with an unusual cargo, U. S. Army Air Force B-25Bs on the way to bomb Tokyo. Two of the escorting destroyers bring up the rear.* (U. S. AIR FORCE)

ous targets were assigned to the five three-plane elements. It was decided to keep the extra B-25. Doolittle would open the attack with his single plane approaching Tokyo at around dusk to bomb the Shiba Ward, an industrial section, about three hours before the other bombers followed. The fires laid by Doolittle's bombs would serve as beacons for the others. Lieutenant Travis Hoover would follow with the first element to bomb factories, warehouses, and gas and chemical installations in northern Tokyo; Captain David M. Jones's second element would concentrate on oil storage tanks, power stations, and several factories in an area to the north of the Temple of Heaven, the Emperor's palace (which was declared off limits as a target). Captain Edward J. York's element was to hit factories and power stations in the southern Tokyo area bordering on Yokohama. Captain Charles Ross Greening's element was given targets in Yokohama proper, with concentration on the dock areas and the Navy Yard. The fifth element, Major John A. Hilger leading, would fan out over the coast and hit targets assigned in Nagoya, Kobe, and Osaka.

Such a distribution would in a sense diffuse the effectiveness of the attack; they could hardly hope to erase an important industry from Japan's war-making potential. They would do some damage, but

The sixteenth, and last, B-25 with its aft section jutting over the Hornet's *fantail. It was this aircraft's propeller that during the takeoffs injured Navy man Robert Wall.*
(U. S. AIR FORCE)

most of that would be to the morale of the people of Japan, who had been assured that their home islands would never be touched by the enemy.

The task group steamed toward the scheduled rendezvous with Task Group 16.1, Halsey's group with the *Enterprise,* on Sunday, April 12. Halsey's return to Pearl Harbor, however, was held up by storms so that the rendezvous was delayed by one day. The days at sea were devoted to sessions with Doolittle on procedure. The crews checked and re-checked their planes. The Navy furnished an intelligence officer, Lieutenant Commander Stephen Jurika, who lectured the crews on the Orient and Orientals. Commander Apollo Soucek, air officer of the *Hornet,* reviewed the subject of carrier takeoff and carrier operations. Until the actual takeoff, therefore, none of the crews would have ever taken off a carrier, nor would they have ever seen a B-25 lifted off a carrier. This did not seem to worry the crews, particularly the pilots.

Commander Frank Akers found the pilots ". . . a carefree, happy group [who] seemed little concerned as to the danger of their mission or what might happen to them if they were shot down over Japan." They were, Akers found in lecturing them on navigation, quite inattentive. Their major prob-

lem was getting the plane off the deck—the rest of the mission would follow in due course.

The still inexperienced gunners managed to get in some practice from the *Hornet's* deck by shooting at kites, the closest they were to come to shooting at an air-borne target until they would be in combat.

Each plane was to carry four five-hundred-pound bombs, in most cases three demolition and one incendiary. In the discussions on bombing Doolittle told them, "You are to look for and aim at military targets only, such as war industries, shipbuilding facilities, power plants and the like." He stressed again that the Emperor's Imperial Palace was to be untouched and that they should keep their bombs out of residential areas.

There still remained the question of where they would land after they had completed their missions. Doolittle had left the United States believing that this problem had been solved, but in truth it was not; also, because of the strict radio silence, it was not possible to inform him of this hitch. In the early stages of the mission's planning negotiations had got under way with both China and Russia. The reaction from both was not encouraging. Russia, despite the tantalizing offer of fifteen only slightly used B-25s on lend-lease, refused upon learning that they were to bomb Japan first. Still at peace with Japan, Russia did not want to become involved with such a project.

Chiang Kai-shek was hardly more co-operative. He was given the merest gist of the First Special Aviation Project, just the fact that Japan was to be bombed. Nothing about how or when. This was for a very good reason: military information in China, including that of Chiang's staff, became Japanese property with disconcerting speed. Chiang offered two objections, suggesting that the mission be delayed. First, he reasoned that the bases being requested for use for American bombers were too close to Japanese-held territory. Second, he feared reprisals upon the Chinese if Japan were attacked. It was a curious point of view, considering the years of "reprisals" which had already been inflicted upon the Chinese. However, his fears were not without foundation, as the aftermath of the mission would prove.

Unknown to Doolittle and his men, therefore, no actual preparations were being made for their arrival as they pored over their target folders at sea.

Aircrews, Doolittle, and Mitscher (left foreground) assemble on the deck of the Hornet *in mid-Pacific.*
(U. S. NAVY)

The verbiage between Chungking and Washington became increasingly frigid. Chiang strongly believed that the aircraft could be better employed against Japanese bases in Burma. But by this time, Washington informed him, it was too late to cancel the mission. By mid-April, Chiang, after frequent changes of mind, gave halfhearted permission for arrangements to be made to receive the B-25s in China. A number of forward bases would be furnished with radios to send out a beam to guide the planes to land; there they would be refueled and flown deeper into China—to Chungking.

IV

Halsey's delay in returning to Pearl Harbor had no effect upon the mission. He left Hawaii, flying his flag on the *Enterprise,* commanded by Captain George D. Murray, on April 8. Halsey's group consisted of a carrier, two cruisers, four destroyers, and a tanker. In addition, two submarines patrolled the areas in advance of and to the flanks of the two groups, which on April 13 merged as Task Force 16 under the command of Halsey.

By this time the Japanese had been aware of an impending action for five days. They had monitored radio signals between Mitscher, Halsey, and Pearl Harbor and could conjecture that a fairly large-scale operation was in the making. It was even surmised that an attack upon Japan itself would take place, the guess being that it would occur around April 14. The radio silence which then descended upon TF 16 threw off that prediction and the Japanese relaxed somewhat, although never completely.

Combined Fleet Headquarters in Tokyo ordered a concentration of naval aircraft from the 26th Air Flotilla into the Tokyo area. The vast network of picket boats, most of them onetime fishing boats, ringing the eastern approach to Japan were alerted. These picket boats, equipped with radios, operated about 650 to 700 miles offshore, beyond the range of carrier-borne aircraft. They could warn of the approach of enemy carriers long before the planes might be launched. Although expecting some form of early warning system, the Americans were not aware of the extent of this floating picket line. Meanwhile, in Tokyo, certain of its efforts, Combined Fleet Headquarters sensed no need for alarm.

Task Force 16 surged due west at sixteen knots for five days (losing Tuesday, April 14, on crossing the International Date Line) without incident. The *Enterprise* maintained a screen of fighters and scout-bombers on combat air patrol, weather permitting—and the weather turned foul. It was as if the theme of the Pearl Harbor attack had returned. Ships tossed and rolled and refueling became a dangerous essential operation. One man was thrown overboard but was pulled from the sea by one of the destroyers. (To this extent the theme varied from the Nagumo operation.) As the bad weather persisted the hope was that the bombers could be launched within five hundred miles of Japan.

Constant vigil was maintained and tension mounted as the launch date, set for April 19, approached. On the fifteenth an English broadcast was picked up from Tokyo:

Reuter's British News Agency has announced that three American bombers have dropped bombs on Tokyo. This is a most laughable story. They know it is absolutely impossible for enemy bombers to get within five hundred miles of Tokyo. Instead of worrying about such foolish things, the Japanese people are enjoying the fine spring sunshine and the fragrance of cherry blossoms.

This was a stunning bit of news, even if not true. Had the Japanese somehow learned of the First Special Aviation Project? Had they been spotted and was the Japanese fleet, plus its formidable armada of aircraft, waiting for them to finish what had been left undone at Pearl Harbor?

Whatever the individual trepidations the broadcast produced, the preparations on the *Hornet* continued. The air patrols spotted no Japanese activity, which was a good sign. There was more than enough to keep the crews busy, with tricky fuel systems, the power turrets, and small mechanical problems with plugs, generators, and the hydraulic systems.

After the tankers and destroyers left the task force, on April 17, the carriers with four cruisers as escort increased speed to twenty knots. The weather continued to be blustery and winds approached gale force. The B-25s were positioned on the flight deck; Doolittle's, which was first in line for take-off, had but 467 feet of runway. White guidelines were painted on the deck, one for the left wheel and the other for the nosewheel. Lining up on these, the pilot would manage to keep his plane's right wing tip about six feet away from the *Hornet*'s island. The sixteenth plane, assigned to Lieutenant William Farrow, was parked at the stern with its tail section protruding. All, with minor mechanical reservations, was ready for the April 19 launchings.

But then, unexpectedly, the tension was released with the expectation of action. At three in the early morning of April 18, the *Enterprise* reported a radar sighting of two enemy surface craft. "General Quarters" reverberated through the entire task force as all ships veered sharply to avoid the enemy craft and all hands peered into the gloom. For a single instant a light flashed in the distance and then nothing. Forty-one minutes later the "All Clear" was sounded and all who could returned to their bunks and the tension returned intensified.

At dawn, despite the squalls, the *Enterprise* dispatched its search flights and fighter patrols— Douglas SBDs (Dauntlesses) and Grumman F4Fs (Wildcats)—which fanned out in advance of the force. At 5:58 A.M. Lieutenant O. B. Wiseman, in an SBD, sighted a Japanese patrol craft. Ducking into cloud he attempted to hide, but was reasonably sure he had been seen. Returning to the task force,

Mission leader Doolittle affixes Japanese medals (which had, in peaceful times, been awarded to Navy men H. Vornstein, J. B. Laurey, D. J. Quigley, and S. Jurika) to a five-hundred-pound bomb which was then loaded into The Ruptured Duck, *piloted by Major Ted W. Lawson.* (U. S. NAVY)

Wiseman flew low in order to enable his gunner to drop a message on the deck in a "beanbag." Again Halsey ordered a shift in the task force's bearing. But by seven thirty-eight, with winds buffeting and waves sweeping across the decks, it was obvious to Halsey that he must do something about the Army bombers. At this time lookouts on the *Hornet* had spotted a Japanese vessel—it was Patrol Boat No. 23—the *Nitto Maru*. If they saw the little boat in the swelling seas, obviously the Japanese could see a great carrier. This was confirmed moments later when the *Hornet* intercepted a signal which had originated nearby. The picket boat had wired, *"Three enemy aircraft carriers sighted our position 650 nautical miles east of Inubo Saki at 0630 [Tokyo time]."*

Aboard the task force ships it was 7:30 A.M. The *Nitto Maru* had seen both the *Hornet* and *Enterprise* (obviously mistaking one of the cruisers for a third carrier). Halsey ordered the *Nashville* to deal with the *Nitto Maru*.

As for the bombers, Halsey realized, there was nothing to do but get them off. This was a real risk (though a lesser one than exposing the men

Japanese fishing boat sighted by American search planes and which was sunk by a Navy ship. The ap-pearance of the Nitto Maru *forced the Tokyo raid to get under way sooner than had been hoped.*

(U. S. AIR FORCE)

and ships of the task force to a full-scale attack) for they were more than six hundred miles offshore —and two hundred miles from a point at which it was hoped they could have launched the bombers. Also, it was a day earlier than Chiang had been informed the attack would occur; perhaps the airfields would not be ready to receive the bombers after the raid. This was assuming they would have enough fuel to reach them. Halsey at this time had no idea that the preparation of Chinese bases had crumbled in a series of disagreements and plane crashes.

At eight o'clock Halsey flashed a message to the *Hornet:*

Launch Planes To Colonel Doolittle and his gallant command Good Luck and God bless you

v

The *Hornet* exploded with activity; signal horns blared and men raced for their action stations. Doolittle, who had been on the bridge with Mitscher, hurtled down the ladder shouting, "This is it! Let's go!" The ship's klaxon boomed, "Now hear this: Army pilots, man your planes!"

The deck swarmed with men rushing about their various businesses. The airmen clambered into their planes, tossing in their baggage, equipment, map folders, and odd personal possessions (one officer carried a small record collection and a wind-up phonograph). The Navy deck-handlers, called "airedales," scurried over the wet, wind-spumed flight deck, taking their positions for the launch. The rough seas would not make the already complex operation any simpler. Soon the deck boomed and roared to the sound of thirty-two engines.

Lieutenant Edgar G. Osborn poised at the end of the tossing bow, checkered flag in hand, eyes on Doolittle's plane, his feet gauging the pitch of the deck and the feel of the sea. The *Hornet* had rolled into a trough and began to rise; Osborne rotated the flag, faster and faster. At the right moment, he hoped, Doolittle would gun the engines, the airedales pull the wheel chocks and drop to the slippery deck. Osborn gave the signal to go. The engines of the B-25, full power on, thundered and the plane moved—all too slowly it seemed. The flaps were down for more lift and the aircraft moved faster and faster, trundling clumsily toward the end of the deck, now being lifted by the swelling sea. The two Wright Cyclones grew louder and the Mitchell picked up speed; even before he ran out of the short span of deck, Doolittle eased the heavily loaded plane off, all but hanging on his propellers, and pulled up and away from the *Hornet,* whose decks resounded with cheers, shouts, whistles, and the merriment of capering men. Doolittle circled, swooped low, and swept over the deck to check his plane's compass—the weeks aboard ship would have undoubtedly thrown the compasses of the B-25s off. Satisfied, Doolittle pointed the aircraft at Tokyo and was quickly enshrouded in the distant mist and out of sight. The next plane, Travis Hoover's, pulled off the deck five minutes later, described the same circle as had Doolittle's, and it too disappeared in the morning haze.

The original plan, of course, had been abandoned; there would now be no three-hour wait for the rest of the planes. The *Nitto Maru* had decided that.

One after the other the B-25s took off from the flight deck, almost without incident. The water spray and unsteady decks, even the powerful gusts of wind, made for anxious moments as men slipped on the deck or staggered dangerously close to the whirling propellers. In the last section of planes, Lieutenant Donald Smith's B-25 nosed into the tail of Hilger's, which preceded his in the take-off line. Smith took off with a gaping hole in the plexiglass nose of his plane.

The last plane (William G. Farrow, pilot) was caught in the roll of the ship and seemed destined for a watery doom. It poised momentarily on the crest of a wave, then began to skid in reverse. Airedales ran to stop its movement, lest it fall into the sea. They succeeded, but as Farrow gunned the plane forward again Seaman Robert W. Wall slipped and fell into the path of one of the propellers. A blade struck him and Wall went down; he lay stunned under the spinning blades for a moment, then oblivious to the danger tried to rise. His crewmates moved in quickly and dragged him away. Farrow, sickened by the implications of the accident, had no recourse but to proceed with the takeoff. (Wall had been struck in the left arm; it was subsequently amputated and he recovered).

The time was 9:20 A.M., exactly one hour from the moment that Doolittle had taken off—Doolittle would have 620 miles to fly to his target, Farrow faced 600 miles of over-water navigation. Now all B-25s were air-borne and bound for Japan. The instant Farrow slipped into the fog, Halsey ordered all ships to turn about and head full speed away from the dangerous waters before they met more potent vessels than picket boats. Like the Nagumo force at Pearl Harbor, Task Force 16 vanished into the Pacific.

Not without some moments of fury. Three Japa-

The order has come from Halsey to "Launch planes," and the deck of the Hornet *becomes alive with the sound of engines. Deck handlers lie on the deck to avoid propeller blades. The day is dark and damp, visibility is poor.* (NAVY DEPT., NATIONAL ARCHIVES)

Doolittle, in the lead Mitchell, begins the take-off run along the wet—and short—deck of the Hornet.
(U. S. AIR FORCE)

Doolittle lifts the B-25 off the Hornet. *White lines painted along left of carrier deck are there to guide the pilots in the alignment of their left undercarriage* *and nosewheels to keep the right wing of the plane from striking the carrier's island.* (U. S. AIR FORCE)

nese patrol boats were sunk, five prisoners were taken, and three American aircraft were lost. The crews of two were rescued, but one, based on the *Hornet*, went down taking its pilots, Lieutenants G. D. Randall and T. A. Gallagher, with it. They were victims of the weather, not enemy gunfire.

Three minutes after Doolittle's plane left the *Hornet*'s deck the *Nashville* succeeded in sinking the *Nitto Maru*. The tiny, bobbing craft proved an elusive target and it required "938 rounds of 6″ ammunition" to sink it. Even dive bombers could not get at it "due to difficulty of hitting the small target with the heavy swells . . ." as the gunnery officer of the *Nashville* later reported. Finally the *Nitto Maru* did sink, and although a search was made, no survivors were found.

It was a small victory, for already Tokyo had put "Tactical Method No. 3 against the United States Fleet" into operation. Vice-Admiral Nobutake Kondo's Second Fleet, just returned from actions in the southern seas, was ordered to confront the U.S. fleet. Kondo's force was to be supported by Vice-Admiral Shiro Takasu's First Fleet out of Hiroshima Bay. Even Vice-Admiral Nagumo's carrier force, at the moment of alarm passing through the Bashi Strait near the southern tip of Formosa upon completion of its operations in the Indian Ocean, was ordered to rush homeward to engage the enemy. More immediately, however, the bombers and fighters from the Kisarazu Air Base near Tokyo were dispatched to begin the search for the American ships.

At Combined Fleet Headquarters in Tokyo, where the bulk of the preparations was under way, all was anxiety and tension. There had been no second message from the *Nitto Maru* to confirm its sighting. The patrol planes had not reported anything (thanks to the covering of bad weather under which Task Force 16 lay). One of the regular patrol planes, however, on its morning patrol had reported seeing a twin-engined landplane about six hundred miles at sea. Such a report could not be taken seriously in Tokyo—no American plane could have reached that point from any American base and, certainly, there were no such carrier-borne aircraft extant. Meanwhile, the weather in the search area deteriorated and the Japanese search planes were forced to return to Kisarazu after a fruitless quest.

If the weather at sea was harsh, the sky over Tokyo was bright and clear. Along the waterfront a few barrage balloons drifted in the brilliant sun. Its rays flashed from the wings of several aircraft also, aloft practicing for a demonstration a week hence celebrating the Emperor's birthday and the dedication of a shrine to the war dead. By coin-cidence that morning at nine o'clock a practice air raid drill took place. The public did not participate, but firemen and air raid wardens did. By noon the drill drew to a close; most of the barrage balloons had been pulled down. The only planes still flying were a few trainers and three Army Defense fighter planes; at this point in the alarums and excursions at Combined Fleet Headquarters the Army was not regarded as particularly essential. The threat to the Empire, as far as the Navy officials were concerned, still lay far out at sea. There was no air of foreboding in Tokyo as its people went about their customary Saturday bustle. It was as if there were no war at all—their great military leaders had assured them of their immunity from enemy attack.

At twelve-thirty that Saturday afternoon the illusion was shattered. The dream drew to an end the moment that James Doolittle raised his B-25 off the deck of the *Hornet*. "Took off at 8:20 A.M. ship time," he was to write in his report later. "Take-off was easy. Night take-off would have been possible and practicable.

"Circled carrier to get exact heading and check compass. Wind was from around 300°.

"About a half hour after take-off, was joined by A/C 40-2292, Lt. Hoover pilot, the second plane to take off. About an hour out passed a Japanese

A Mitchell leaves the Hornet *as the others await their turns. Note the choppiness of the water in the fore-ground.* (U. S. AIR FORCE)

Yokosuka Naval Base from the right-hand cockpit of No. 40-2247 (Crew No. 13), Lieutenant Edgar E. McElroy, pilot, and Lieutenant Richard A. Knobloch, copilot and photographer. (U. S. AIR FORCE)

camouflaged naval surface vessel of about 6000 tons. Took it to be light cruiser. About two hours out passed a multi-motored land plane headed directly for our flotilla and flying at about 3,000 ft.—2 miles away. Passed and endeavored to avoid various civil and naval craft until landfall was made north of Inubo Shuma.

"Was somewhat north of desired course but decided to take advantage of error and approach from a northerly direction, thus avoiding anticipated strong opposition to the west. Many flying fields and the air full of planes north of Tokyo. Mostly small biplanes apparently primary or basic trainers.

"Encountered nine fighters in three flights of three. This was about ten miles north of the outskirts of Tokyo proper. All this time had been flying as low as terrain would permit. Continued low flying due south over the outskirts of and toward the east center of Tokyo.

"Pulled up to 1,200 ft., changed course to the southwest and incendiary-bombed highly inflammable section. Dropped first bomb at 1:30 (ship time).

[It was twelve-thirty in Tokyo when the first bombs fell.]

"Anti-aircraft very active but only one near hit,"

Having released its bombs, McElroy's Mitchell pulls away from Yokosuka as machine shops burn from a bomb hit. (U. S. AIR FORCE)

Doolittle noted. "Lowered away to housetops and slid over western outskirts into low haze and smoke. Turned south and out to sea. Fewer airports on west side but many army posts. Passed over small aircraft factory with a dozen or more newly completed planes on the line. No bombs left. Decided not to machine gun for reasons of personal security. Had seen five barrage balloons over east central Tokyo and what appeared to be more in the distance.

"Passed on out to sea flying low. Was soon joined by Hoover who followed us to the Chinese coast. Navigator plotted perfect course to pass north of Yaki Shima. Saw three large naval vessels just before passing west end of Japan. One was flatter than the others and may have been converted carrier. Passed innumerable fishing and small patrol boats.

"Made landfall somewhat north of course on China coast. Tried to reach Chuchow on 4495 [kilocycles] but could not raise.

"It had been clear over Tokyo but became overcast before reaching Yaki Shima. Ceiling lowered on coast until low islands and hills were in it at about 600'. Just getting dark and couldn't live under overcast so pulled up to 6000' and then 8000' in it. On instruments from then on though occasionally saw dim lights on ground through almost solid overcast. These lights seemed more often on our right and pulled us still further off course.

"Directed rear gunner to go aft and secure films from camera. [Unfortunately, they were jerked out of his shirt front where he had put them when his chute opened.]

"Decided to abandon ship. Sgt. [Fred A.] Breamer, Lt. [Henry A.] Potter, Sgt. [Paul J.] Leonard and Lt. [Richard E.] Cole jumped in order. Left ship on AFCE (automatic pilot), shut off both gas cocks and I left. Should have put flaps down. This would have slowed down landing speed, reduced impact and shortened glide.

"Left airplane about 9:30 P.M. [ship time] after about 13 hours in the air. Still had enough gas for half hour flight but right front tank was showing empty. Had transferred once as right engine used more fuel. Had covered about 2,250 miles, mostly at low speed which more than doubled the consumption for this time.

"All hands collected and ship located by late afternoon of 19th. Requested General Ho Yang Ling, Director of the Branch Government of Western Chekieng Province to have a lookout kept along seacoast from Hang Chow Bay to Wen Chow Bay and also to have all sampans and junks along the coast to keep a lookout for planes that went down at sea, or just reached shore.

"Early morning of 20th, four planes and crews, in addition to ours, had been located and I wired General Arnold, through the Embassy at Chungking: *Tokyo successfully bombed. Due bad weather on China coast believe all airplanes wrecked. Five crews found safe in China so far.* Wired again on the 27th giving more details.

"Discussed possibility of purchasing three prisoners on the seacoast from Puppet Government and endeavoring to take out the three in lake area by force. Believe this desire was made clear to General Ku Cho-tung (who spoke little English) and know it was made clear to English-speaking members of his staff. This was at Shangjao. They agreed to try to purchase of three [American prisoners] but recommended against . . . due to large Japanese concentration.

"Bad luck:

"(1) Early take-off due to naval contact with surface and air craft.

"(2) Clear over Tokyo.

"(3) Foul over China.

"Good luck:

"(1) A 25 mph tail wind over most of the last 1,200 miles.

"Take-off should have been made three hours before daylight, but we didn't know how easy it would be and the Navy didn't want to light up. Dawn take-off, closer in, would have been better as things turned out. However, due to the bad weather it was questionable if even daylight landing could have been made at Chuchow without radio aid.

"Still feel that original plan of having one plane take off three hours before dusk and others just at dusk was best all-around plan for average conditions."

When he dropped out of the B-25, Doolittle, like the others in the crew, fell into the unknown. There was no certainty that they had been over Chinese-held territory, nor even that they were over inhabited country. Prepared for anything in the deep blackness, Doolittle remembered, once his chute had jerked open, to come down in a knees-up attitude. He had broken both his ankles in a youthful accident and did not want to chance it again. His landing, however, was "soft" in the extreme, for he landed in a rice paddy, up to his neck in fertilizing night soil. Reeking and cold from the dampness, Doolittle set out to find refuge from the night winds. He soon learned that the phrase they had been taught aboard the *Hornet,* "*Lushu hoo megwa fugi*" ("I am an American"), did not exactly open doors (he later learned that it was the wrong dialect for the section in which he had come down). He found refuge finally in an old water mill, although sleep was an impossibility because of the cold.

In the morning he found a farmer who led him to a military outpost and trouble. The Chinese major in charge, who understood some English, found it difficult to believe Doolittle's story. He had not heard of the mission because the word had not been transmitted because of the breakdown in the preparations. Doolittle then led a group of soldiers to the farmhouse whose door had been bolted to him the night before, and the frightened people inside denied the whole tale. Hoping to furnish his parachute as evidence Doolittle led the major and three soldiers to the rice paddy in which he had come down in the night. It was gone. The soldiers began muttering among themselves and the major looked more doubtful than ever. But at this moment two of the other soldiers emerged from the farmhouse carrying the parachute; the farmer would have willingly exchanged Doolittle's life for such a great quantity of high-grade silk.

Finally convinced, the major smiled, shook Doolittle's hand, ordered food, and sent word back to the outpost to send out search parties for the rest of the crew. All by this time had experienced their own little dramas. Crew chief Paul Leonard had been fired upon by a small patrol and took to the woods; navigator Henry Potter and bombardier Fred A. Breamer were taken prisoner by a band of guerrillas and robbed. They were aided by an

Disheartened, Doolittle sits beside the wing of his B-25 the morning after the Tokyo raid.

(U. S. AIR FORCE)

English-speaking Chinese boy. The guerrilla chieftain returned their valuables and arranged for them to be taken to the outpost. The search went on until all of the crew had been found, all luckily unhurt except for bumps and bruises.

Doolittle, accompanied by Leonard, clambered up the mountain on which the B-25 had crashed. It was a depressing sight, for it was nothing now but a mangled pile of junk. Silently the two men picked through the debris. Doolittle found his oil-soaked Army blouse—someone had already clipped off the brass buttons. It then all caught up with him; dejected, he sat down.

Leonard spoke gently. "What do you think will happen when you go home, Colonel?"

"Well," Doolittle replied, "I guess they'll send me to Leavenworth."

"No, sir," Leonard offered. "I'll tell you what will happen. They're going to make you a general."

Doolittle managed a weak smile at Leonard's obvious attempt to cheer him up. He had lost sixteen planes and at this gray instant, he had no idea where seventy-five men could be.

". . . and," Leonard persisted, "they're going to give you the Congressional Medal of Honor."

Doolittle worked up another smile at the extravagance. Even Leonard recognized that and added, "I know they're going to give you another airplane and when they do, I'd like to be your crew chief."

Tears, a rare Doolittle commodity, filled his eyes. This was the highest tribute of all, from one professional to another. He was never to forget Leonard's request on that mountaintop. (All of Leonard's predictions came true: Doolittle was awarded the Medal of Honor and promoted to brigadier general—skipping a colonelcy—and when he returned to active duty in north Africa flying a Martin B-26, Master Sergeant Paul Leonard served as his crew chief. Leonard was killed on January 5, 1943, during an air raid on an Allied base near Youks les Bains, Algeria.)

Within hours after Doolittle had wired Arnold of the completion of their mission, the news of the bombing of Tokyo and the other cities was flashed across the nation. Affecting an air of mystery President Roosevelt announced that the B-25s had taken off from Shangri-La, a Tibetan never-never land in the popular novel *Lost Horizon* by James Hilton. A full year went by before it was revealed that the Mitchells had been launched from the deck of the *Hornet*. Meanwhile, a wave of jubilant excitement swept the country with a resultant quickening of morale.

Morale in Japan sank, despite the fact that the military damage inflicted by Doolittle's crews was light. The Japanese war leaders had lied to their people about their invulnerability to American attack. This introduced an uneasy air of doubt where once all had been optimistic. Hoping to regain this optimism, the Japanese leaders quickly flooded the media with further deceits.

The official voice of the militarists was the Tokyo

Asahi Shimbun, which, in part, printed of the Doolittle raiders that "While fleeing helter-skelter to avoid the curtain of shells which burst forth from our antiaircraft batteries, the enemy planes chose innocent people and city streets as their targets. They did not go near military installations. They carried out an inhuman, insatiable, indiscriminate bombing attack on the sly, and the fact that they schemed to strafe civilians and non-combatants demonstrates their fiendish behavior."

Radio Tokyo added its permutations: "The cowardly raiders purposefully avoided industrial centers and the important military establishments and blindly dumped their incendiaries in a few suburban districts, especially on schools and hospitals." The motif of the bombardment of schools and hospitals was developed into a major theme in the propaganda following the raid. Claims were also made for nine American planes shot down.

VI

Of the sixteen aircraft participating in the First Special Aviation Project only one made a safe, intact, wheels-down landing, the one piloted by Captain Edward J. York. During their flight to Tokyo York had noted that fuel consumption had been alarmingly high. Upon bombing a factory in the Tokyo area, York asked navigator Lieutenant Nolan A. Herndon for a heading to Russia instead of China. Thanks to the carburetor switch made at Sacramento they could hardly anticipate better than ditching in the sea three hundred miles off the China coast. Russia remained their only chance, even if they had been told (not ordered) to stay away.

After an uneventful flight York brought the B-25 down onto an airfield about forty miles north of Vladivostok in a perfect landing. Perhaps, York hoped, since they and the Russians were allies they might be permitted to refuel and get out of Russia in the morning to rejoin the others in China. Instead, the five men were interned and the plane confiscated. Although the Americans were reasonably well treated, they remained virtual prisoners until they escaped (by arranging bribes) into Iran about a year later.

Eleven crews, including Doolittle's, bailed out and four attempted crash landings. The crews which bailed out generally fared best. Corporal Leland Faktor, engineer-gunner in Lieutenant Robert M. Gray's plane, however, died of injuries sustained when he landed in mountainous country in his parachute. His burial was attended to by an American missionary, the Reverend John M. Birch. Most of the others who bailed out, and who were injured, suffered sprained ankles, leg and back injuries. Faktor was the only fatality.

Lieutenant Dean Hallmark attempted to ditch his plane in the water near Hanchang, on the China coast. The impact threw Hallmark through the windshield and injured the others. Hallmark, however, in company with Robert J. Meder and Chase J. Nielsen, despite their injuries, set out for the beach. Meder turned back when he saw William J. Dieter and Donald Fitzmaurice floundering in the surf. He pulled Fitzmaurice onto shore and, though injured and exhausted, returned to the ocean to look for Dieter. He found the bombardier on the beach, face down in the water. Both Fitzmaurice and Dieter were dead of injuries and possibly drowning. But the three surviving officers were fated for worse: all three fell into the hands of the Japanese.

Ted Lawson also attempted to bring his plane down in the coastal waters and, like Hallmark, was flung through the windshield, along with navigator Charles L. McClure and copilot Dean Davenport. Robert Clever, the bombardier, smashed through the plexiglass and metal nose of the aircraft. Of the five-man crew only engineer-gunner David J. Thatcher was not seriously injured, or rather, was the least injured. Lawson, whose left leg was ripped open terribly, was in the worst state. Limping and in pain himself, Thatcher attended to the injuries of the others. With the aid of Chinese he had the men moved inside a nearby hut (though not without hideous pain to all), for once the news of the Tokyo raid was known and the B-25s came crashing down, Japanese patrol activity became intense.

By various means, ranging from junk to improvised stretcher, the men were spirited into unoccupied China, to a small hospital in the village of Linhai. By this time Lawson was so far gone with infection that he could neither eat nor speak. Thatcher informed Chungking of their state and

The Chinese, civilians as well as soldiers, rallied to the aid of the Tokyo raider crews. Those Chinese who were suspected of helping the Americans suffered terribly at the hands of the Japanese soldiers.

(U. S. AIR FORCE)

was joined in a few days by Lieutenant Thomas R. White.

White was the unique member of the mission; he was not an airman at all but a doctor who had volunteered for the raid. He was permitted to go as a gunner member of the crew of Lieutenant Donald Smith. The latter had crash-landed his plane in the same vicinity, so White, once informed of the fate of Lawson's crew, made his way to Linhai. To keep out of the path of the Japanese, Smith, his crew, and the remarkable Thatcher of Lawson's crew moved on to Chungking. White remained with Lawson, McClure, and Davenport, treating them skillfully with the primitive means at hand. He also doubled as a dentist for the Chinese villagers. In time, White was forced to amputate Lawson's left leg, which saved the pilot's life. When some recovery was made, White had the three men evacuated out of the path of the vindictive Japanese.

Lieutenant William Farrow's crew, of the ill-fated

After the mission: Madame Chiang awards the Tokyo raiders decorations in appreciation for their feat. With her are Doolittle (now a brigadier general; he had been a lieutenant colonel when he took off from the Hornet), *Colonel John A. Hilger (pilot of the fourteenth plane), and Lieutenant Richard E. Cole, who had been Doolittle's copilot.* (U. S. AIR FORCE)

sixteenth plane (the propeller of which had gashed Seaman Wall's arm), bailed out near thc China coast at Shipu, in Japanese-occupied territory, and fell into the waiting arms of the Japanese. Along with the survivors of Hallmark's crew these men were "tried," after a long period of hideous treatment, by a Japanese military court. This mockery, held on August 28, 1942, in Shanghai, decreed that all eight prisoners were to be executed because they had "suddenly exhibited cowardice when confronted with opposition in the air and on the ground, and with intent of cowing, killing, and wounding innocent civilians, and wreaking havoc on residences and other living quarters of no military significance whatsoever" and further "did carry out indiscriminate bombing and strafing." The early themes of press and radio were worked up in the "trial" as a full-fledged symphony.

The eight prisoners, who had been tortured and starved and were in poor health (Hallmark, for example, was unable to sit up and attended the proceedings in a cot), had no conception of what it was all about. They were made to sign blank papers which were subsequently filled in in Japanese. They even signed "confessions," also in Japanese, without the slightest conception of content. All men were in a state of befuddlement as well as physically weak.

Ultimately the death sentence was applied to only three of the eight—Hallmark, Farrow (both pilots) and Harold Spatz (engineer-gunner), all three having unwittingly signed their own death warrants; their portions of the "confessions" admitted to bombings of civilians and strafing. The remaining five, George Barr, Robert Hite, Jacob DeShazer (all of Farrow's crew), Nielsen, and Meder, were "spared" through the alleged god-given leniency of the Emperor. Their sentence was life imprisonment as "war criminals."

This meant forty months of solitary confinement for the five men. During this tortuous period Meder died of maltreatment, disease, and sheer neglect. Nielsen, Barr, Hite, and DeShazer were rescued by an American parachute team on August 20, 1945, at Peiping. Of the survivors, DeShazer eventually returned to Japan—as a missionary, an exemplification of compassion in the highest degree.

Substantial, if not definitive, damage was done by the Doolittle mission. Possibly the greatest injury was to the self-esteem of the Japanese Samurai. Although it had not bccn hit, the very fact that the air over and around the Emperor's Imperial Palace had been violated by enemy aircraft was a gross affront to those who had sworn their very lives to keep this from happening. The militarists, with a keen professional eye, tended to denigrate the raid—English-speaking members referred to it as the "Do Nothing Raid"—but they knew better. It was a harbinger of things to come.

The reaction to the raid was savagery unleashed. The mistreatment of the eight prisoners was reprehensible, but the slaughter of the Chinese which followed the raid was manic barbarism without military justification. Fifty-three battalions of Japanese troops moved inland, ravaging the land, and in about three months they had killed 250,000 Chinese—soldiers as well as civilians—in the rampage. Villages in which the American airmen had hidden or were cared for were all but deracinated. Chinese who had taken small token gifts—coins, gloves, a scarf—or who had taken parts from the planes were tortured and killed. Wang Poo-fang, a village schoolteacher from Ihwang, near which the plane of Lieutenant Harold Watson had crashed, related a single incident which could be multiplied a thousand times over.

"We fed the Americans," Wang said, "and carried them to safety so that they could bomb Tokyo again. Then the dwarf-invaders came. They killed my three sons; they killed my wife, Angsing; they set fire to my school; they burned my books; they drowned my grandchildren in the well." The schoolmaster, too, had been flung into the well, but managed to climb out after the Japanese had moved on. There was little of his village left to him.

All airfields, which might have served as landing spots for possible future raids, were destroyed, ridged with trenches (all work being done by Chinese), and rendered unusable. And then the Japanese troops moved back from a wasteland of twenty thousand square miles.

Another unreasonable means of vengeance was the so-called "balloon bombs," the Japanese equivalent to the German V-weapons of the later months of the European war. The balloon bombs, however, were much less sophisticated though equally senseless. They were constructed of rice paper and potato paste by Japanese civilians in their homes. Carrying

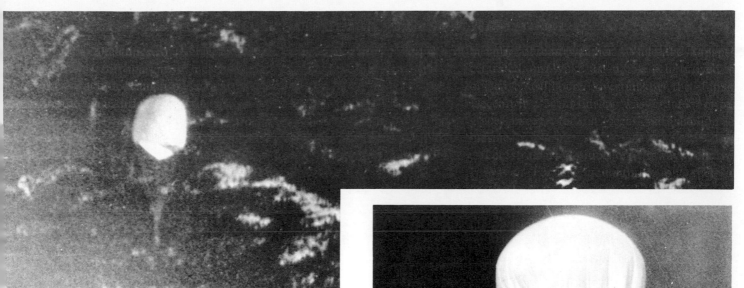

Made in Japan: vengeance balloons released over the Pacific to drift on the winds to the United States. At top left is one of the balloons in flight over the northwest United States. Below it is a close-up demonstrating the workings, theoretically, of the balloon. Balloons did not always work and, in the lower photograph, woodmen chop a tree in which one had become lodged. Others worked, however, and killed several people, haphazardly and senselessly.

(U. S. AIR FORCE)

booby-trap bombs, about ten thousand of these giant balloons were released near Tokyo to be carried across the Pacific at high altitudes by prevailing winds. Many actually completed the voyage—about 280 were found in the American Northwest, Canada, and Alaska. Six picnickers were killed in a forest near Lakeview, Oregon, when they came upon one of these homemade balloon bombs. As late as 1955, a decade after the last of the balloons had been released, one was discovered in Alaska and tested by the Department of Defense, which found the device "still highly explosive and dangerous."

The Doolittle raid had not been, as Imperial General Headquarters in Tokyo implied, a "Do Nothing Raid." Perhaps its most strategic consequence was that it settled a bitter controversy. This argument had been under way for weeks between Combined Fleet and the Imperial Naval General Staff. Yamamoto had been pressing for an early, full-scale, decisive battle with the U. S. Pacific Fleet.

That the carriers had escaped the Pearl Harbor attack never ceased to vex him. The truth was emerging that aircraft, not battleships, would decide the Pacific war, but the Imperial Naval General Staff did not wish to rush into a major fleet engagement.

The coming of Doolittle decided the issue. Yamamoto sensed that the bombers had come from an American carrier—and he reminded his critics that the failure to keep Doolittle from Tokyo was a reflection upon the General Staff as well as Combined Fleet. Consequently by the end of April Yamamoto's controversial plan was completed and approved by the General Staff. On May 5, 1942, Admiral Osami Nagano issued, in the name of the Emperor, Imperial General Headquarters Navy Order No. 18, directing Yamamoto "to carry out the occupation of Midway Island and key points in the western Aleutians in co-operation with the Army."

4

MIDWAY: TRAGIC VICTORY

BY THE SPRING of 1942 the virus that came to be called the "Victory Disease" infected the Japanese. Few were immune, from the man in the street on up into the honored and seemingly invincible purlieus of Combined Fleet and the Naval General Staff.

Invincible indeed—from Pearl Harbor through the fall of Wake Island, the destruction of the British ships *Prince of Wales* and *Repulse,* the surrender of Hong Kong and Singapore—the uncoiling of the Greater East Asia Co-Prosperity Sphere into the southern Pacific had gone unchecked for nearly six months. Then came news of the fall of the Philippines with the surrender of Corregidor on May 6, 1942. Yamamoto had truly "run wild." His leadership had been as good as his word, but the question was, in early 1942, what were the long-range plans to be? Even the most optimistic among his admirers had not expected so unremitting a succession of victories.

Should they consolidate their cheaply won holdings, or should they extend their "security perimeter"? In Yamamoto's mind there was little question of the next move. He knew they could not dig in and wait for the American industrial machine to grind into action and take it all away. Several plans had been under consideration by the middle of January. One favored an all-out attack upon Hawaii, another pointed toward India and Ceylon, and a third advocated an Australian offensive. This last originated from the Naval General Staff, the argument being that Australia must be cut off as a future springboard for an Allied counteroffensive against Japan. The attack upon Hawaii had originated from the Chief of Staff, Combined Fleet, Rear Admiral Matome Ugaki, who based his thinking upon the possibility of such an attack luring the American fleet to its destruction by the Imperial Navy.

The Navy's plan to take Ceylon was rejected by the Army, which did not have the troops to back up the amphibious landings proposed. Ugaki's Hawaii plan was shot full of holes by his own staff because of the impossibility of achieving another surprise attack. Also, there was the formidable job it would pose for carrier-borne aircraft to maintain air superiority over so large an area as the Hawaiian Islands. The Australian plan was scuttled also by the Army High Command, which insisted it would be unable to supply the required ten divisions. However, there was obvious merit in isolating Australia.

Yamamoto, however, favored another plan—related to Ugaki's Hawaii proposal, but not so formidable in terms of area. In early April he introduced his Operation MI, the major point of which appeared to be the occupation of the Midway atoll. In truth, the occupation of the atoll was secondary in

Yamamoto's mind; his wish, his dream, was to lure the American fleet, and especially its carriers, into one massive decisive battle with the Imperial fleet. Once over—with a Japanese victory, inevitably— the reeling Americans must ask for peace before they had properly geared for war.

Yamamoto's proposal set off another round of debate. The Naval General Staff rose in opposition to the plan. One of the most serious objections was: Even if the atoll were taken, how would it be kept supplied, if, for some reason, the U.S. fleet had

Before the storm: flight deck of the U.S.S. Enterprise, *Pacific 1942.* (NAVY DEPT., NATIONAL ARCHIVES)

not been destroyed? Could Midway truly function as an advance base for Japanese air patrols, considering the range (six to seven hundred miles) of patrol planes? Would the United States actually sue for peace merely because Midway had fallen? Finally, Midway was within bombing range of Hawaii; would not the long-range U.S. bombers menace the occupation force as well as attempts to supply it?

But these arguments were beside the point, for Yamamoto's dream, incited by the fever of the Victory Disease, visualized the mass sinking of American carriers. Despite the objections, Yamamoto—as he had before the Hawaii Operation— made it clear what he desired. The Naval General

Staff, bludgeoned, halfheartedly assented to the operation. Arguments, even opposition, continued on into April until the Doolittle raiders appeared over the sacred soil of Nippon. Debate was ended and Operation MI went into active preparation.

II

If the Doolittle raid was a portent, during the planning of the Midway operation another occurred of even greater immediate significance to Yamamoto, the Battle of the Coral Sea. This was the first naval battle in history in which the ships themselves did not exchange a shot. All the fighting was done by aircraft and in this battle, though ostensibly "won" by the Japanese, Japan suffered its first setback of the war.

This crucial engagement was ignited by Japanese operations aimed at the dual-pronged invasions of Tulagi, in the Solomons, and Port Moresby, in strategic proximity to Australia, in southern Papua, New Guinea. From the first of February the American carriers *Enterprise* and *Lexington* had been making hit-and-run raids upon Japanese-held positions in the Marshalls, the Solomons, and northern New Guinea. Yamamoto recognized the importance both of clearing this area of the American carriers and of the establishment of bases for future operations.

What Yamamoto did not know was that, thanks to Army cryptographers, the Japanese codes were no secret to the enemy and his plans, in turn, were no secret to Admiral Nimitz. By mid-April Nimitz was aware of the impending operations; by the twentieth he even knew the date: May 3. Whereupon he sent Task Force 17, built around the *Yorktown* and *Lexington* and under the command of Rear Admiral Frank Jack Fletcher, to counter the Japanese move.

To accomplish this Fletcher had only about half the force that was at the disposal of Vice-Admiral Shigeyoshi Inouye, Commander in Chief, Imperial Fourth Fleet. This massive force was, it is true, divided into three parts, each of which was assigned its special task in the Port Moresby-Tulagi invasions. The Tulagi Invasion Group (twelve assorted ships) was to occupy that base, which was defended by a few Australian troops, and establish an air base there for future operations. The Port Moresby Invasion Group consisted of eleven troop transports covered by several heavy cruisers, light cruisers, and the light carrier *Shoho*. Also covering the two invasions was the main Carrier Striking Force (carriers *Zuikaku, Shokaku*) with its protective heavy cruisers and screen of destroyers. The plan envisioned was that the invasions would bring out the American carriers, which, when they ventured into the Coral Sea, would be destroyed by the Japanese forces.

The already alerted Nimitz was ready with Task Force 17, to which had been added a support group (two heavy cruisers, a light cruiser, and two destroyers) of what was then called "MacArthur's Navy" under Rear Admiral Crace, Royal Navy.

On May 3 the Japanese opened the battle by taking Tulagi; on the following day planes from the *Yorktown* bombed the Japanese positions at Tulagi. This revealed that an American carrier was indeed somewhere in the area. The *Zuikaku* and *Shokaku* were headed south from Rabaul (where they had gone to deliver fighter planes) to engage the enemy task force. Meanwhile, the Port Moresby Invasion Group continued on its course.

Not until dawn of May 7 did search planes make contact—in the Coral Sea. Japanese scouts reported sighting the American task force, specifically "a carrier and a cruiser." Rear Admiral Chuichi Hara, commander of air operations, under orders from Vice-Admiral Takeo Takagi, commander of the Carrier Striking Force, sent out the entire bombing strength of the two Japanese carriers (a total of seventy-eight bombers, torpedo planes, and fighters) to make an all-out attack. The "task force" turned out to be the destroyer *Sims* and the oiler *Neosho*, neither really worth the wholesale effort. Both were sunk, the *Sims* first (almost within minutes); the *Neosho*, which had been spared at Pearl Harbor, was scuttled a few days later, after smoking and drifting helplessly. But the loss of these ships had pulled the Japanese planes away from the *Lexington* and *Yorktown*, whose planes had been launched. While the Americans were off on their own wild-goose chase ("two carriers and four heavy cruisers"—actually two outdated light cruisers, three gunboats, and a seaplane tender) they unexpectedly came upon the light carrier *Shoho*. The *Lexington*'s Scouting Squadron 2 led the assault, followed by a torpedo squadron and a bombing squadron. All

three had scored hits, but the *Shoho* had turned into the wind to launch its planes. The *Yorktown* planes arrived at this moment, catching the *Shoho* in a position where evasive action was impossible, and soon the word went out in the excited voice of Lieutenant Commander Robert Dixon, commander of the *Lexington*'s scout bomber squadron: "Scratch one flattop!"

Within minutes the *Shoho,* a burning shambles, sank into the sea, taking five hundred crewmen to

Below decks of a carrier, the hangar deck, where engineers work on a fighter, the Grumman F4F "Wildcat." (NAVY DEPT., NATIONAL ARCHIVES)

the bottom. This development unnerved Vice-Admiral Inouye so much that he called off the Port Moresby invasion and recalled the transports to Rabaul. Until he was certain the American carriers had been cleared out of the Coral Sea, Inouye felt that he could not expose the invasion forces to aerial attack. This was a decision that later greatly displeased Yamamoto, for Inouye could not exploit the advantages that came his way later in the battle.

On May 8, finally, the Japanese spotted the American carriers and launched another full-scale attack. The Japanese had the advantage of heavy weather cover, but the *Lexington* and *Yorktown*

Prelude to Midway: the Battle of the Coral Sea, the first major sea battle in which surface ships did not exchange a shot. Fought by aircraft in the vicinity of the Solomon Islands, the Coral Sea battle blocked the Japanese in their drive toward Australia and New Zealand. One of the American losses was the carrier Lexington. Wildcats on the flight deck following bomb hits by Japanese planes.

(NAVY DEPT., NATIONAL ARCHIVES)

A destroyer moves in to pick up Lexington crew men after the order to abandon ship has been given. Japanese torpedo planes and dive bombers caused fires and internal explosions; the "Lady Lex" was finally sunk by the American destroyer Phelps.

(NAVY DEPT., NATIONAL ARCHIVES)

lay in bright day. The Americans missed finding the *Zuikaku* but did locate the *Shokaku* and succeeded in hitting it with two bombs. Seventy Japanese aircraft, meanwhile, attacked the American carriers savagely. The *Yorktown,* struck by a single bomb, lost sixty-six men, but the *Lexington,* torpedoed and bombed, was left burning and listing after the encounter. Damage-control parties seemed to bring the three fires which blazed under control, but internal explosions doomed the "Lady Lex." New fires spread as gasoline poured into the flames. Captain Frederick Sherman ordered "Abandon Ship," the wounded were evacuated, and the *Lexington,* rather than be abandoned to the Japanese, was sunk by American destroyers.

Trading the *Lexington* for the *Shoho* was no true victory, but the invasion of Port Moresby was canceled. Also, both the *Shokaku,* which would be out of commission for two months being repaired, and the *Zuikaku,* which had lost many of its pilots, were to be denied to Yamamoto for his Midway operation. This fact did not trouble him, for his pilots had sunk the *Lexington* and claimed to have sunk the *Yorktown.*

Nimitz, however, was concerned over the temporary loss of the *Yorktown* in his planning to counter Yamamoto's Midway assault. It was estimated that three months would be required to return the carrier to fighting trim. However, at the Pearl Harbor dry dock a miracle occurred. An army of workmen swarmed over the carrier, working night and day, and within two days the patched-up, scarred *Yorktown* was ready for action.

Despite his losses, Yamamoto was ready, afflicted as he was by then with singleness of purpose and the Victory Disease. He wanted those other American carriers.

III

Midway atoll lies about 1150 miles to the northwest of Hawaii. Its two major islets, Sand and Eastern, were not impressive land masses—Sand Island, the largest, was barely two miles long. In 1859 one Captain N. C. Brooks claimed the two islands for the United States; Secretary of the Navy Gideon Welles placed it under informal U. S. Navy jurisdiction in 1867. Two years later the Congress author-

ized channel dredging between the two islands. In 1900 the Japanese arrived for the first time to prey on the islands' bird population, killing the terns, gannets, and goonies for their feathers. In 1903, fearing that Japan would claim the atoll, President Theodore Roosevelt again placed it under naval jurisdiction and the Japanese poachers were driven off. Midway became a link in the trans-Pacific cable between the Philippines and Hawaii in the same year.

Americans recalled Midway best before the war as one of the way stations for Pan American Airways' *China Clipper* in 1935. Four years later the Navy's Hepburn Board, along with other recommendations, found that Midway was "second in importance only to Pearl Harbor." By August 18, 1941, Midway was commissioned as a Naval Air Station with a complement of around eight hundred men. Dock facilities and airstrips were built and gun positions installed. Although shelled on December 7, 1941, Midway had escaped serious damage and invasion. The planned air strike was canceled

Frank J. Fletcher, Task Force 17 commander—and victor—in the Battle of Midway.
(NAVY DEPT., NATIONAL ARCHIVES)

because of bad weather. While the Japanese concentrated on Wake Island, which proved no easy objective (although overrun by the Japanese on December 23), Midway was granted a period of grace, except for an occasional shelling by submarine.

The strategic position of Midway, relative to the Hawaiian Islands, would bring out the American fleet, which was Yamamoto's most feverish dream. It was no fantasy, however, for his Hawaii Operation, having put most of the U.S. battleship strength out of consideration, placed the Americans in the position of the underdog. Even though the Coral Sea Battle had "scratched" one light carrier and sent the *Shokaku* and the *Zuikaku* into temporary retirement, Yamamoto was capable of amassing a large number of ships for his Midway Operation— nearly two hundred. Among these were eight carriers (four heavies), eleven battleships, twenty-two cruisers, sixty-five destroyers, and twenty-one submarines. About seven hundred aircraft, dive bombers, torpedo bombers, and fighters, were at Yamamoto's disposal.

Rear Admiral Frank J. Fletcher had to counter this force with 3 carriers (including the hastily repaired *Yorktown*), 7 heavy cruisers and 1 light cruiser, and 15 destroyers. Aboard his carriers, Fletcher carried about 230 aircraft; in addition, there were a number of Midway-based planes, Marine fighters and scout bombers, Navy torpedo bombers and patrol bombers, totaling 98. The Army Seventh Air Force, too, had moved 17 B-17s up from Hawaii and 4 B-26s, converted into torpedo bombers. Although handicapped in terms of sheer weight, Fletcher enjoyed certain advantages: he knew Yamamoto was coming, he knew where Yamamoto would strike and when, so that he could concentrate his meager forces at the point at which they would prove most effective.

Yamamoto, on the other hand, split his forces in a characteristic attempt at a diversionary feint. This took the form of what was called the Northern, or Aleutians, Force under Vice-Admiral Moshiiro Hosogaya, who was to spearhead the Midway Operation by an attack upon American installations at Dutch Harbor and the invasion and occupation of Attu and Kiska. Two carriers, *Ryujo* and *Junyo*, whose air commander was Rear Admiral Kakuji Kakuta, accompanied the Northern Force. It was

hoped that this attack, so close to the American homeland, would bring out the American fleet, send it scurrying off into the northern Pacific, and leave Midway more or less unguarded for the main attack.

If not, Yamamoto planned to meet the American fleet and planes, after Midway itself had been struck, when they came out of Pearl Harbor to meet the surprise Japanese thrust. Yamamoto's forces consisted of the 1st Carrier Force, under command of Admiral Chuichi Nagumo, who had led the Hawaii strike upon Pearl Harbor. Nagumo had, in addition to screening and support groups of battleships, cruisers, and destroyers, four great carriers, *Akagi* (his own flagship), *Kaga, Hiryu,* and *Soryu.* That the temporary loss of the *Shokaku* and *Zuikaku* denied him one third of his air power did not disquiet Nagumo. He was certain, after six months of victory, that he and his carriers were invincible.

Yamamoto, aboard his flagship, the giant battleship *Yamato,* would command all the Midway-Aleutians forces, from what was named the "Main Body of the Main Force." This force, consisting of three large battleships, the light carrier *Hosho,* cruisers, destroyers, and seaplane carriers, would be situated about six hundred miles northwest of Midway, ready to come to the aid of Nagumo and the Midway Invasion Force or the Aleutian Invasion Force, as the course of the battle demanded.

Before the strikes were made various submarines of the Advance Submarine Force were to be dispersed northwest of Hawaii to spot the American ships as soon as they left Pearl Harbor to meet Nagumo's challenge at Midway. That, at least, was the plan—on paper. In practice, it did not work out quite as Yamamoto had expected.

The submarines were to have been in position by June 1, but because of delays in overhauling some of them and poor weather, the sub cordon was not established until June 4. By this time the great armada of Combined Fleet had been steaming toward its several objectives for ten days, ten days of nearly complete ignorance of the movements of the U.S. fleet.

The elaborate preparations required for the Midway-Aleutians Operation filled the airwaves with messages, most of which U. S. Intelligence intercepted, decoded, and flashed to Pearl Harbor. Thus two of the favorite Japanese techniques, surprise and feint, were rendered pointless from the beginning.

Task Force at sea, spring 1942: a view from the aft flight deck of the Enterprise *bearing TBFs; bringing up the rear are a destroyer, a tanker, and, in the distance, the* Hornet *and a tanker.*

Not that every step of the proposed operation was lucidly outlined for Nimitz. His guess was that, in view of the massive preparations which were under way, the objective must be Midway. But there was no absolute certainty that the "AF" to which the Japanese referred so frequently in their messages was, indeed, Midway. Admiral King, in fact, was equally certain that it was Oahu, Hawaii.

Naval Intelligence then tricked the Japanese into the identification of AF. Dutifully, as ordered, Midway sent a message in the clear to Pearl Harbor reporting that its water distillation apparatus had broken down. Within days a Japanese radio message was intercepted reporting that AF was low on water. Midway it was!

This was only the first in a series of unanticipated errors which would beset Yamamoto. Another occurred when the submarine squadrons were delayed in taking up their positions to the north and northwest of Hawaii. By the time they had arrived, the

The lost Zero of the Aleutians; Tadayoshi Koga's Reisen *on its back in the tundra of Akutan Island. The Americans now had a nearly intact, once mysterious, Zero.* (NAVY DEPT., NATIONAL ARCHIVES)

two American task forces had already crossed the assigned cordon lines. When the time came for opening the Midway-Aleutians Operation, Yamamoto had no idea of the whereabouts of the American fleet, nor of its composition, however disproportionate compared to his.

Even while the several Japanese task forces approached their targets the American task forces lay in wait at "Point Luck," about 350 miles northeast of Midway. On May 28, the day the last Japanese ship left port, Rear Admiral Raymond A. Spruance's Task Force 16 (the *Enterprise* and *Hornet*) left Pearl Harbor for Point Luck. Two days later Rear Admiral Frank J. Fletcher, aboard the expeditiously rejuvenated *Yorktown,* left for Point Luck to join forces with Spruance and to take tactical command of the task forces. Nimitz would oversee the battle from his headquarters at Pearl Harbor. Thus he would be able to watch the progress of the battle from a central point. Yamamoto, on the other hand, would be aboard the *Yamato,* and thanks to the need for radio silence, would frequently be completely out of touch with the progress of the battle.

Nimitz was taking one risk in assuming that the main force was aimed at Midway and not the Aleutians. He concentrated his main striking force, therefore, in the vicinity of Midway, leaving the defense of the Aleutians to a small token force, mainly cruisers, under the command of Rear Admiral Robert A. Theobald. Fortunately for Nimitz his guess had been right, and although the Japanese succeeded in landing troops on Attu and Kiska, they neither gained strategic ground nor succeeded in luring the main American forces away from Midway. In fact, they suffered one serious loss in the Aleutians. This occurred on May 3, 1942, with an inconclusive attack by a formation of Kates, escorted by a half-dozen Zeros, upon Dutch Harbor. After leaving the carrier *Ryujo,* the Japanese planes encountered no opposition but heavy rain and thick fog. Over Dutch Harbor it was clear enough for the Kates to bomb and the Zeros to strafe the harbor installations and moored flying boats. There was some return fire from the few Americans based there, but Dutch Harbor was left a smoking shambles as the Japanese formation completed its attack and pulled away to reassemble for the return flight to the *Ryujo.*

It was then that Flight Petty Officer Tadayoshi

The crew of the Navy Catalina that spotted the Japanese fleet approaching Midway. Back row (*left to right*): *R. J. Derouin, Francis Musser, Ensign Hardeman, Jewell H. Reid (pilot), R. A. Swan. Front row: J. F. Grammell, J. Goovers, and P. A. Fitzpatrick.*
(NAVY DEPT., NATIONAL ARCHIVES)

Koga, flying an A6M2 *Reisen,* noticed that his aircraft trailed fuel in his wake. By radio he informed the bomber leader, Lieutenant Michio Kobayashi, that he did not have enough fuel to return to the *Ryujo* and would attempt to land at one of the designated emergency landing sites in the area. He would then await a pickup by Japanese submarine, according to the plans made for such emergencies.

Koga came in upon Akutan Island, a small island to the east of Dutch Harbor. Choosing a smooth, clear area, Koga lowered the wheels, opened his canopy, and cranked up his seat for the landing approach. Kobayashi, meanwhile, had scouted the landing area, which he later described as perfect. Koga skillfully brought the Zero lower, touched his wheels down, and with a great splash the Zero whipped over onto its back. The "flat and clear" landing spot was actually spongy tundra. Kobayashi circled over the wrecked Zero and assumed that Koga was either dead or seriously injured. He also assumed that, because of the marshy terrain, it would be impossible, or extremely difficult, to retrieve the "heavily damaged" plane. Five weeks

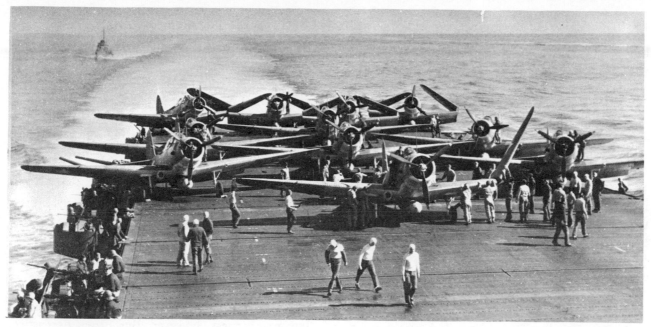

The Enterprise, *with the Douglas TBD-1s ("Devastator") of VT-6 on deck, races from "Point Luck" toward Midway.* (U. S. OFFICE OF WAR INFORMATION)

later, however, after the Zero was spotted by a Navy reconnaissance plane, the U. S. Navy sent a party to Akutan Island. There they found Koga hanging from his seat straps in the cockpit. He had evidently struck his head when the plane turned over and was killed. But the Zero was not as damaged as Kobayashi had supposed. It was in fact virtually intact, the first Zero to fall into American hands in so good a condition. Koga's plane was salvaged and shipped to the Naval Air Station, North Island, San Diego, and restored to flying condition. Tested by American pilots, the Zero revealed all of its secrets, good points as well as bad. It also led to the production of a plane specifically designed to deal with the Zero, the Grumman F6F ("Hellcat"). The loss of the single plane in the Dutch Harbor attack, the hoped-for diversion opening the Battle of Midway, was to cost the Japanese dear and ended the reign of the Zero over the skies in the Pacific.

Assuming that the Aleutian attacks were feints, the Americans awaited the main thrust at Point Luck. From Midway itself scouting planes were sent out to search for the oncoming Japanese fleet. It was around nine in the morning of June 3 that Ensign Jewell H. Reid, pilot of a Midway-based Catalina, flying about seven hundred miles to the

west of Midway, spotted a large number of Japanese ships. He had found the transports of the Midway Invasion Force. Reid tracked the ships, dodging in and out of clouds, counting, checking direction and speed. For nearly two hours Reid and his crew observed what they believed was the main Japanese fleet headed for Midway at nineteen knots; the eleven ships were pointed east. As Reid reported his find to Midway and Pearl Harbor, Rear Admiral Raizo Tanaka, commanding the transport group, informed Yamamoto that all hopes for surprise were over. Yamamoto had counted upon unleashing an aerial attack upon Midway before the Americans ever realized the battle had begun. The initiative had now fallen into enemy hands. A heavy antiaircraft barrage forced Reid away from the Japanese surface force, but he had seen enough.

Midway, so long under the tension of waiting, came alive with preparation. Nine B-17s, led by Lieutenant Colonel Walter Sweeney, took off shortly after noon and reported that "Late in the afternoon, at a distance of 570 miles south of west of Midway, interception of the Japanese force was effected."

Sweeney's reaction upon seeing the vast Japanese fleet was less phlegmatic. "Good God," he said to his copilot Everett Wessman, "look at 'em!" It seemed that as far as the eye could see the waters below were dotted with ships trailing thin white wakes, like skates on a frozen pond. Smaller escort ships circled around the armada describing less regular patterns, like nervous water insects. It was an awe-inspiring sight; Sweeney estimated (erroneously) no less a force than forty-five ships.

The B-17s attacked in elements of three, Sweeney leading the first, dropping his six-hundred-pound bombs at the gyrating ships from an altitude of eight thousand feet. Antiaircraft fire flashed up at them furiously, appearing to one crewman "like a Times Square electric sign gone haywire." The next three Flying Fortresses followed, dropping their bombs from ten thousand feet; the last three dropped theirs from an altitude of twelve thousand feet. All three elements claimed either direct hits or near misses, and as all nine B-17s wheeled away from the antiaircraft fire, Sweeney looked back to see a battleship and a transport, seemingly still in the water, with "huge clouds of dark smoke mushroomed above them."

Although a total of thirty-six bombs were dropped by the B-17s, not one struck the dodging Japanese ships. The claims, plus others to follow, as well as the newspaper headlines attributing great feats to the Air Force bombers, would lead to much wartime feuding between the U. S. Navy and the Air Force.

Vice-Admiral Nagumo, meanwhile, was literally in a fog. His huge carrier striking force lay under a blanket of heavy weather, screening him from enemy search planes. At the same time it rendered navigation hazardous and also prevented Nagumo's search planes from being launched. One nagging question haunted him, one which he blurted out finally to his by now apprehensive staff; "But where is the enemy fleet?"

Some of the fog under which Nagumo proceeded was man-made. Yamamoto's staff, aboard the *Yamato,* had picked up radio transmissions in the Hawaii area which led them to suspect unusual enemy activity and the possibility of an American sortie. But Yamamoto did not inform Nagumo of this activity. He assumed that Nagumo was aware of it, which he was not, because Nagumo's ships were hundreds of miles closer to the enemy. Yamamoto was also all but fanatical upon maintaining radio silence. Meanwhile Nagumo glared into the swirling fog, hoping that the American carriers were still in the vicinity of the Solomon Islands, where Japanese intelligence had last placed them. The 1st Carrier Striking Force plunged through the fog toward Midway. Tomorrow, June 4, would re-

solve all things when Nagumo sent his planes off to bomb Midway.

Admiral Fletcher, in the area of Point Luck, had considered Ensign Reid's report of the sighting of the main force of the Japanese fleet. If Reid was right, then Fletcher's task forces were ill situated to challenge the invasion attempt. But Fletcher, judging from Reid's report of the location of the Japanese ships, concluded that they must be part of the invasion fleet and not the main attack force at all. There had been no carrier detected. And Fletcher's sixth sense told him that the air strike would materialize out of the area of murky weather to the northwest of Midway; further: the Japanese would, according to previous practice, launch their planes at dawn. So far, there was no sighting of Japanese carriers, however. But Fletcher's carriers would be in place, about two hundred miles north and slightly east of Midway, when morning came.

Dawn began to break at around four that morning. Though still under cloud, Nagumo's carriers came into a clearing. Despite the broken clouds and intermittent showers, stars were visible for the first time in days. A light wind blew from the southeast, which would aid the launch of the first attack wave. Nagumo could find some comfort in that. They would be precisely on schedule and Nagumo was aware of Yamamoto's addiction to timetables.

A Dauntless is given the signal to take off on a search mission. (DOUGLAS AIRCRAFT)

At almost the same moment that attack preparations were under way on the Japanese carriers, Midway too resounded to the roar of engines. Eleven Navy Catalinas were about to take off on search missions; streaks of light fanned into the dark eastern sky—it was 4:30 A.M. when the Catalinas, already fifteen minutes air-borne, prodded the western darkness in search of the Japanese ships. The PBYs were followed shortly after by bomb-laden planes from the Seventh Air Force's 5th and 11th Bombardment Groups, ready to attack the oncoming ships of the invasion force, which had been attacked the day before. Obviously, Nagumo was not aware of the attack, for before he ordered the first attack wave launched, he issued an estimate of the situation which revealed an unwonted optimism in Nagumo's generally conservative outlook. Two items, in retrospect, were tragically ironic: "The enemy is not yet aware of our plan, and he has not yet detected our task force," Nagumo had observed. And "There is no evidence of an enemy task force in our vicinity." According to all of the intelligence at his command, Nagumo could send his airmen off to bomb Midway believing that which he hoped was true was, indeed, true.

Marine SB2Us (Vought-Sikorsky "Vindicator") leave Midway in search of the Japanese fleet, June 4, 1942.
(U. S. NAVY)

At a point about 240 miles northwest of Midway the 108 planes of the first attack wave took off from the four Japanese carriers. Thirty-six Zeros served as escort for the 36 Vals (dive bombers) and 36 Kates (torpedo bombers). The first wave was led by Lieutenant Joichi Tomonaga, on his first mission in the Pacific war. By 4:45 A.M. the formation had taken off and headed for Midway. The Vals and Kates flew in V-shaped echelons and the faster Zeros darted here and there over the formations to stay with them. As soon as the first wave was under way, Nagumo ordered the second wave, also 108 aircraft, to be readied. These would attack an enemy task force if it should appear, or if a second strike upon Midway were necessary, they would be ready. Eighteen Zeros circled over the striking force on air combat patrol.

Although not expecting American carriers or warships until after the Midway attack had begun, Nagumo, as an extra precautionary measure, dispatched several search planes to scour the seas to the south and east of his four carriers. Even so, the measure was much less systematic than usual. Of the seven planes, two took off on schedule; one developed engine trouble and returned before completing its search pattern and others returned early upon flying into the squally weather which clung to

Nagumo's ships. The critical planes, as it turned out, those which were to be launched from the cruiser *Tone*, were delayed a half hour because of a malfunctioning catapult. The search pattern of one of the planes would have carried it over the American carriers—had it been launched.

Fletcher, too, was sending off search planes, ten Dauntlesses from the *Yorktown*, but they also missed the enemy carriers, still hidden under heavy weather. But the pilots of PBY Flight 58, Lieutenants Howard Ady and William Chase, churning through patches of clear and cloudy sky, spied a thin feather on the water to the north. It was a ship's wake; then another, another—and more. They dipped down and saw Japanese carriers below. They immediately radioed a maddeningly laconic message to Midway, intercepted by Fletcher waiting in the dark, "Enemy carriers." That was all. This answered very few of the questions racing through Fletcher's mind. Where were the carriers? How many were there?

These questions were not immediately forthcoming, for the Catalina had been spotted and anti-aircraft fire rose up from the ships. Zeros, too, began climbing to intercept the American plane. Ady and Chase dipped into a cloud bank and were lost to the Japanese gunners, as well as to the fighter pilots. After some moments, they selected another break in the clouds and circled back for another look. Almost directly below them they saw Tomonaga's bombers and fighters, halfway to Midway. Their radio crackled, "Many planes heading Midway, bearing 320°, distance 150." And then Fletcher began accumulating his answers when a third message came in, "Two carriers and battleship bearing 320°, distance 180, course 135, speed 25." Because he had to wait for the search planes, Fletcher ordered Spruance to "proceed southwesterly and attack enemy carriers when definitely located. I will follow as soon as planes recovered."

At Midway too all hands prepared for action. Shortly after the message "Many planes heading Midway," the radar picked up the Japanese formation. Air raid sirens blared, aircraft lifted into the air, and men rushed to gun positions and shelters. The B-17s headed for the transports were reached by radio and directed to strike at the carriers. The four B-26s armed with torpedoes and six Grumman TBFs ("Avengers"), making their first combat sortie,

The Brewster F2A ("Buffalo"), no match for the Zero, made its single U.S. combat effort at the Battle of Midway and was hopelessly outperformed—to the tragic cost of Marine pilots. (NAVY DEPT., NATIONAL ARCHIVES)

were vectored toward the Japanese carriers. In addition Marine dive bombers, sixteen SBD-2s (Dauntlesses) led by Major Lofton B. Henderson, and eleven SB2U-3s (Vindicators) led by Major Benjamin Morris, all of VMSB-241, were also sent to deal with the carriers.

As for the oncoming Japanese bombers and fighters, within ten minutes of their first sighting Marine fighters of VMF-221 were air-borne for interception. There were twenty-five fighters, nineteen of which unfortunately were the hopelessly inferior Brewster F2A Buffalos; the remaining six were Grumman F4F Wildcats. Major Floyd B. Parks led the first attack upon the Japanese formation with a dozen planes. Thirty miles out at fourteen thousand feet Parks sighted a Japanese formation twenty thousand feet below him. The Zeros, evidently assigned to strafe Midway and not expecting interception, flew beneath the dive bombers. Parks led a diving attack upon the unsuspecting bombers. Within minutes he was joined by Captain Kirk Armistead with the other thirteen Marine fighters and a general melee ensued. The Zeros swarmed over the Buffalos and Wildcats and of the twenty-five which had gone into the battle, only ten Marine fighters returned. In exchange for five or six Japanese planes the Marines lost thirteen Buffalos and two Wildcats,

Midway following the Japanese air attack by Tomonaga's first wave of Vals and Kates. Two of the island's *indigenous inhabitants, gooney birds, nest in the foreground.* (NAVY DEPT., NATIONAL ARCHIVES)

and of the ten planes which returned only two were operational.

Tomonaga pressed on to Midway and at six-thirty the first bomb fell; bombs continued falling, despite the heavy antiaircraft fire, for the next twenty minutes. Hundreds of bombs tumbled down upon both Sand and Eastern islands. Several buildings were left burning on both islands; the powerhouse on Eastern was struck, so was the post exchange; a bomb crashed into the command post of Major William W. Benson, killing him and several other men. Bombs fell along the northeastern edge of Sand also, demolishing barracks, setting a seaplane hangar aflame, and detonating fuel storage tanks. Very little damage was done to the airstrip and, of course, since most of the Midway-based aircraft were out searching for Nagumo's carriers, very few planes went up in smoke. Thirteen Americans lay dead and eighteen were wounded. Although unaware of the small casualty toll, Tomonaga saw that not enough damage had been done to Midway—and that

Midway flag raising. The Japanese attack came simultaneously with the raising of the colors, which proceeded as scheduled despite the "bombs bursting in air." (Note: this was not a posed photograph.)
(U. S. NAVY)

Grumman TBF ("Avenger"), which made its battle debut at Midway. (NAVY DEPT., NATIONAL ARCHIVES)

Of the six new Avengers that had been dispatched from Midway, only one returned; this is it.

(U. S. NAVY)

antiaircraft fire was savagely profuse as he led the formation away from Midway, now marked by curling columns of black smoke and fire. He radioed to Nagumo on the *Akagi,* "There is need for a second attack. Time: 0700."

When this message was received Nagumo was in a state of passive perturbation; the Catalina piloted by Ady and Chase had been seen and clearly it had seen them. The Americans must now be aware of the presence of Japanese carriers. What to do? Should he send another strike against Midway, or should he hold his planes in readiness for a possible attack from enemy carriers, if they were around?

A bugle blared announcing "Air Raid!" At this time the Japanese had no radar system. It was just five minutes after Tomonaga's request for a second Midway attack. A flag whipped up the mast of one of the destroyers: "Enemy planes in sight." Shortly after, a bridge lookout on the *Akagi* shouted, "Six medium land-based planes approaching! Twenty degrees to starboard. On the horizon." Nearly ten miles away were the four Army Marauders, "their bellies cut and sutured to carry torpedoes," a detachment from the 22nd Bombardment Group (Medium) and the 38th Bombardment Group (M). Leading the four B-26s was Captain James F. Collins. As he sighted the Japanese ships he saw also six Navy Avengers, low on the water, swarming with Zeros.

The Avengers were a detachment of Torpedo

Squadron 8, the main body of which was based on the *Hornet* at Point Luck. Caught by the impending battle at Midway en route to join the rest of the squadron, they had to operate from the islands rather than from the *Hornet.* The six TBFs were led into the battle by Lieutenant Langdon K. Fieberling. He and Collins had sighted the Japanese carriers at about the same time.

Leading the attack, Fieberling bore down upon the carriers through a virtual curtain of antiaircraft fire and a trio of Zeros, the pilots of which took the chance of being struck by their own shellfire. Within moments three of the Avengers were aflame and cartwheeled into the water. But the survivors pushed onward, through the all but impenetrable gunfire. By this time the Marauders, too, had joined in the attack, flying through the barrage of gunfire. Even the big guns on the larger ships were depressed to fire into the onrushing planes, raising great waterspouts in their flight paths as dangerous as the fire itself. It was near suicide, as the planes and crews were chopped to bits in the unescorted attempt at the carriers.

When the torpedo bombers came within range only three planes of the original six remained. One of the Marauders was shot down, then another. The last, which had managed to release its torpedo, flashed over the deck of the *Akagi,* burst into flame, and plunged into the sea. When the attack was over, only two B-26s and one TBF returned to Midway. Not one of the torpedoes had hit its target. The ferocity of the Japanese defense had forced the Americans to release the torpedoes from too great a distance, which enabled the ships to maneuver out of their paths. Nagumo watched one of the torpedoes pass harmlessly by the *Akagi* in a curling white wake.

As soon as it was clear that the Americans had either been driven off or had crashed into the sea, Nagumo made his decision. As Tomonaga had suggested, there would be a second attack upon Midway itself. Evidently the land-based torpedo bombers would give them no further trouble.

This decision entailed complications for the deck crews of the *Akagi* and *Kaga,* for the planes then ready on their flight decks were armed with torpedoes in readiness for an attack upon American carriers. But to this moment none had been sighted. So the planes were brought below decks and the torpedoes removed and replaced with conventional bombs. The aircraft of the *Hiryu* and *Soryu* were not affected by Nagumo's decision, for they were already armed for dive-bombing. The torpedo bombers from these carriers were part of Tomonaga's first attack wave; the dive bombers for this wave had come from the *Akagi* and *Kaga.*

As this changeover was being feverishly made, the carriers came under another attack, this time from Sweeney's Flying Fortresses. From the *Akagi* great water geysers could be seen rising around the *Hiryu* and *Soryu* as the fourteen B-17s, untroubled by the Zeros, whose pilots seemed wary of the big bombers, dropped their full load of bombs. Again, upon their safe return to Midway, claims for hits upon the carriers were made, but actually no bomb from the B-17s hit any of the carriers.

Nagumo could take pride in the effective manner in which the men in his force dodged the American missiles or destroyed their planes. But to his surprise, the delayed *Tone* search plane had wired back a report of "Ten ships, apparently enemy. . . ." But what kind of ships? Nagumo wished to know. This was an unexpected turn, for American surface ships, hundreds of miles from Midway, were not anticipated for another day or two. Nagumo sent orders below and to the *Kaga:* Stop rearming the bombers with conventional bombs and begin arming with torpedoes.

There was another interruption in the rapidly developing battle. The Marine Dauntlesses and Vindicators from Midway, led by Henderson and Morris, arrived to make glide-bombing attacks upon the carriers. Henderson led, with his sixteen Dauntlesses, an attack upon the *Hiryu.* Because of his pilots' unfamiliarity with the Dauntless, Henderson decided upon a glide attack rather than a dive-bombing. At eight hundred feet he was met by a swarm of Zeros and within minutes eight of the Dauntlesses, including Henderson's, went down in flames. There were no hits made on any enemy ships.

Major Morris's slower Vindicators came upon the Japanese ships shortly after Henderson but not in a position for an attack on any of the carriers. They attacked battleships instead and although claiming to have hit the *Haruna* or *Kirishima,* may have only succeeded in a near miss. Two of the Vindicators were lost in the attack and a third crashed in the sea five miles from Midway. The pilot was alive,

Enterprise *Wildcats prepare for takeoff to escort the bombers and torpedo planes of the U.S. fleet.*
(NAVY DEPT., NATIONAL ARCHIVES)

but the gunner, Private Henry I. Starks, was dead; he had never fired a machine gun before in his life until the Battle of Midway. Major Morris later took over the command of VMSB-241, upon the loss of Henderson, but was himself lost later in the day during a search flight for "a burning enemy carrier," which was never found.

Once again the Japanese carriers had fought off heroic but ineffectual American attacks, and Nagumo could take some consolation in that. But then the *Tone* search plane wired another report on the American surface fleet it had found: "Enemy ships are five cruisers and five destroyers."

There was a break in the tension on the *Akagi*'s bridge.

"Just as I thought," said intelligence officer Lieutenant Commander Ono, expressing everyone's sense of deliverance; "there are no carriers."

Eleven minutes later the *Tone* plane reported, "Enemy force accompanied by what appears to be aircraft carrier bringing up the rear." The imprecision—"what appears to be aircraft carrier"—was hopeful, but maddening. Ten minutes later the plane reported, "Two additional ships, apparently cruis-

ers. . . ." Nagumo realized he must face reality; so great a number of ships must contain at least one carrier. If so, however, where were the carrier aircraft?

Nagumo now decided that he must launch his torpedo-armed aircraft against the American surface fleet, whatever its composition. The Japanese would then however, be without proper fighter escort, for all of the Zeros from the projected second wave had been sent aloft to fight the several waves of attackers which had come from Midway. The Zeros would need to land to refuel. And any moment would bring the return of the first attack wave; Tomonaga's bombers and fighters would need the deck space for landing—and they too would require refueling and rearming. While Nagumo pondered his next move, he received a message from Rear-Admiral Tamon Yamaguchi, whom many regarded as the heir of Yamamoto and who led the 2nd Carrier Division (the *Hiryu* and *Soryu*). "Consider it advisable," Yamaguchi radioed, "to launch attack force immediately." Yamaguchi, having successfully dodged the B-17s, was concerned with the *Tone*'s search plane's reports of the American surface fleet and the probable carrier. The enemy task force must be attacked immediately.

But Nagumo continued to vacillate. He was aware of the importance of attacking the American ships, but he could not send off the torpedo planes without escorting Zeros—or with Zeros on the verge of running out of fuel. He had himself witnessed the virtual butchery of the American attackers without escort. Then he made up his mind: they would recover the Midway returnees, rearm, and be ready for the enemy surface fleet. Another order went to the hangar decks below as the readied planes were cleared from the flight decks to receive the incoming aircraft. The bombs were to be changed to torpedoes—again. As this proceeded Nagumo sighted the first of the returning planes. He signaled the *Kaga, Soryu,* and *Hiryu:* "After completing recovery operations, force will temporarily head northward. We plan to contact and destroy enemy task force." He then radioed Yamamoto, hundreds of miles away aboard the *Yamato,* and Vice-Admiral Nobutake Kondo, with his Midway Invasion Force, of his decision. Finally, after nearly forty minutes, all of the first attack wave planes had been recovered and were being feverishly refueled and rearmed. Nagumo ordered the carrier force to steam away from Midway to a position from which the second attack wave could be sent against the American fleet. Meanwhile, his carriers were in their most vulnerable state: decks and hangar decks crowded with planes, bombs, and fuel hoses. But this nagging thought was overlooked in the excitement of preparing to finish off the American fleet.

Spruance, in the *Enterprise,* with the *Hornet* as company, had steamed toward the Japanese carrier force as soon as word had come of its location. Spruance, like Nagumo, had difficult decisions to make. He had planned to launch planes about a hundred miles from the Japanese carriers, but his chief of staff, Captain Miles Browning, described by Samuel Eliot Morison as "one of the most irascible and unstable officers ever to earn a fourth stripe, but a man with a slide-rule brain," suggested an earlier launch. Browning's thinking told him that Nagumo would attempt to launch a second attack upon Midway. Why not catch him while he was refueling his

John Waldron, dedicated commander of VT-8, "Torpedo 8" of the Hornet, *which was wiped out at Midway; right: Clarence W. McClusky, air group com-* *mander of the* Enterprise *who led the attack on the Japanese carrier* Kaga.

planes? Decisive, brilliant, even enigmatic, Spruance took the advice, and further, he decided to launch a full-scale attack (knowing that Fletcher would follow later with reinforcements from the *Yorktown*).

About 7 A.M. the *Hornet* and *Enterprise* turned into the wind; they were nearly two hundred miles away from the expected position of the enemy carriers, but Spruance believed the risk of the long distance would be worth it, indeed, if Browning were proved correct. At this same moment, Tomonaga's planes had begun their return flight from Midway and Nagumo's carriers had come under the attack of the Army B-26s and the Navy Avengers.

Among the first aircraft off the *Hornet*'s flight deck were the torpedo bombers of the main section of Torpedo 8, fifteen ancient Douglas Devastators. Leading this squadron was a Navy career pilot, tough, aggressive, sharp-eyed, proud of his Sioux Indian forebears, Lieutenant Commander John C. Waldron. A devoted Navy man, Waldron had welded his men into a well-disciplined unit without ever losing their devotion. Along with the Torpedo 8 (VT-8) planes, the *Hornet* launched thirty-five bombers and ten fighters. The total of sixty *Hornet* aircraft were led by the carrier's Air Group Commander, Commander Stanhope C. Ring.

Lieutenant Commander Clarence W. McClusky led an equal number of aircraft (actually thirty-seven bombers, fourteen torpedo bombers, and ten fighters) off the *Enterprise*. The air reverberated to the roar of more than a hundred planes, which formed into units and headed for the expected point of interception with the Japanese carriers. Fletcher too followed these planes up with a dozen torpedo bombers, seventeen dive bombers, and six Wildcats—these last under the leadership of Lieutenant Commander John S. Thatch. The dive bombers were under the command of Lieutenant Commander Maxwell F. Leslie, who suffered an ironic mishap early in the flight. When the planes had climbed to an altitude of ten thousand feet, he signaled the squadron to arm their bombs. Leslie himself pushed the newly installed electrical device and, to his dismay, experienced the unmistakable lurch of a suddenly lightened aircraft. He soon learned through hand signals from his number two man on the left (whose rear gunner joined in the frantic wigwagging) that the squadron commander had lost his thousand-pound bomb. From the right another

Dauntless veered over, pilot and gunner signaling. Obviously a short or some other mechanical quirk had caused the bomb to fall instead of merely arming it. There was nothing for Leslie to do but to lead his squadron into the battle without a bomb. Within minutes, to his further dismay, he learned that three other planes had suffered the same accident. All seventeen planes pushed on, though only thirteen were properly armed. Lieutenant Paul Holmberg, Leslie's number two man, laconically commented, "When this bad news was confirmed, the skipper made many frustrating motions with his hands and lips. . . ."

Meanwhile, the *Hornet* and *Enterprise* planes neared the point of interception. Nagumo's decision to turn north, away from Midway, while his planes refueled actually took the carriers out of the line of interception. Intermittent cloud cover, too, played its role. For as Ring led the *Hornet* planes along the line, he saw none of the Japanese carriers, then hidden under cloud. He continued farther, along the line, followed by the bombers and fighters, until he saw nothing but ocean or clouds. Perhaps Nagumo had turned southward, toward Midway, Ring thought, and turned toward the atoll. But he found nothing there but the smoking reminders of the Japanese bombings. He had made a wrong guess. Although some of his planes managed to return to the *Hornet,* some, dangerously low on fuel, had to put down at Midway; some did not make it and splashed into the waters around Midway.

Waldron, leading Torpedo 8, on the other hand, sensed that Nagumo would change course. To Waldron's left, a few miles to the south, flew Lieutenant Commander Eugene F. Lindsey's fourteen Devastators of Torpedo Squadron 6. Above him, at twenty thousand feet, zigzagged the ten Wildcats led by Lieutenant James S. Gray as fighter escort of the *Enterprise* bombers. The agreement between Gray and Lindsey was that when the torpedo bombers found the Japanese carriers, Lindsey would signal Gray for fighter protection during the attack. However, in flying through cloud Gray's fighters attached themselves inadvertently to Waldron's Devastators. There was no agreed signal, of course, between the *Hornet*'s Waldron and the *Enterprise*'s Gray.

Thus, because of a series of small twists and turns of fate, Waldron's slow-moving Devastators were the first of the carrier planes to find the Japanese car-

Ensign George H. Gay (recuperating in the U.S. naval hospital at Pearl Harbor), the lone survivor of Waldron's Torpedo 8.

(NAVY DEPT., NATIONAL ARCHIVES)

riers. Certainly one of the reasons was Waldron's mystical determination. When his men received their attack plan that day, attached to it was a letter from Waldron:

Just a word to let you know that I feel we are ready. We have had a very short time to train and we have worked under the most severe difficulties. But we have truly done the best humanly possible. I actually believe that under these conditions we are the best in the world. My greatest hope is that we encounter a favorable tactical situation, but if we don't, and the worst comes to worst, I want each of us to do his utmost to destroy our enemies. If there is only one plane left to make a final run in, I want that man to go in and get a hit. May God be with all of us. Good luck, happy landings and give 'em hell.

Waldron led the Devastators to the point of interception, and when he found nothing, some sixth sense told him to turn north. This brought them around the edge of the large bank of cloud through which they had passed. And there—about eight miles distant, off his starboard wing—lay Nagumo's carrier striking force. Ordering Torpedo 8 into bat-

tle formation, Waldron descended to within a few yards above the Pacific, assigning targets to the various elements, barking commands in a dry, emotionless voice. The fifteen Devastators lined up on their targets, Waldron selecting the nearest carrier.

Fifty Zeros which had been circling over the Japanese fleet dropped down to intercept the intruders. Without fighter protection they should be relatively simple to deal with. The Devastator was slow, underarmed (one .50-caliber and one .30-caliber machine gun: the pilot controlled the forward firing gun and the radio-gunner manned a flexible gun); the Douglas TBD-1 was obsolete by 1942. It could barely manage two hundred miles an hour top speed, and when on its torpedo run, the plane lumbered along, a moving target.

Even before Waldron reached anywhere near a torpedo release point, the swift Zeros thronged around the hapless Devastators. In seconds, the Pacific erupted with the blazing splashes of fiery Devastators. The Zeros closed in from all sides and shot the torpedo bombers literally to pieces. Ensign George Gay, the squadron's navigator, piloted the fifteenth Devastator and watched the decimation of Torpedo 8 with horror. One after the other the burning planes careened into the water, crumbling in the impact, spurting foam, smoke, and flame. Gay saw Waldron still pressing on although both his wingmen had been shot down. A Zero flashed across the Devastator's path, spraying it with machine-gun fire, and Gay saw flame licking from a ruptured fuel tank; then the tank burst into an orange-red blossom. Waldron, evidently trying to get away from the scorching flames, clawed the canopy open and stood up. At full speed, with torpedo still slung under the fuselage, the blazing Devastator slammed into the Pacific.

Gay continued on his run. The skipper was gone, he realized; as he darted his eyes over the water, he realized too everyone was gone but him. His was, in Waldron's tragically prophetic phrase, the "only one plane left." The Zeros whirred in to attack the fifteenth Devastator. Gay tried to ignore them as he centered his sight on a carrier, even then maneuvering out of his line of sight. He sensed the thud of Japanese machine-gun fire striking the plane; there was stinging pain in his left arm. A spent slug had dug into the flesh of the arm; another fragment of steel, possibly a piece of the cockpit torn away, cut his hand. His gunner, Robert Huntington, shouted, "Mr. Gay, I'm hit!" Through the frenzied, unremitting attack of the Zeros, Gay prodded the Devastator toward his target.

The single aircraft became the center of attention of the ship's antiaircraft guns as well as of the converging Zeros. Bits of cockpit burst in around Gay's feet, control cables severed, and he had trouble keeping the Devastator under control. He had to release that final "pickle," as Waldron called the torpedoes. Gay, of the thirty men who had begun the attack, was the only man alive. Huntington sprawled lifelessly in the rear cockpit.

Gay had further trouble with his torpedo release mechanism, undoubtedly shot up by the Zeros. Unable to use his left hand, Gay gripped the control column between his knees and with his right hand pulled the emergency release lever. The torpedo dropped and the lightened plane leaped up into the air and within minutes skimmed barely ten feet over the bow of the carrier. Gay kicked the rudder, turning south, now barely above the waves. It was over for Ensign Gay, so he flattened out the Devastator and stalled into the sea. He splashed in with great force, tearing away the right wing, which bounced along the surface like a flat rock. Gay tore open the canopy as water poured in on him. He glanced again at the rear cockpit. There was nothing to do for Huntington. Quickly Gay swam away from the sinking plane, concerned over what would happen when the Zeros came around to investigate.

Inflating his life jacket, Gay bobbed around the waters strewn with the debris of battle. He found a boat bag, which contained an inflatable rubber raft, holding onto it for future use. It would not be healthy to use it now, with the Zeros whipping over now and then. Then he found a floating cushion which had been knocked free of the Devastator. Placing the cushion over his head, Gay found refuge from the searching Zeros and for the next few hours watched the unfolding drama of the Battle of Midway. (After dark Gay inflated his rubber boat and was found the next day, the sole survivor of Torpedo 8's attack, by a Navy PBY. Upon being taken to Pearl Harbor for medical attention, Gay was asked by a doctor how he had treated his wounds. In his Texas-inflected speech Gay replied that he had soaked his wounds in "salt water for several hours.")

A Dauntless, dive brakes down, drops a bomb.
(DOUGLAS AIRCRAFT)

It was a jubilant Zero leader who could report to Nagumo that all fifteen American torpedo bombers had been sent burning into the sea. Not one torpedo strike had been made. The war gods smiled, indeed, upon Nagumo.

But Nagumo hardly had time for an impassive smile, for a lookout shouted, "Enemy torpedo bombers, thirty degrees to starboard, coming in low!" This was followed by another exclamation, from the opposite lookout, "Enemy torpedo bombers approaching forty degrees to port!" The tempo was accelerating. The starboard attackers were Lindsey's fourteen Devastators of VT-6 (the *Enterprise*), which had flown parallel to Waldron's squadron, but some miles to the south. Like Waldron, Lindsey sensed that the carriers lay to the north instead of closer to Midway, as Ring had thought. Also like Waldron, Lindsey swooped in to attack (his major target being the *Kaga*) without fighter escort. For some reason Lindsey never called Gray, still circling over the the scene of the battle at twenty thousand feet. Instead, he plunged into the attack and was cut to

Dauntlesses at Midway: as a Japanese ship burns following an earlier attack, another wave of SBDs close in for the kill. (NAVY DEPT., NATIONAL ARCHIVES)

ribbons by antiaircraft and the swarms of Zeros. In minutes, ten of Lindsey's fourteen planes (including his own) were sent spinning and flaming into the sea. The four remaining planes released their torpedoes, but again not one struck home.

Almost stimultaneously the *Yorktown*'s VT-3, commanded by Lieutenant Commander Lance E. Massey, a dozen Devastators in all, in company with Thatch's six Wildcats, arrived upon the scene. As they hurtled toward the Japanese carriers, some of the Zeros could be seen landing. Obviously the earlier fighting had depleted the fuel and ammunition of the Japanese fighters. But this did not prevent others from swamping Thatch's little band and also Massey's Devastators on their torpedo run-ins. The air once again filled with puffs of smoke and machine-gun fire crisscrossed above the water, breaking the surface with evenly spaced, vicious geysers. Like Waldron and Lindsey before him, Massey raced headlong into certain devastation. His and six other planes were quickly shot into the sea. The five remaining planes continued on the run-in and

splashed their torpedoes into the churning water. Three planes were flamed by the Zeros just moments after. Of the twelve TBDs Massey took into the attack, only two returned to the *Yorktown*.

In about a half hour, roughly from 9:28, when Waldron's VT-8 had attacked, until 10 A.M., when the last of Massey's torpedoes went astray, Nagumo's carriers had been attacked by forty-one American aircraft and had destroyed thirty-five. Not one torpedo struck any Japanese ship. Now at last the battle-churned skies were free of enemy aircraft and the sea, here and there, emitted rising smoke. But the destroyed planes did not stay afloat long and all that remained was oil-soaked, scorched flotsam. Under one of the insignificant dots floated Ensign Gay.

Now Nagumo could give his full attention to launching the counterstrike. All during the attack by the doomed torpedo bombers preparations had gone on to get the planes ready to strike at the carriers, the source of the thirty-five planes they had just annihilated. Soon after, the planes were bombed-up and ready for take-off. The four carriers turned into the wind. Within five minutes their bombers would be air-borne and racing for the American carriers. The gods continued to smile. At ten-twenty Nagumo gave the order to begin launching the attack.

At ten twenty-four the air officer on the *Akagi* signaled, and a Zero gathered speed and roared off the deck. A lookout screamed, "Hell-divers!"

Plummeting out of a nearly cloudless sky were several Dauntlesses. The men on the deck of the *Akagi* watched this sudden materialization with stunned horror. The dive bombers plunged toward the *Kaga,* almost unopposed except for sporadic machine-gun fire from a few alert crews and some splotches of antiaircraft fire. The Zeros had been pulled down to the water by the attack of the torpedo bombers, whose sacrifices now would begin to assume implications beyond blind heroism.

The Dauntlesses were the *Yorktown* dive bombers led by Maxwell Leslie, whose own bomb had been accidentally dropped into the sea. He and the sixteen others arrived not long after the Japanese carriers had scurried out of the way of Massey's torpedo attack. Leslie had his eye on the nearest two, the *Soryu* and the *Kaga*. The latter, with more than twice the tonnage of the *Soryu,* impressed Leslie as the more tempting target. Signaling his wingmen, he led the bombers into a seventy-degree dive. Although bombless, Leslie contributed to the general destruction by firing his .50-caliber machine gun, beginning at ten thousand feet and pulling out at four thousand because the gun had jammed. On the decks of the *Kaga* he saw many planes apparently ready for take-off.

Leslie was followed by Lieutenant Paul Holmberg, who like his commander aimed the Dauntless at the great red circle painted on the *Kaga*'s flight deck. The wind screamed over the Dauntless as Holmberg dived down to twenty-five hundred feet. He pushed the electric bomb release and, just to make certain, also snatched at the manual release. Holmberg's thousand-pound bomb burst near the *Kaga*'s superstructure, spilling flame, flinging shattered metal, ripping and tearing across the deck, leaving a screaming, red trail of horror in its wake. More planes dived, some achieving only near misses, but three other bombs followed across the flight deck. Planes were flung over the side into the sea by the force of the explosions. Fuel tanks burst and poured flame into the holocaust, fires enveloped the flight deck and poured onto the men and planes below. Within minutes, the *Kaga* was a hopeless flaming pyre, despite the efforts of damage-control crews.

As Leslie and his men attacked the *Kaga* Mc-Clusky and his thirty-seven Dauntlesses from the *Enterprise* came upon the scene. McClusky had followed the wake of a destroyer which had left the main carrier group to deal with an American submarine, the *Nautilus,* which had been harassing it. The destroyer, moving at a fast clip would head, McClusky was certain, for the carriers—and he was right. McClusky's planes came in from the southwest, almost at right angles to Leslie's. The *Akagi,* which had been fleeing northwestward, was nearest to McClusky's formation; the giant carrier made a sharp turn to the south. The smaller *Soryu,* which had been passed over by Leslie in favor of the *Kaga,* was also in McClusky's view. The first bomb had already burst on the *Kaga*'s deck, billowing black smoke. McClusky felt certain it would need no further attention. The remaining two carriers (the *Hiryu* was farther to the north and out of sight) had turned into the wind to launch aircraft.

Two minutes after Leslie dropped down upon the *Kaga,* the *Enterprise* Dauntlesses, divided into two formations, dived on the *Soryu* and the *Akagi.* Mc-Clusky led the *Soryu* attack and Lieutenant Wilmer E. Gallagher led the attack upon the *Akagi,* Nagumo's flagship. Unopposed by the Zeros, the Dauntlesses whipped through the air toward their targets, dropped their bombs, and pulled away. Two direct hits smashed onto the *Akagi*'s deck—neither of which would have normally seriously stopped the carrier. But the detonations flared the fuel in the waiting planes; the intense heat, in turn, detonated the bombs and torpedoes the Japanese planes carried. The air became deadly with metal splinters and flame. Pilots died in their cockpits, or were blown overboard burning into the sea. Deck hands became screaming torches. The helpless wounded were literally roasted to death on the twisted, scorching decks.

Three direct hits transformed the nearby *Soryu* into a similar inferno; within twenty minutes Captain Ryusaku Yanagimoto ordered the carrier abandoned. Men leaped into the water away from the searing heat and explosions. Because of the several order changes of the bombers' bomb loads, many bombs and torpedoes had been left lying about the decks, which added further hazard. The *Soryu* was obviously doomed. His men tried to force Yanagimoto, who was an extremely popular officer, to leave the bridge, but the captain refused. A burly petty officer, a Navy wrestling champion, was sent to take Yanagimoto by force if necessary. He was prevented by the determined look in his captain's eyes—he left without touching the officer. The last known act of Yanagimoto was his singing of *"Kimigayo"* the national anthem, as he remained on the smoke-obscured bridge. Shortly after 7 P.M., following nine hours of drifting and blazing, the *Soryu* sank steaming under the sea. It was the first of the Japanese carriers to be lost.

The *Kaga* followed within twelve minutes—at 7:25 P.M. During its fiery death throes the carrier came under a submarine attack. Three projectiles streaked for the stricken carrier; two missed and one struck a glancing blow. It was a dud which broke in two; the warhead sank harmlessly into the depths but the buoyant rear portion of the torpedo remained afloat to serve as an improvised floatboard for several of the *Kaga*'s crew. But eight hundred others went to the bottom when the burning hulk, torn by severe explosions, sank to the bottom.

Nagumo found the realities difficult to grasp.

Japanese torpedo bombers race through heavy anti-aircraft fire for the American ships. Shrapnel splashes in the foreground. A cruiser (left) and a destroyer (right) fire at three approaching enemy planes.
(U. S. NAVY)

From the *Akagi*'s bridge he could see the smoke of the *Kaga* and *Soryu* staining the distant skies. Around him there were confusion, shouting, the acrid stench of burning metal; Rear Admiral Ryunosuke Kusaka, Nagumo's chief of staff, was shouting something to him. In the noise of explosion, the confusion, the smoke, Nagumo stared at him. Kusaka said something about leaving the *Akagi*. Nagumo seemed oblivious to the sense of Kusaka's statement; he nodded and turned away from his chief of staff. The *Akagi*'s deck was a flaming shambles, but Nagumo did not wish to leave.

"Sir," Kusaka pleaded, "most of our ships are still intact. You must command them." The old man, ashen, found it all very difficult to believe: in two minutes a handful of planes had wiped out three quarters of his carrier force. Captain Taijiro Aoki joined the men, added his voice gently to the argument. The *Nagara,* a light cruiser, had pulled up alongside and the two men convinced Nagumo that he should retire to the *Nagara*. Aoki assured Nagumo, "I will take care of the ship. Please, we all implore you, shift your flag to the *Nagara* and resume command of the force."

Aoki also argued that since there were no communications systems working, Nagumo must leave the ship in order to carry on. The old admiral realized the sense of this statement and consented to leave. By this time the fires had spread so heavily that Nagumo could leave the bridge only by sliding down a rope to the deck. He was then led along an outboard passage to the anchor deck, where he stiffly climbed down a rope ladder into a waiting boat, which took him to the *Nagara*.

Yamamoto, who had positioned the ships of the main force too far away from Nagumo's carriers to be of any help to him, found it difficult also to comprehend the meaning of what was happening. When Captain Aoki, still aboard the doomed *Akagi,* wired for permission to sink the carrier after ordering the survivors off, Yamamoto, upon intercepting the message, ordered the scuttling delayed. Aoki then lashed himself to the anchor, on the only fire-free portion of the ship, and waited. Eventually, Yamamoto sensed the inevitable and gave the order to sink the carrier. A rescue party went aboard and convinced Aoki he should not go down with the ship. Rather than permit the ship to fall into enemy hands, even

The Yorktown *under attack by torpedo bombers led by Tomonaga, whose plane was destroyed by American* guns *after it had released its torpedo. The* Yorktown *lists, the result of earlier strikes.*

in derelict form, Japanese destroyers sent torpedoes into its sides. At 4:55 A.M. in the morning of June 4, Nagumo's flagship sank bursting into the sea, carrying 263 dead with it. That was the third carrier to go.

Aboard the *Hiryu,* the fourth and last carrier of Nagumo's striking force, Admiral Yamaguchi prepared to attack the American ships. Because of his position to the north of the other three carriers, he had escaped attack from the dive bombers. Gazing around the horizon, Yamaguchi was readily aware of his responsibilities: his planes only could strike at the American fleet.

Just four minutes before a reluctant Nagumo abandoned the *Akagi,* the resolute Yamaguchi launched eighteen dive bombers and six Zeros against the now known position of an American carrier. The small force was led by Lieutenant Michio Kobayashi, a veteran of Pearl Harbor. On the flight Kobayashi lost two of his escorting fighters, whose overzealous pilots darted away to attack a

formation of American Dauntlesses returning from the battle scene. These may have been Leslie's planes triumphantly finished with the *Kaga.* Kobayashi lost further to an American Wildcat attack, so that by the time he came within the vicinity of the carrier, only eight of the original eighteen bombers continued to follow him.

Meanwhile, just before noon of that June 4, the radar aboard the *Yorktown* detected the approach of Japanese aircraft, and all preparations were made to meet an enemy attack: refueling of aircraft was stopped, watertight doors were slammed closed, an auxiliary tank on the stern holding eight hundred gallons of aviation fuel was pushed over the side, fuel lines were drained and filled with carbon dioxide. Fighters were sent out to meet the attack, and returning planes, including Leslie's flight, already low on fuel, were waved off and ordered out of antiaircraft fire zones.

Kobayashi swept in for the attack with his decimated forces; two of the eight planes went down before the guns from the ships and the remaining six swept through the murderous wall of fire. Three bombs struck the *Yorktown,* the second of which caused the most serious damage because it had pierced the side of the carrier and detonated within the ship. A rag stowage compartment burst into flames, sending harsh black smoke out of the *Yorktown.* The other two bombs also caused intense fires, but working quickly and efficiently, the damage-control parties soon checked the most serious blazes. However, by twelve-twenty the *Yorktown* stood dead in the water, the engines stopped. Fletcher knew he would be out of communication with his other ships if he remained aboard the stricken, burning *Yorktown.* He transferred with his staff to the cruiser *Astoria.* Meanwhile, damage-control work continued on the *Yorktown.*

While Kobayashi led the attack upon the *Yorktown,* Yamaguchi finally learned the full measure of the American carrier strength. A *Soryu* scout plane had returned to the Japanese fleet and, finding its home carrier ablaze, landed upon the *Hiryu.* The pilot's radio had gone out on him and he was unable to report that he had seen three carriers, naming them—the *Enterprise,* the *Hornet,* and the *Yorktown!* which was supposed to have been sunk at the Coral Sea.

Only five bombers of the original eighteen and three fighters of six returned to the *Hiryu.* Among the missing was attack leader Kobayashi. From the surviving pilots Yamaguchi ascertained that the elusive *Yorktown* was dead in the water and spouting smoke. With two more carriers in the vicinity Yamaguchi ordered an immediate attack. All available aircraft must seek out and strike the two remaining carriers. It was not a very impressive array of air power: ten bombers (one of them an orphan from the *Akagi,* burning in the distance) and six Zeros (two of them strays from the *Kaga,* also smoldering), sixteen planes altogether to be led by Joichi Tomonaga, who had led the morning's attack upon Midway. In that attack the left-wing fuel tank had been punctured, but Tomonaga ordered his plane readied despite this. When he took off he knew he was on a one-way flight. Even if not struck down by the enemy, he would not have enough fuel in the single intact tank to bring him back to the *Hiryu.*

All sixteen planes had cleared the *Hiryu's* decks by twelve forty-five. During this period between attacks, the fires on the *Yorktown* were brought completely under control. The decks were cleared of wreckage, holes patched up, and four boilers warmed to life. Within two hours, no longer smoking, the *Yorktown* moved under its own steam. The planes circling overhead were signaled to land, although some, with fuel too far gone, splashed into the waters near other ships. Among these were the aircraft flown by Leslie and Holmberg. Their two Dauntlesses stalled into the water near Fletcher's new flagship, the *Astoria,* and the pilots and gunners were taken from the sea.

About an hour later—at 2:42 P.M.—Tomonaga's small force swarmed in upon the *Yorktown* from all sides. The air boomed and cracked to the sound of gunfire, antiaircraft bursts, and the engines of planes. American fighters attempted to intercept the bombers and tangled with the Zeros. Japanese torpedo bombers were blasted out of the air, but some broke through once again. Tomonaga weathered the storm of fire, dropped his torpedo, and disintegrated under a direct hit. The Japanese force was cut precisely in half: of the ten bombers which took off from the *Hiryu* only five returned; of the six Zeros, three returned. But they claimed two hits upon "a carrier of the *Yorktown* class." Having found the newly restored *Yorktown* moving through the Pacific, apparently unharmed, Tomonaga mistook it for another carrier.

But of the five bombers which had survived the attack, two had indeed sunk a torpedo each deep in the port side of the *Yorktown.* Within minutes the great carrier listed dangerously. The power had gone off and counterflooding, to correct the list, was impossible. There was nothing for Captain Elliott Buckmaster to say but "Pass the word along to abandon ship."

Back at the untouched *Hiryu,* Yamaguchi learned that a second carrier—as his by now exhausted pilots believed—lay dead and smoldering in the water. To Yamaguchi it meant that only one more carrier remained; there was still the chance to snatch some fraction of victory out of their frightful losses. He still had five dive bombers, four torpedo bombers, and six Zeros—with these Yamaguchi would launch a twilight attack upon the "last" American carrier.

But the surviving pilots, many of whom had been active since the morning Midway strike, must rest.

Around five o'clock in the afternoon, during a lull, they were served sweet rice balls (for many the first meal since dawn). A search plane was made ready to find the last carrier for the twilight attack.

Fletcher, meanwhile, realizing he was cut off from on-the-scene reports from pilots, placed Spruance in command of the carrier activities. At almost the exact moment that Tomonaga's bombers came in to attack the *Yorktown* for the second time, a *Yorktown* search pilot, Lieutenant Samuel Adams, spotted the *Hiryu*. He radioed its position back to the carriers and Spruance prepared for an attack on Yamaguchi's ship. Twenty-four Dauntlesses warmed up on the *Enterprise;* they were armed with thousand-pound and five-hundred-pound bombs. Some of the aircraft were from the listing *Yorktown;* all were led by Lieutenant Wilmer E. Gallagher, who had taken part in the earlier attack upon the *Akagi* and *Soryu* with McClusky. On the *Hornet* Captain Marc Mitscher watched sixteen Dauntlesses ready to take off in search of the *Hiryu*. The first planes began taking off around three-thirty in the afternoon.

Gallagher's force found the *Hiryu* at five o'clock, just as the weary pilots wolfed down their sweet rice balls. The scout plane was about to leave the deck when the dread cry rang out, "Enemy dive bombers overhead!" Gallagher's Dauntlesses hurtled down upon the carrier. Antiaircraft fire was pumped up at them as the carrier's captain, Tomeo Kaku, ordered full right rudder in an evasive turn. Three bombs fell into the sea, but there were more and four of them crashed explosively along the flight deck. Flame and gouts of smoke heaved into the air. As on the other three carriers, gassed-up and bombed-up planes burst into flame, spreading the fiery, consuming havoc.

When the *Hornet*'s planes arrived they found the *Hiryu* burning and turned to attack the other ships in the area. But their attacks upon the *Haruna, Tone,* and *Chikuma* were fruitless. Likewise, once again, some of the B-17s from Midway arrived and dropped bombs without making any hits. The *Hiryu,* however, was, like all of the other Nagumo carriers—the *Akagi,* the *Kaga,* the *Soryu*—doomed. The entire carrier force was erased from the Pacific. Attempts were made to bring the fires under control, to get into the engine rooms—but to no avail. Before dawn on June 5 Yamaguchi ordered all the survivors—about eight hundred men—to

Raymond A. Spruance, commander of Task Force 16 at Midway. (NAVY DEPT., NATIONAL ARCHIVES)

come on deck. He had decided to order abandonment of the *Hiryu*.

"As commanding officer of this carrier division," he told them, "I am fully and solely responsible for the loss of the *Hiryu* and *Soryu*. I shall remain on board to the end. I command all of you to leave the ship and continue your loyal service to His Majesty the Emperor." Characteristically, his staff pleaded to be allowed to share his fate, but Yamaguchi ordered them to leave the ship also. Captain Kaku, the ship's skipper, was also determined to remain and begged Yamaguchi to leave; it was the captain's place to go down with the ship. But Yamaguchi was firm, saying merely, "The moon is so bright in the sky."

Kaku, taking his place beside Yamaguchi, said, "We shall watch the moon together." Thus, poeti-

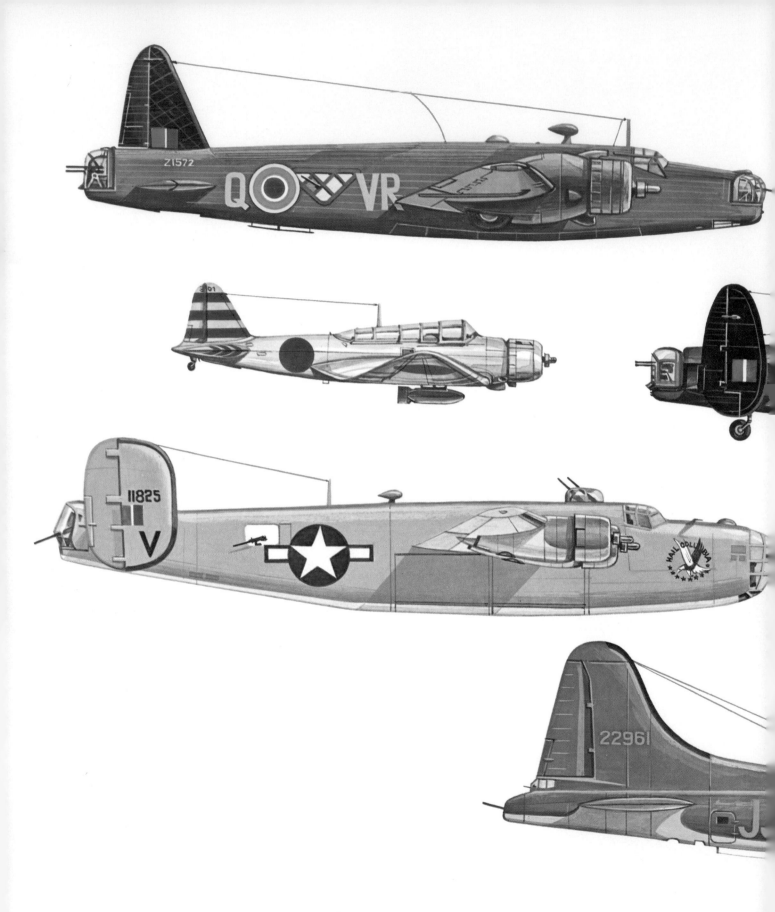

Various aircraft that participated in "victories" of dubious consequence but of remarkable valor. Counterclockwise, beginning from top left: Vickers *Wellington* III of No. 419 Squadron (RCAF) which participated in the Thousand Bomber Raid; Nakajima "Kate," in the markings of Commander Mitsuo Fuchida who led the air attack on Pearl Harbor; Consolidated B-24-D *Liberator,* "Hail Columbia" of the 98th Bomb Group flown by Major John R. Kane to and from Ploesti; Boeing B-17F *Flying Fortress* of the 305th Bomb Group which lost thirteen (of sixteen)

aircraft over Schweinfurt; Curtiss P-40B Tomahawk in the markings of the American Volunteer Group of the Chinese Air Force better known as "The Flying Tigers;" Douglas SBD *Dauntless* of VS-2 from the *Lexington* which participated in the Battle of the Coral Sea, the prelude to Midway; Avro *Lancaster* B.III of No. 617 ("Dam Busters") Squadron, flown by leader Guy Gibson; North American B-25B *Mitchell* flown by Lieutenant Colonel James H. Doolittle on the Tokyo Raid from "Shangri-La."

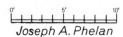

Joseph A. Phelan

cally, did they face the end. Yamaguchi had ordered the final scuttling of the *Hiryu,* which occurred around dawn of the next day, June 5, when four torpedoes were shot into the carrier's sides. However, a search plane which Yamamoto had sent off from the carrier *Hosho* (the single light carrier which had been attached to the main force) to find Nagumo's force located the *Hiryu* still afloat an hour and a half later. The pilot also saw several men still alive on the derelict. Immediate orders went off to Nagumo to send a rescue ship, but when it arrived after daylight no trace of the *Hiryu* remained. (The survivors, members of the engine-room crew who had been trapped below decks, were freed when the Japanese torpedoes blasted open a passage for them. When the *Hiryu* sank they floated around in an abandoned lifeboat they had found until rescued by an American ship. None of these men saw either Yamaguchi or Kaku, who may have already committed suicide.) More than four hundred crewmen went down with the *Hiryu,* along with Yamaguchi and Kaku.

The last of Nagumo's impressive carrier force was gone; the few surviving aircraft, those Zeros which had been in the air when the dive bombers struck, fluttered helplessly over the burning ships, unable to land. As the fuel ran out, the planes fell into the sea.

The fate of the *Hiryu,* if it totally depressed Nagumo, did not take the fight out of Yamamoto, miles from the battle arena aboard the *Yamato.* He had no real idea of what ensued hundreds of miles east. Battle reports were all but incoherent, but one fact was clear: Nagumo's carriers were suffering at the hands of the American airmen. Reacting forcefully, Yamamoto, shortly after noon on June 4, ordered the carriers of the Aleutians Force to race down to Midway; he ordered the heavy cruisers, which were to cover the Midway invasion, to close with the American fleet—and he too would move in to engage the enemy in a last-ditch surface battle. Yamamoto hoped that the cruisers of the Kondo force might meet the Americans in a night action.

But the wary Spruance did not wish to press his luck. Instead of pursuing the Japanese fleet, and risking a night engagement, he reversed course. "I did not feel justified," he reported, "in risking a night encounter with possibly superior enemy forces,

but on the other hand, I did not want to be too far away from Midway the next morning [June 5]. I wished to have a position from which either to follow up retreating enemy forces or to break up a landing attack on Midway."

Yamamoto continued to receive grim news from the scene of action. Even after he had heard that the *Hiryu* had been stricken, he transmitted orders of unbelievable optimism:

(1) *The enemy fleet has been practically destroyed and is retiring eastward.*

(2) *Combined Fleet units in the vicinity are preparing to pursue remnants of the enemy force and, at the same time, to occupy Midway.*

But Nagumo persisted in afflicting him with oppressive information. At each successive report the American forces seemed to increase until Nagumo reported on the evening of June 4 that "Total enemy strength is five carriers, six heavy cruisers, and fifteen destroyers. They are steaming westward. We are retiring to the northwest escorting *Hiryu.* Speed, eighteen knots."

"The Nagumo force," Chief of Staff Rear Admiral Matome Ugaki bitterly and wearily said, "has no stomach for a night engagement!" But Yamamoto, whose stomach literally churned and pained, did and he continued to plan for such an engagement. He relieved Nagumo of his command, except for the still floating but burning *Akagi* and *Hiryu,* and turned the surface fleet command over to Vice-Admiral Nobutake Kondo, who commanded the ships of the Midway Invasion Force (Second Fleet). Kondo managed to instill some of the lost aggressiveness to the fleet and made plans for the night action. But soon, what with Spruance's evasive move to the east, it became obvious that the action could not possibly take place until dawn. Once again in daylight their ships would be at the mercy of the American carrier planes. Various alternative plans were discussed by Yamamoto's staff, each one more impractical than the previous one. One suggestion was that all possible large Japanese ships approach Midway on the following day, June 5, and shell it, a suicidal and therefore attractive solution to the problem of defeat. It would have placed most of the Japanese Navy within the reach of shore-based batteries and shore-based aircraft as well as of the remaining carrier planes. Admiral Ugaki disabused the staff of this idea. He suggested that they wait

The Japanese heavy cruiser Mikuma, *its eight-inch guns useless after attacks by Marine and Navy Vindicators and Dauntlesses, lies helpless in the water. The Vindicator of Richard Fleming smolders on the aft turret (right). The* Mikuma *was sunk soon after by Navy carrier Dauntlesses.*

for the Aleutian carriers and then perhaps launch another attack. "But even if this proves impossible," he asserted, "and we must accept defeat in this operation, we will not have lost the war."

There was a gloomy silence following this statement, for Ugaki had voiced the unspeakable. Who among them could face the prospect of defeat? "But how can we apologize to His Majesty for this defeat?" someone inquired.

"Leave that to me," Yamamoto interjected sharply. "I am the only one who must apologize to His Majesty." He recognized the fruitlessness of

attempting to engage the Americans at night. The *Kaga* and *Soryu* were gone; he then had to turn to the scuttling of the *Akagi*. It would be the first time in history that a Japanese warship was scuttled. It was a difficult decision; at 2:50 A.M. on June 5, Yamamoto gave the order. Within five minutes he issued another, the first sentence of which read:

"THE MIDWAY OPERATION IS CANCELED."

But the drama was not ended simply because its author so decreed; events and characters had taken on their own dynamisms. Within an hour after Yamamoto had canceled the Midway Operation an American submarine, *Tambor,* under the command of Lieutenant Commander John W. Murphy, Jr., patrolling about ninety miles west of Midway, spotted several Japanese ships. They appeared to be heading away from Midway at high speed; they were, in fact, four heavy cruisers, in company with two destroyers, which had been dispatched to carry out a night bombardment upon Midway. When the cancellation order came, the ships, under the command of Rear Admiral Takeo Kurita, turned around and steamed northwest. Upon sighting them, Murphy, still uncertain of the ships' nationality, began to stalk them. In the dark, it was all but impossible to identify the cruisers, so Murphy stalked them until dawn. He then identified the ships as Japanese, but almost simultaneously the Japanese spotted the *Tambor* and the alarm went out. Murphy ordered a dive and the Japanese ships began emergency maneuvers. The first two cruisers, the *Kumano* and *Suzuya,* turned hard to port as ordered. So did the *Mikuma,* next in line, but the *Mogami,* the last ship in line failed to read the emergency turn signal and plowed into the *Mikuma.* The *Mogami,* in ramming into the *Mikuma,* suffered a serious slicing away of a portion of the bow and was forced to stop. The *Mikuma,* although not as seriously damaged, left a telltale trail of oil in its wake. Eventually both ships continued under way, but at reduced speed.

When the morning's searches began on June 5, the oil slick of the *Mikuma* was picked up by Midway-based dive bombers of Marine Aircraft Group 22, six Dauntlesses under Captain Marshall A. Tyler and six Vindicators under Captain Richard E. Fleming. Tyler led the Dauntlesses in a diving attack upon the *Mogami,* but scored only near misses. Almost simultaneously B-17s dropped bombs from high altitudes but without success.

Fleming brought his flight in upon the *Mikuma* in a glide attack. As he headed for the target his Vindicator burst into flame from heavy antiaircraft fire. Fleming managed to drop his bomb, but could not pull away, for the old plane was blazing furiously. It crashed at full speed into a turret just aft of the bridge. Flames from the fiery wreck were sucked into an air-intake system and detonated fumes in the starboard engine room, killing all the men inside. Fleming's crash, mistaken for a suicide attack by the Japanese, caused more damage to the

Mikuma than the near misses (two men were killed on the *Mogami*) and its collision with the *Mogami.* Now both cruisers limped away from the fury of the avenging Americans.

At dawn the following day, June 6, Spruance dispatched the last air strikes of the Battle of Midway. Around eight in the morning Mitscher's *Hornet* dispatched twenty-six dive bombers with fighter escort; at ten forty-five the *Enterprise* sent off thirty-one dive bombers, three torpedo bombers, and a dozen escorting Wildcats. The final sortie was launched at one-thirty, after some of the earlier planes had returned to relate the successes of the initial strikes. The *Hornet's* twenty-six dive bombers, upon returning to the scene of battle, found little to do. The first wave from the *Hornet* attacked both cripples, with the heaviest casualties being suffered by the bow-less *Mogami.* The *Hornet* and *Enterprise* Dauntlesses finished off the *Mikuma* with five direct hits. Spreading fires set off internal explosions, which sent the ship to the ocean bottom. The *Mogami,* despite its rent bow and the six hits which rendered it a floating vessel of anguish, eventually reached Truk, although it was to be out of operation for a year. The *Mikuma* (discounting the four lost carriers) was the heaviest warship lost by Japan since the war's opening. In addition, there were many dead and wounded aboard the destroyers, the *Arashio* and *Asashio,* assigned by Yamamoto to stand by the damaged cruisers. These too came under bombing and fighter attacks. With no Zeros to oppose them the Wildcats strafed at will.

The *Yorktown,* which the Japanese had claimed three times to have destroyed, had not sunk after being abandoned on June 4. Fletcher directed that the *Hughes,* a destroyer captained by Lieutenant Commander Donald J. Ramsey, "stand by *Yorktown.* Do not permit anyone to board her. Sink her if necessary to prevent capture or if serious fire develops."

By the morning of the fifth Ramsey saw that the *Yorktown* was not sinking; the list was stabilized at twenty-five degrees. He suggested that salvage operations be attempted and several ships were dispatched to assist. A burst of machine-gun fire from the tilting deck of the *Yorktown* revealed that two crewmen, left for dead, had recovered slightly from their wounds; they were taken off the *Yorktown.* A further search revealed that in the abandon-

The Yorktown *in distress at Midway with destroyer* Hughes *at "Stand by." Although badly hit, the York-* town *seemed capable of being saved and taken under tow.* (NAVY DEPT., NATIONAL ARCHIVES)

Men of the Yorktown *walk the slanting deck of their carrier; Japanese torpedoes from submarine I-168* *ended all hope of saving the* Yorktown.
(NAVY DEPT., NATIONAL ARCHIVES)

ment a number of secret papers and decoding devices had been left aboard. The minesweeper *Vireo* arrived around noon and took the *Yorktown* in tow. It was a great burden for the little ship and little speed was made, but the wounded ship moved slowly toward Pearl Harbor.

Buckmaster, the *Yorktown*'s skipper, asked for a volunteer salvage crew to board the carrier. Soon, with 141 enlisted men and 29 officers, he boarded the destroyer *Hammann,* which in company with destroyers *Benham* and *Balch,* pushed off for the crippled *Yorktown.* They arrived at daybreak on June 6 and immediately began working according to the plan drafted by Buckmaster. The various parties were hard at work; cooks prepared lunches, gunners were on duty at their antiaircraft guns, a medical group attended to the identification and assembling of the dead. Electrical power was drawn off the *Hammann,* directly alongside, to run the pumps to drain the flooded engine rooms. Water was pumped aboard to quench the fire in the rag-stowage room. By midafternoon the list had decreased by two degrees. Destroyers circled around the *Yorktown* and *Hammann.*

Suddenly a hoarse cry went out: "Torpedoes!" Men aboard the *Hammann* opened up with their

Hit in the same torpedo attack as the Yorktown, *the* Hammann *sinks into the Pacific.* (U. S. NAVY)

Midway secured; it belongs again to the goonies, the Marines, the Navy, and the Seventh Air Force, whose B-24 approaches for a landing. (U. S. AIR FORCE)

Isoroku Yamamoto, who, as he had promised, "ran wild" in the Pacific "the first six months" after the initiation of the Hawaii Operation. His time began running out at Midway and ended over the jungles of the Solomon Islands. (U. S. NAVY)

guns on the four white streaks in the water rapidly closing from the starboard side. One streak missed completely and continued on harmlessly, but one detonated into the side of the *Hammann* and the other two, passing underneath the destroyer, smashed violently into the *Yorktown.*

The torpedoes had come from the Japanese submarine I-168, commanded by Lieutenant Commander Yahachi Tanabe. Originally sent by Yamamoto to "shell and destroy enemy air base on Eastern Island" in the vain attempt to deal with Midway with surface ships, Tanabe had attempted that but with little success. Later, when the drifting *Yorktown* was found by a float plane, Yamamoto ordered Tanabe to attack the carrier. Having found it, Tanabe delivered his torpedo attack. The I-168 soon came under attack also, but despite the heavy depth charging (Tanabe counted sixty near misses),

the submarine escaped. His was the only decisive Japanese naval action of the Battle of Midway.

Within five minutes the *Hammann,* all but broken in half, sank to the bottom. The *Yorktown,* which had been listing to port, lost a good deal of the list because of the hits in the starboard side, but the carrier now lay deep in the water. Buckmaster continued to hope to salvage the ship, but during the night the *Yorktown* again listed to port. At dawn, June 7, 1942, it could be seen that the *Yorktown* was finally doomed. The ships flew their colors at half-mast; men, many in tears, removed their hats. The death rattle from the *Yorktown*— the sound of loose gear that slipped along the decks, the other equipment and furniture below—echoed over the still waters. The flight deck rolled under the oil-slicked waters, then the gallant *Yorktown,* heaving and shuddering, vanished into the Pacific.

The Battle of Midway was over.

EPILOGUE

A great mantle of secrecy descended upon the outcome of the Battle of Midway in Japan. Only the mildly successful, though inconsequential, Aleutian Operation was mentioned in the newspapers. Nothing was said of the Midway encounter itself and all references to it were deleted from diaries and official reports. The wounded were even held incommunicado and brought into naval hospitals after nightfall. Captain Mitsuo Fuchida, who had led the aerial attack upon Pearl Harbor and was prevented from leading the attack upon Midway by illness, was taken wounded from the *Akagi,* and tells of his stealthy evacuation from a hospital ship ". . . after dark . . . on a covered stretcher and carried through the rear entrance [of the hospital at the Yokosuka Naval Base]. My room was in complete isolation. No nurses or medical corps men were allowed in and I could not communicate with the world outside. All the wounded from Midway were treated like this. It was like being a prisoner of war among your own people."

Yamamoto too went into isolation. He had led the Imperial fleet of Japan into its first major naval defeat in three hundred years. Four of Japan's finest carriers had been sent to the bottom of the Pacific —3500 Japanese seamen (among them about 100 first-line, irreplaceable pilots) died, ten times the number (307) of Americans lost. More than 300 aircraft were lost (the total number based on the carriers, plus some which were being ferried to be based on Midway as soon as it was under Japanese domination); American aircraft losses numbered 147. The course of the Pacific war was completely changed at Midway.

As the Japanese fleet sped out of the range of Spruance's planes, the latter called for a halt of the pursuit. After several days of intense fighting he knew the pilots must be near nervous and physical exhaustion; his ships were running dangerously low on fuel and they were approaching dangerous waters. They had destroyed about half of Japan's carrier strength, but little of the remainder of the surface fleet. Wisely Spruance ordered a return to port.

Yamamoto, ill with severe stomach cramps, remained in his cabin unable to eat anything except gruel for several days. In the wake of the retreating *Yamato*, the *Nagara* too sped toward safer waters. Aboard the cruiser was Admiral Nagumo, dispirited, broken, a man without a ship—the man who had led the Pearl Harbor attack had failed at Midway. Though he returned to sea, Nagumo was a depleted man and did not find peace until July 6, 1944, when he committed suicide on an island named Saipan. His body was never found.

Yamamoto recovered from his mysterious illness and regained his powers sufficiently to press for the occupation of Guadalcanal in the Solomon Islands. This was Japan's southernmost conquest. After hard and painful fighting it was taken back by the Americans—the Greater East Asia Co-Prosperity Sphere was gradually, and bloodily, shrinking. But despite these setbacks, the Japanese continued to revere Yamamoto and to respect his leadership. The very presence of the man in a distant outpost —and no matter how primitive the outpost, the man was invariably immaculate, composed, dedicated— inspired all who saw him.

So it was that following the fall of Guadalcanal Yamamoto planned to fly to Rabaul, New Britain, headquarters of the Seventeenth Army—which had fought at Guadalcanal—and then to proceed eastward to inspect naval bases near Bougainville in the Solomon Islands. Bougainville was the northernmost of the Solomon group and still held by the Japanese; Guadalcanal, the southernmost island, lay about four hundred miles away. According to the planned schedule, Yamamoto, in company with several officers including his chief of staff, Vice-Admiral Matome Ugaki, would leave the main naval base at Truk, spend an evening at Rabaul, and then leave for Kahili airdrome, on the southern tip of Bougainville, arriving at precisely 9:45 A.M.

As before, all preparations for this "secret" move were known by American cryptologists within hours after the coded messages were sent to the Japanese forward bases alerting them of Yamamoto's impending inspection. Word was flashed to Washington; Secretary of the Navy Frank Knox immediately issued orders to intercept Yamamoto's party and "destroy it at all costs." The loss of Yamamoto would tell heavily upon the Japanese and upon the future development of the war. Along with the order arrived a most meticulous itinerary indicating Yamamoto's exact position during his entire tour. Admiral William Halsey, commanding the southern Pacific, assigned the mission to Rear Admiral Marc A. Mitscher, COMAIRSOLS (Commander Air Solomons), who turned it over to Major John W. Mitchell of the Air Force's 339th Fighter Squadron.

A total of eighteen Lockheed P-38s (Lightnings) were to take part in the mission. Mitchell would lead the sixteen-plane cover section and Captain Thomas G. Lanphier the four-plane attack unit. It was decided that the best means of carrying out the mission was to intercept Yamamoto as he came into the Kahili airdrome. It was not without hazards, for the Kahili-Buin area swarmed with Zeros (or Zekes, as the newer models were called). Only the P-38 had the range—a round trip of nearly a thousand miles—taking into consideration the circuitous route which would be necessary to escape detection. Navigational as well as flying skill was essential to the mission.

Mitchell's timetable was carefully geared into that of the punctual Yamamoto's. At exactly seven twenty-five in the morning of April 18, 1943, Mitchell led his planes off the runway of Henderson Field, Guadalcanal. The field was named for Major Lofton R. Henderson, who had died in the Battle of Midway. Two of the eighteen P-38s were forced to turn back almost immediately; one had malfunctioning auxiliary fuel tanks and the other blew a tire during the take-off run. These two planes cut Lanphier's attack section in half, leaving himself and Lieutenant Rex T. Barber (of the 70th Fighter Squadron) to carry out the attack. Mitchell then assigned Captain Besby Holmes and Lieutenant Raymond Hine to the attack section.

The sixteen P-38s flew for two hours and nine minutes, about 30 feet above the Pacific, a distance of 435 miles, dodging small islands which might be harboring enemy coast watchers. At 9:35 A.M., if all had gone well, they would meet Yamamoto about 35 miles west of Kahili. All through the flight absolute radio silence was observed; Mitchell's navigation was superlative. As the time drew near

the hazy mountains of Bougainville appeared out of the sea. The P-38s swung inland. It was nine thirty-three.

Suddenly the silence was broken by the voice of Captain Douglas S. Canning in the cover section. "Bogey. Ten o'clock high!" About five miles distant Lanphier made out a flight of two Mitsubishi (Betty) bombers, escorted by six Zekes. This was one hitch: they had hoped to have gained altitude before attacking. Now they had to climb, which

The Lockheed P-38 "Lightning," selected as the instrument of Yamamoto's destruction.

(LOCKHEED-CALIFORNIA)

Thomas G. Lanphier, "credited" with shooting down Yamamoto's plane. (U. S. AIR FORCE)

placed them at a disadvantage. All aircraft released their belly tanks in preparation for the attack. Besby Holmes of the attack section, however, could not drop his tank. Raymond Hine stayed with him for protection—with auxiliary tanks the P-38 lost speed and could not maneuver properly in an air battle. Lanphier and Barber, at full throttle, roared in on the Japanese formation. Mitchell's top cover climbed to be on the lookout for possible Zero reinforcements.

The Japanese suddenly became aware of the P-38s; the two Bettys dived for the jungle and three of the Zeros turned upon Lanphier's plane. The Lightning was by this time on a level with the lead Betty and met the assault of the lead Zero head on. Both pilots exchanged wasted shots and then, more calmly, Lanphier took careful aim and the Zero spun into the jungle burning and minus a wing. The other two Zeros flashed by the P-38 as Lanphier made a sharp turn away. He was next aware of the shadow of one of the Bettys moving rapidly over the treetops.

Lanphier lunged the P-38 into a full power dive, then realized he would overshoot the bomber. By this time the duo of Zeros had whipped around to attack him again. To Lanphier it seemed that all were on a collision course, with all four aircraft des-

Lieutenant Besby Holmes, center, is congratulated by Brigadier General Dean G. Strother, commander of

Thirteenth Air Force Fighter Command, after the Yamamoto mission. (U. S. AIR FORCE)

tined to meet at an imaginary point over the jungle. He maintained his course, however, eyes upon the Mitsubishi, racing in almost at right angles to the Betty's flight path. When it came into his sights he pushed the gun release button. In an instant the right engine of the Betty burst into flame; seconds later the entire wing was ablaze. The two Zero pilots, seeing that the Betty was doomed, no longer considered suicide. They pulled up sharply and away from Lanphier's Lightning.

The stricken Betty, dripping flame, suddenly lost its wing and crashed into the jungle. The ball of fire erupted into a savage explosion and only thick black smoke and red flame remained of the Betty.

The other Mitsubishi, carrying Ugaki, was attacked by Barber, who pursued it over the jungle toward the sea. Ugaki had observed the crash of his chief's Betty and knew that within minutes he too must share Yamamoto's fate. Barber's gun's decimated the crew, spattered the interior of the plane with bits and pieces of metal, killing the passengers also. A cannon hit in the right wing crippled the Betty so that the pilot brought it into the water at full speed. Only three men, one of them the injured Ugaki, survived the attack. With the aid of Mitchell's top cover, the Zeros, which attempted to avenge the attack, were driven off. Holmes, having finally dropped his tanks, shot a Zero off Barber's tail.

Lanphier and Barber raced from the vicinity of the crashed bombers by hedgehopping, dodging, and skidding. Of the sixteen aircraft which participated in the mission, only one, Lieutenant Raymond K. Hine's, failed to return. He had assisted Holmes in driving the Zeros away from Barber's P-38. (Although Lanphier was credited at the time with the victory over the Betty carrying Yamamoto, this victory was questioned by Barber, who thought he had shot down the critical Betty. Holmes also claimed a Betty, the one which fell into the sea, and thought that the bomber which fell into the jungle had been shot down by Barber. Lanphier, however, also claimed a Betty which fell into the

jungle. Unless there was a third Betty, which the Japanese claim there was not, the victory claims cannot be clarified.)

Whatever the dispute over the honors of having assassinated Admiral Yamamoto—honors which should be shared by all pilots who participated in the remarkably executed raid—there is no doubting that his loss was grievous to the Japanese. Their most gifted strategist was gone—and there was no one of equal stature to replace him. The one man who might have, Yamaguchi, had, in an excess of vainglory, chosen to go down with the *Hiryu* at Midway.

Yamamoto was succeeded by Admiral Mineichi Koga (who died within a year in an air accident), but the Japanese fleet had long since stopped "running wild." After Midway, a battle in which not one surface ship exchanged a shot with another, and yet which was the most decisive naval battle of the Second World War, the doom which Yamamoto had predicted for Japan should the war be prolonged was inevitable. After Midway, also, Yamamoto spoke of his own death, which he predicted with a curious wistfulness. Shortly before the interception near Kahili, Yamamoto composed a poem, a sequel to one he had written on the day of the Pearl Harbor attack. In the earlier quatrain he expressed contempt for the world's opinion of the brilliant attack he had engineered; even his own life was insignificant except as "the sword of my Emperor." In his final poem, translated by John Deane Potter, Yamamoto rhapsodized

> *I am still the sword*
> *Of my Emperor*
> *I will not be sheathed*
> *Until I die.*

The sword of the Emperor had been sheathed at Midway by a small band of courageous men in their Buffalos, Vindicators, Marauders, Wildcats, and Dauntlesses. No one knew that better than the wise Yamamoto.

BOOK II
The Big League

Hitler built a fortress around Europe but he forgot to put a roof on it.

—FRANKLIN DELANO ROOSEVELT

5

MILLENNIUM

Winston Churchill arrived in Washington within two weeks of the Pearl Harbor attack for the "Arcadia" conferences with President Franklin D. Roosevelt and other political and military chiefs. On the day of Churchill's arrival—December 22, 1941 —Japanese troops landed on Luzon in the Philippines to begin the inexorable crushing of MacArthur's outnumbered and ill-equipped Filipino and American troops. By New Year's Day 1942, when Arcadia ended, the Allies agreed that, despite the Japanese conquests, Nazi Germany prevailed as the prime enemy.

But until the United States was capable of joining the British in the offensive, it would be necessary for the Empire to carry on alone as before. True, the situation had brightened somewhat: the Battle of Britain had proved abortive and now the Germans had embarked upon Barbarossa, the attack upon Russia which Hitler, with a love for coining phrases, termed the "eight-week war." The nightly terror which had fallen upon Britain was pretty much over by 1942. Hitler's neat little timetable was off a bit in the east so that he was forced to drain off much of the Luftwaffe strength from France and the Low Countries to pour it into the Balkans, north Africa, and the capacious Russian maw. Nearly half of the Luftwaffe was in Russia by the spring of 1942. A quarter of the Luftwaffe's strength remained on the Western Front and in Ger-

many. Although the bombers of Luftflotte 3 were few and aging, the fighters were modern and formidable. Among these were the late-model Messerschmitt 109 and the new Focke-Wulf 190. Some of the latter were converted eventually into fighter-bombers which made harassing "tip and run" raids upon Channel shipping and English seaside towns. These raids were not decisive, merely bothersome and deadly on a small scale. It was, in effect, a kind of stalemate.

Although the Russians clamored for a "Second Front," the only means by which the Allies could possibly bring the war directly to Germany in the spring of 1942 was via British Bomber Command. In February 1942 a new commander in chief, Air Marshal Arthur T. Harris, was appointed to replace Sir Richard Peirse, who had endured a hard and frustrating year as Chief of Bomber Command. Bomber crew losses had increased; bombing accuracy, primarily because of inadequately trained crews, had decreased. During the same period Bomber Command's forces were diverted to the Middle East and effective bombing missions into Germany became more academic than real. Without men and aircraft equal to the task such missions were hardly better than the German tip and run raids—and wasteful in terms of men and machines. So although he was not responsible for the situation, Peirse as commander in chief must serve as scapegoat. But it by no means improved the state of Bomber Command simply because Peirse was dispatched to the Pacific to head the all but non-existent Allied Air Forces there.

Harris had been absent from the battle scene since May of 1941, when he had been placed at the head of an RAF delegation and was sent off to Washington. It was the function of the delegation to acquire American aircraft for the RAF, but the attack on Pearl Harbor, for some time at least, quickly placed the American Air Force high on the priority list, and Harris had little to do.

When he was recalled to command the bomber offensive, Harris had inherited not only the afflictions of the depleted Bomber Command, but also an outstanding senior air staff officer, Air Vice-Marshal Robert H. M. S. Saundby, an old friend from early flying days. Both men were advocates of the "strategic bombardment" concept—the direct attack upon the enemy's warmaking facilities. In less guarded language: an attack upon Germany's industrial cities. If such assaults could be made regularly and in force, both Harris and Saundby believed, they would have a serious effect upon the future of the war.

The job facing Harris was a tough one indeed. He had been handed the task of dealing with several of Germany's greatest industrial concentrations at a time when his forces were being drained away to fight in the critical Battle of the Atlantic and to be used by the Army for close support in north Africa. In brief, while Bomber Command was expected to operate with greater impact than before, almost at the same time this was made difficult, or even impossible, by denying its expansion. Just three days after Harris had taken over, Sir Stafford Cripps, then Lord Privy Seal, spoke in the House of Commons touching upon the subject of whether or not "the building up of this bombing force is the best use that we can make of our resources." It being wartime, Cripps refrained from encouraging a public debate on the subject; he hinted, however, that if "the circumstances warrant a change, a change will be made."

While the semipolitical arguments proceeded and reams of paper were consumed for memos and minutes, Air Marshal Harris went on with his own plans undisturbed. He realized that only decisive accomplishment could save Bomber Command from

High Command conference at Bomber Command: Air Vice-Marshal R. Graham, Air Vice-Marshal Robert Saundby, and, seated, Air Marshal Arthur T. Harris, Commander in Chief. Harris and Saundby planned the Bomber Command attacks on Germany's war industries from 1942 until the end of the war.
(IMPERIAL WAR MUSEUM, LONDON)

complete dispersal and, in his view, waste. He believed too that unless a target was saturated with a series of concentrated blows, there would be little result from several scattered missions. Saturation could be achieved only if a target were correctly identified and bomb loads concentrated within a reasonably small area. By using "Gee," a new electronic navigational device, and by employing both advance aircraft to drop flares to mark the target and other early-wave planes to follow with incendiaries, the area would be clearly, even accurately marked for the succeeding waves of the main force bombers carrying high-explosive and incendiary bombs. It was a page torn from the book of the Luftwaffe, but the system was applied with greater intensity.

By early March Harris had initiated his campaign, although the first targets were not primary ones necessarily. The Renault works near Paris, which supplied war materials to the Germans, was struck by 235 bombers using Gee, which succeeded in knocking it out for about four months. A few days later Essen, home of a giant Krupp arms complex, was bombed using Gee for navigation and the flare system (later to be known as "pathfinder"); in all, 211 bombers were dispatched, but Harris found, upon studying the post-raid photographs, that the mission was not a success. The Krupp works was barely touched (many incendiaries were not dropped until after the flares had burned out; the resulting fires, scattered as they were, misled the succeeding waves of bombers). One bomber, struck by flak, had jettisoned its bomb load, which fell upon Hamborn, not Essen, causing fires which appeared to following bomber crews as signals for a target area. By pure accident many of the bombs intended for Krupp fell instead upon the Thyssen steelworks.

But Harris could not operate on such luck and he soon learned that Gee was not a foolproof device. Within limitations it was fine, but in order to work properly a good clear moonlit night was essential. It could bring a bomber force within reasonable proximity to a target, but the rest of the mission depended upon the human eye.

It was not until the end of March 1942 that Bomber Command could claim a truly successful raid. This was the March 28/29 strike upon the city of Lübeck, a Baltic port of great importance to the German supply system. The dwellings in Lübeck were predominantly wood and Air Staff pressed Harris upon the use of incendiaries. In the resulting attack nearly half of Lübeck was destroyed. Bad weather interfered with subsequent missions dispatched to Essen, Dortmund, Cologne, and Hamburg.

Hitler, meanwhile, issued his Baedeker order on April 14, in which the term *Terrorangriffe* ("terror attacks") appears. These, the Führer pointed out, were to be made upon targets which might "have the greatest possible effect on civilian life." Thus such raids were aimed at undefended, or lightly defended, cathedral cities such as Bath, Norwich, and York, beginning late in April. As Goebbels confided to his diary, Hitler "shares my opinion absolutely that cultural centers, health resorts and civilian centers must be attacked now. . . ." So much for philosophy and morality.

Harris contributed to Hitler's fury with a series of attacks upon Rostock beginning on the night of April 23/24 and continuing through the following three nights. Rostock was, like Lübeck, a port city on the Baltic and also the site of a Heinkel aircraft factory. Over the four nights a total of 521 aircraft were sent to bomb (468 claimed they had succeeded; twelve aircraft were lost) and severely crippled the city, besides damaging the Heinkel works and devastating nearly three quarters of Rostock.

Throughout these tentative, almost experimental early weeks of his tenure, Harris pondered a daring plan. What with the "successes" obtained upon Lübeck and Rostock, which greatly improved the morale of the bomber crews besides giving Hitler a jolt, what might be accomplished by a truly massive force concentrating upon a major target? Say a thousand bombers over a city like Hamburg or Cologne. He spoke of this fancy to Saundby, who immediately and quietly undertook the research to learn if it was not so much a fancy after all.

The next time Harris broached the subject, Saundby informed him that it was indeed feasible at that time, in May 1942. Harris was skeptical, though he continued to listen to Saundby's statistics. If they put up all of their first-line operational units plus training units and borrowed a few aircraft and crews from Coastal Command and perhaps from the Army, a total of a thousand bombers could be dispatched against a single target. Thus assured of at least one aspect of the plan, Harris turned to the others.

These would include target selection, weather, the use of Gee, the risk of collision, and, of course, the inevitable political backing. Harris was quite aware of the implications of failure; but if successful, the "result of using an adequate bomber force against Germany would be there for all the world to see, and I should be able to press for the aircraft, crews and equipment we needed with far more effect than by putting forward theoretical arguments, however convincing, in favour of hitting the enemy where it would hurt him most. . . ." In addition, "from such an operation we should also learn a number of tactical lessons of the greatest possible value, lessons which could not be learned any other way and without which we could not prepare for the main offensive."

By a main offensive Harris visualized hundreds of such massive raids upon the industrial cities of

Germany, which might possibly eliminate the need for an invasion of Europe.

However much exhilarated by the concept, Harris (who was no dreamer) realized also that "if anything went seriously wrong . . . then I should be committing not only the whole of my front-line strength but absolutely all of my reserves in a single battle." Using instructors and trainees from the Operational Training Units further risked, if the losses were great, the crippling of the training program for years to come. But then, since Bomber Command was being picked to pieces and dwindling away anyway, the dramatic conception of a thousand planes over a single target in one raid might make the impression that could save the Command.

To obtain official backing Harris approached his chief, Sir Charles Portal, who guardedly approved, although cautioning that Air Staff also must recognize its "usefulness" and that proper political backing was important. Harris immediately found his backer: Winston Churchill. The Prime Minister's home, Chequers, was but a ten-minute drive (at the high speed at which Harris generally drove his battered old Bentley) from Harris's home, Springfield. This was a handsome Victorian mansion situated near High Wycombe, headquarters of Bomber Command, about twenty miles directly west of London.

The two men, the flamboyant Churchill and the reserved but tough Harris, got along very well. After dinner on a Sunday evening in mid-May 1942, Harris broached the subject of a thousand-bomber raid. The very grandeur of the conception impressed Churchill. For all the romanticism, however, Churchill pressed for concrete details. The target? Hamburg or Cologne. Why not Essen (then regarded as the most important target in Germany)? Because of the limitations of Gee, it was necessary to strike at an easily identified city, Hamburg because it lay on the estuary of the Elbe River (although out of Gee range), and Cologne because of its location on the Rhine River.

There was the delicate point: How many aircraft did Harris expect to lose? Even this eventuality was taken into consideration. Fifty aircraft, or about 5 per cent of the force.

"I am prepared for the loss of a hundred," Churchill told Harris.

The Thousand Plan (Operation Millennium) was on.

II

On May 19 Harris received a letter from Portal informing him that the Prime Minister "warmly approved" of the plan and that it seemed that there was all likelihood of "the co-operation of Coastal Command unless they have special operations on hand." Within two days Harris had a letter from Sir Philip Joubert, Chief of Coastal Command, telling him that "I can go your 250 . . ." in answer to Harris's request for 250 aircraft. Thus Coastal Command would supply one quarter of the total force.

Rapid planning and preparation became essential, for the raid had to take place within the next period of full moon (May 26–30), a week away. Counting Coastal Command's promised 250 planes, Harris had by this time accumulated via his four operational groups, two bomber training groups, and Flying Training Command (with 21 aircraft) a total of 1081 planes and crews. With a force of this size, consisting of a large number of inexperienced crews, a serious possibility of many collisions over the target had to be faced. Although much was to be gained by concentrating a large force over a small space in a short time, there was still this nagging problem.

He asked Dr. B. G. Dickins, head of Bomber Command's Operational Research Section, to work out the probabilities scientifically. He quickly learned that with a single aiming point the risk of collision was very high, but that with three, which divided the forces into three parallel streams, the risk came down to just a little more than one an hour. There were chances also of aircraft being hit by the bombs of other aircraft because the different waves would come in at staggered altitudes, which to some extent lessened the chance of collision. But, theoretically at least, even these possibilities were less than those of being hit by flak or being shot down by night fighters.

With so great a concentration over the target in so short a time—if Cologne, which Harris had already decided would be the target, it would be for ninety minutes—it was hoped that the defenses would be saturated. Radar plots would pile up, gun crews would become confused, and the entire defense system in the area of Cologne would be swamped.

The night of May 27/28 was set for the attack, a night which promised a good moon. But it was just before this that Harris suffered his first blow. Coastal Command was forced to defect from the raid on orders from the Admiralty. A quarter of the total force was gone. Clearly the Admiralty did not wish to place so large a proportion of their planes in jeopardy. If Harris failed, they too would fail; if Harris carried off his scheme, the Admiralty would lose also. Harris would have proved his point and the Admiralty, which clamored for a diminished Bomber Command, would lose their appeal for bombers in the Battle of the Atlantic. There was little that Harris could do but curse the Admiralty. The Bomber Command planes, by May 26, stood ready at fifty-three airfields; training had ceased and the mission must go on.

The weather next turned on Harris. Thunderstorms and clouds over northern Germany made the mission impossible. The next night it was the same. Meanwhile hundreds of bombers and thousands of men waited for something to happen. The mission was postponed for a third time. In order not to make the Germans suspicious of an impending large mission, Harris sent a force to bomb targets in France and another to lay mines. As each wasted day went by, the chance of a security leak became greater.

The extra days, however, gave the ground crews the opportunity to put more aircraft on the Operational Forms. By the morning of Saturday, May 30, thanks to the hard work of these men, Harris actually had his thousand aircraft; more, in fact. On that morning, with good weather promised on home bases, there were 1046 bombers awaiting the signal to take off. Other planes, from Army Co-operation Command and Fighter Command, although not participating directly in the raid, would provide diversionary attacks along the way.

But the full moon period was drawing to a close, and unless the force took off that night, it would have to wait another month before the Thousand Plan could be attempted again. The continental forecast—again thunder and cloud, with chance of clearing—was less than ideal. Hamburg was curdled over with cloud. However, Harris's weather expert,

Magnus Spence, predicted that Cologne might clear around midnight. Also, by the time the bombers returned to England some of their bases would undoubtedly be fogged in. But planes from those bases could be diverted to the still clear fields. It was the weather over Germany which most troubled Harris. With cloud over the target, the mission might very well prove fruitless, and with fog over England, with hundreds of milling aircraft, the mission could be disastrous. Still, to Harris, who had but that night and the next before the favorable moon period ended, Spence's prediction sounded better than any they had had so far.

Harris was alone now. It was up to him, however much Saundby sympathized, and he did, for Harris had seen it in an instant in which their eyes met as he lit a cigarette, stalling for time perhaps. He placed the cigarette into a holder, which he clenched in his teeth, and then leaned over the map that lay on his desk. Harris said, "Thousand Plan tonight. Target Cologne."

The word was flashed out immediately to the fifty-three bases scattered northward from London along the east coast of England, with a few farther inland and west of the capital. Unless the weather changed considerably during the remainder of the day, Operation Millennium would take place. With incredible efficiency the more than a thousand aircraft were readied for the mission—the English countryside, especially in East Anglia, resonated to the "dreadful note of preparation." There were shouts and curses; engines shuddering into life barked, snorted, and died, inspiring more curses and activity. Bomb loads ranged from 4-pound and 30-pound incendiaries to be used by the advance force marking the target area (nearly 500,000 incendiaries would fall on Cologne that night) through 4000-pound high-explosive bombs. In between were 2000-pound, 1000-pound, 500-pound, and 250-pound high explosives —about 1300 of these assorted bombs to sow destruction in the marked areas and to disrupt firefighting attempts by German Civil Defense units.

Nearly half of the force consisted of the Vickers Wellington, the "Wimpy" to crews (named for the "Popeye" cartoon character J. Wellington Wimpy). The Wellington was a favorite among aircrews because of its rugged ability to absorb battle damage and remain airworthy. It was reliable, tough, and a good plane to fly. The Wimpy, though designated

Vickers "Wellington," the "Wimpy," favorite of Bomber Command pilots. Its remarkable geodetic construction, the conception of Barnes N. Wallis of Vickers, made it a rugged aircraft capable of withstanding battle damage. Nearly six hundred Wellingtons participated in the thousand-plane raid on Cologne (although not these pictured: Wellington 1s of No. 311 [Czechoslovakian] Squadron).

(IMPERIAL WAR MUSEUM, LONDON)

as a heavy bomber, was powered by two engines rather than four. So was the Avro Manchester, a few of which also participated in the raid. Also a heavy bomber, the Manchester proved to be underpowered, and when two additional engines were later added, it was transformed into the four-engined Lancaster, one of the best bombers of the Second World War. A few of the early Lancasters, fitted with their four engines (Rolls-Royce Merlin), also went to Cologne that night.

The Short Stirling, Bomber Command's first four-engined heavy bomber, delivered the 2000-pound bombs, hundreds of the 500-pounders, and thousands of the incendiaries. By 1942 the Stirling, not a very popular aircraft among pilots, was gradually being retired to such less hazardous operations as minelaying and glider towing. Bomber Command's second four-engined heavy, the Handley Page Halifax, was second in weight of numbers to the Wellington of the participating aircraft. The Halifax was assigned mainly to the incendiary force which initiated the raid.

The two-engined bombers, besides the Wellington and the Manchester, were the Armstrong Whitworth Whitley and the Handley Page Hampden, both early designs which had formed the backbone of Bomber Command during the early months of the war. Both took part in the target-marking phase of the operation. Both aircraft soon after Millennium were gradually withdrawn from heavy bombing operations. Training aircraft, such as the de Havilland Tiger Moth and the Avro Anson did not take part

"Short Stirling," the RAF's first four-engined heavy bomber. Designed in the late 1930s according to curious specifications (the wing span was determined by the width of RAF hangar doors: a hundred feet; the span of the Stirling was ninety-nine). The performance of the plane was affected by the wing design, restricting its operational ceiling. On missions to Italy, Stirlings were forced to fly through the Alps, rather than over them.

(IMPERIAL WAR MUSEUM, LONDON)

in the Thousand Plan, although popular legend has long contended so.

All through the morning and afternoon of Saturday, May 30, the 1046 Wellingtons, Stirlings, Whitleys, Hampdens, Manchesters, Halifaxes, and Lancasters—each with its own special bomb load—were serviced, armed, and standing ready for the signal to take off.

The aircrews, totaling about six thousand men, came from all corners of the Empire, from Australia and New Zealand to Canada, and even from the United States. The Americans ranged from the inevitable boy from Brooklyn (Charles Honeychurch; although he was not a boy, being then in his thirties) to the equally inevitable representatives of the "Royal Texas Air Force," Bud Cardinal of Fort

Worth and Howard L. Tate, Jr., of Dallas. Gunner-radio operator R. J. Campbell came from Pawling, New York. One American, Flying Officer Frank Roper, piloted a Lancaster of No. 207 Squadron.

The British crewmen characteristically ranged across the spectrum of personalities, ranks, attitudes, and ages. For example, flying in one of the leading waves was a fifty-year-old air vice-marshal, J. E. A. Baldwin, Air Officer Commanding, No. 3 Group. During the First World War Baldwin had bombed Cologne; he could not let the opportunity slip by in Millennium, for obvious reasons. "I'm going to see for myself," he announced simply. As AOC, No. 3 Group, he was not supposed to take part in operations, but since he received no definite order to that effect (possibly because he had never both-

H. M. King George VI, in RAF air marshal uniform, visits a Bomber Command base and inspects a typical Lancaster crew. (IMPERIAL WAR MUSEUM, LONDON)

ered to mention it at HQ), Baldwin flew as second pilot in a Stirling of No. 218 Squadron. The pilot was Wing Commander Paul Holder, a South African, who commanded the squadron.

Alongside such veterans as Baldwin and Holder, there were also young men still in their teens, some of them pilots, some gunners, others navigators. Many first pilots had only been promoted from second (in U.S. usage, copilot). By the curious workings of the British system, several pilots in command of aircraft were non-commissioned officers, technically outranked by navigators and bombardiers. Inevitably, most pilots were called "Skipper," a reminder of Britain's seafaring traditions. The pilot was in complete charge of the plane, whatever his rank.

Leslie Manser, with the rank of flying officer, was skipper of a Manchester. A gentle, sensitive young man of twenty, his appearance was deceiving. When first encountered by one of his crew, Manser

quickly came under suspicion: he was too pretty to be the skipper of a bomber. At the controls of his plane, however, the youthful Hertfordshire man was as tough as any man in his crew. A superb pilot, extremely cool, competent and at the same time fully dedicated to the safety of the other five in the crew, Manser left no doubt in their minds as to his authority and competence. His copilot was Sergeant Leslie Baveystock, older than Manser, married and the father of an infant daughter. The navigator was Flying Officer Richard Barnes, the radio operator Pilot Officer Norman Horsley. The latter had finished his tour of duty, but was ordered to make one more operation before being posted to a training unit as an instructor. Barnes was a pilot, but was also a skilled navigator (his nickname was "Bang On" because of his reputation for directing his aircraft bang on the target). Neither man had any misgivings about flying with Manser, although Horsley sensed that "making one more ops" might be stretching his luck a bit far.

The rest of Manser's crew was made up of the two gunners: in the Manchester's tail was B. W. Naylor and in the nose, A. M. Mills. Horsley, in addition to operating the radio, also manned the top-turret guns of the plane.

All five men would, by Sunday morning, owe their lives to Manser.

Rumor had spread early throughout Bomber Command that on that Saturday night the "Big Show" would be on. So long as Bomber Command's chief meteorologist Magnus Spence could promise a reasonably stable weather situation, Harris permitted the preparations to continue through the day. By six in the evening the formal briefings on the various stations could officially begin. The scene was similar in all fifty-three stations. The men jammed into the briefing rooms, some diffident, some boisterous, some silent, all apprehensive. At one station the briefing room was furnished with folding seats which had been salvaged from a bombed London movie theater. The station commander entered with what appeared to be a smile on his face. After quiet had settled upon the room, he told the men, "You may have guessed there's something special on tonight. Well, this is what it is. We're bombing Germany tonight with over a thousand aircraft."

The men sprang to their feet, cheering, pounding each other on the back, and danced about. The tension of the past few days was over—and all believed that they would take part in a worthwhile operation. When calm had been restored, the station commander read them a message from Harris.

The force of which you form a part tonight is at least twice the size and has more than four times the carrying capacity of the largest air force ever before concentrated on one objective. You have an opportunity, therefore, to strike a blow at the enemy which will resound not only throughout Germany, but throughout the world. In your hands lie the means of destroying a major part of the resources by which the enemy's war effort is maintained. It depends, however, on each individual crew whether full concentration is achieved. Press home your attack to your precise objective with the utmost determination and resolution in the foreknowledge that, if you individually succeed, the most shattering and devastating blow will have been delivered against the very vitals of the enemy. Let him have it—right on the chin!

While the incendiary vanguard, primarily consisting of Gee-equipped Wellingtons and Stirlings from several squadrons of No. 3 Group, began taking off for Cologne, aircraft of the intruder forces also took off. These were the Blenheims of No. 2 Group and of Army Co-operation Command as well as Bostons,

Havocs (American-built Douglas A-20s), and Hurricanes of Fighter Command. Altogether these totaled eighty-eight aircraft, which were to "intrude" along the route to Cologne, bombing night fighter airfields, hopefully to draw the night fighters away from the main bomber stream. The Luftwaffe fields in northern France, Belgium, and Holland lay adjacent to the route of the thousand bombers. During this phase of the operation the weather proved to be a formidable hindrance. Coming in low over the Continent the men in the intruder aircraft found the German airfields hidden under heavy cloud and all but impossible to find. In some instances the bombers were unable to find the airfields at all, and if they did, the small bombs they dropped (250- and 40-pounders) had little permanent effect upon the targets.

All through the hours of the mission, from the time the first bomber took off for Cologne until the final bomb fell upon Cologne (theoretically at 2:25 A.M. Sunday morning), the intruders did all they could to harass the Luftwaffe, but with no great success. Of the eighty-eight aircraft which took part, however, only three were lost.

Nor did the major part of the operation proceed

Avro "Manchester," the predecessor of the four-engined Lancaster. The Manchester was regarded as a failure and plagued with engine problems until powered by four Merlins, which led to the highly successful Lancaster, Britain's most potent bomber. The Man- *chester pictured has not had an upper gun turret installed; this was done at about the point where the letter "E" is painted. "EM" is the code for No. 207 Squadron; an American, Frank Roper, was a pilot in this unit on the thousand-plane raid.*

Handley Page "Hampden," an advanced aircraft for its time—it first flew in 1936—but afflicted with shortcomings by 1942. A few Hampdens carried bombs in the Cologne mission, as well as other succeeding thousand raids, but it was not retained as a night bomber and went into Coastal Command operation as a tor- *pedo bomber. These aircraft, of No. 185 Squadron (which by the night of the raid had been converted into an operational training unit and did not participate), illustrate why the Hampden was frequently called "the Frying Pan."*

(IMPERIAL WAR MUSEUM, LONDON)

according to plan. Many heavily laden bombers struggled to achieve altitude and their pilots found themselves all but blind in the cloud. Icing too became a serious problem, rendering the planes sluggish and straining the already laboring engines even more. Some planes were forced to turn back before getting away from England because of straining engines, inability to gain altitude, or other mechanical problems. The first planes of the incendiary force, the Wellingtons and Stirlings of No. 3 Group, began lumbering down the flare paths of their runways around 10 P.M. Within a half hour all aircraft were ready to begin the flight to Cologne. Very soon it was clear that there would never, in actuality, be a thousand bombers over the target. Boomerangs, the planes with various mechanical problems, began to return with crestfallen and genuinely disappointed crews. About a hundred planes were thus forced to return.

Others were stopped by other mishaps. A Wellington of No. 12 Squadron, obviously suffering engine trouble, simply burst into flame and crashed in Norfolk, killing all aboard. Others, unable to gain the altitude and the safety of the larger formations, ran into German night fighters and were shot down over Holland. Or, despite overheating engines, pilots continued on, hoping for the best—such a pilot was Pilot Officer Reece Reed of No. 101 Squadron—only to lose an engine and be forced to bail out.

Flying on Gee, the leading Wellingtons pushed on through the disconcerting overcast toward Co-

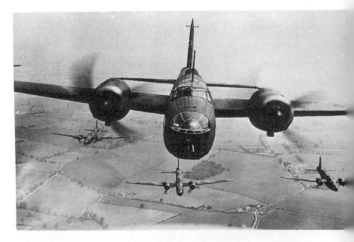

Wellingtons, which flew in the vanguard of the thousand-plane attack on Cologne.

(IMPERIAL WAR MUSEUM, LONDON)

logne. The conditions promised little success. The air was bumpy and with so many planes in the air, pilots became especially sensitive to the chance of collision. Around midnight the leading bombers were within less than an hour's flying time from Cologne and the cloud was still dense and rough.

In Cologne, veteran of 106 bombings, the routine Yellow Alert had been sounded; minutes later, one minute before midnight in fact, the Red Alert was flashed. It was still too early to tell where the British bombers were heading, but the efficient Warning Control of Cologne was on the job as usual. There was still no reason to sound the sirens.

When the vanguard Wellingtons approached within sixty miles west and slightly north of Cologne, the weather miraculously began to clear. In minutes the night sky flooded with moonlight and below the force glistened the Rhine. Germany lay in darkness, except for the glimmer of a lake and the bright curling Rhine pointing toward Cologne. The river, running generally north and south, intercepted the flight path of the bombers, coming from almost due west now, at right angles. The two lines crossed at the Hindenburg Bridge. About a mile to the west of the bridge lay that quarter of the city known as the Neumarkt, in the center of the Old City on the left bank of the Rhine. The Neumarkt was the aiming point for the first of the incendiaries.

At seventeen minutes after midnight the sirens

Night Mission to Germany: Lancasters await the signal to start engines. (IMPERIAL WAR MUSEUM, LONDON)

keened in Cologne. The dutiful, the experienced, the expectant, and the cynical moved into shelters. They had done it before—so many times, it was becoming a bore. And Göring had promised them that there would be no English bombers. . . .

Two Stirlings of No. 15 Squadron, one piloted by Wing Commander J. C. Macdonald and the other by Squadron Leader R. S. Gilmour, approached Cologne at an altitude of fifteen thousand feet. They had first skirted the city, turning north, in order to make the bombing run on the Neumarkt from the north. Off their starboard wing the Rhine glittered in the bright moonlight, the river gracefully arching eastward above the Hindenburg Bridge. The moonlight and intense shadows brought out the city's details. Less than a half mile northeast of the Neumarkt lay the famous cathedral of Cologne, begun in the thirteenth century and completed six hundred years later. The cathedral was not a target. However, just above it lay the main station on the rail line which crossed the Rhine over the Hohenzollern Bridge. The other two aiming points lay a mile to the north and a mile to the south of the Neumarkt.

As the two Stirlings settled on their bomb runs the first burst of flak came up. They were neither accurate nor numerous. Precisely, one half hour after the air raid sirens sounded in Cologne—at 12:47 A.M.—the first incendiary bombs fell from the two Stirlings and spattered across the Neumarkt. The fires these 4-pound and 20-pound bombs ignited would serve as aiming points for the bombers of the main force. During the next hour and a half Cologne would suffer bombing attacks by no less than nine hundred bombers—not the spectacular thousand perhaps, but tragically sufficient.

When the bombers in the train of Macdonald and Gilmour started on their bombing runs, the Germans had already lit dummy fires away from the critical centers of Cologne, hoping to confuse the attackers. In addition, the midnight sky was sliced with heavy flak and blindingly vivid with searchlights. If there was a beginning of terror on the ground, it was as terrifying at eighteen thousand feet. Within minutes after the initial bomb drop, even before the first conflagrations erupted in the Old City, the bombers had begun to take antiaircraft hits; some flared and fell out of the crisscross of the searchlights. The atmosphere bounced with flak, tossing the planes around as pilots, flying on instru-

Night Mission II: A Handley Page "Halifax" (105 attacked Cologne in the night of May 30/31, 1942) gets the signal to begin its takeoff.
(IMPERIAL WAR MUSEUM, LONDON)

ments to keep from being blinded by the lights, weaved to distract the flak-directing instruments, dodged lights, and worried about collision. Quite soon pilots discarded the carefully laid plans for the operation and proceeded under the desperation of the moment. Bombers struck by flak jettisoned bombs as quickly as possible; others, awed by the lights, the flak, and the sight of Cologne burning, bombed directly rather than proceeding according to the briefings on definite bomb runs. Some pilots, even after bombing, circled Cologne to watch in horrified fascination the great sheets of flame which appeared to engulf the city.

Aircraft, therefore, converged over the target area from many directions at different altitudes, some assigned and some enforced by the bomb loads and overtaxed engines. The first collision occurred during the incendiary phase. As one pilot approached the aiming point in a confusion of light, noise, and concussion, he saw one bomber nearby suddenly dissolve in one burst of flame, a great orange ball which remained in place for a moment as small pieces of dripping metal scattered away from it. Keeping directly on his run to give his bombardier the highest chance of accuracy, the pilot found him-

self dangerously close to a Stirling just above and ahead. There were about four hundred yards between him and the Stirling, so he kept a wary eye on his airspeed as well as the Stirling. From below, almost directly under the Stirling, loomed the form of a Wellington.

Night Mission III: Halifax lifts off the runway. Later "Marks" (Halifax III et seq.) were powered with air-cooled Rolls-Royce "Merlins" in place of liquid-cooled "Vultures." (IMPERIAL WAR MUSEUM, LONDON)

Night Mission IV: Lancaster I of No. 61 Squadron; sixty-seven Lancasters bombed Cologne the night of the raid. The only known collision over the target *involved a 61 Squadron Lancaster and a Halifax.*
(IMPERIAL WAR MUSEUM, LONDON)

"There were aircraft everywhere," one bombardier later reported. "The sky over Cologne was as busy as Piccadilly Circus. I could identify every type of bomber in our force by the light of the moon and fires."

The Stirling and the Wellington flew on toward

Night Mission V: A No. 50 Squadron Lancaster, barely off the ground, has already retracted its undercarriage. (U. S. AIR FORCE)

the center of the fires, their crews oblivious to the hazardous proximity of their aircraft. Besides "jinking" (taking evasive action) they were also being bounced by the slipstreams of the planes which had preceded them. The Stirling dropped down and the Wellington rose, but nothing happened and they continued flying with only a few yards separating them. And then they came together again. The Stirling had gained a fraction in speed so that, with a dazzling shower of sparks, the Wellington's propellers cut off its tail section. For a moment the two great planes hovered in unreal suspension; the next moment the Wellington blew out of existence; the four-engined Stirling gyrated down into the holocaust of Cologne, taking its crew with it.

When the incendiary force concluded its job of seeding with flame, there was no doubt as to the location of the target. The stricken city could be seen as far as two hundred miles away. "It was almost too gigantic to be real," one pilot observed. "But it was real enough when we got there. Below us in every part of the city buildings were ablaze. Here and there you could see their outlines, but mostly it was just one big stretch of fire. It was strange to see the flames reflected on our aircraft.

*Night Mission VI: A Stirling heads for Germany—
seventy-one bombed Cologne.*
(IMPERIAL WAR MUSEUM, LONDON)

It looked at times as though we were on fire our-
selves, with a red glow dancing up and down the
wings."

The airspace over Cologne churned with the heat
of the fires, aircraft slipstreams, and the sporadic
burst of antiaircraft fires. Under the unremitting onslaught—about eleven planes crossed over the city
every minute—the defenses had indeed been saturated. The guns ringing Cologne could not keep up
with the great numbers of aircraft. Night fighters
operating on the edge of the flak areas could deal
with but a few of the bombers—and these frequently only after the bomb load had been dropped
into Cologne's inferno. Halfway through the attack
crews noticed a decided confusion and debilitation
on the part of Cologne's flak guns—of which there
were around five hundred.

The bombers of the main force, scheduled to follow the incendiary force, came over and bombed
for an hour. The first plane to arrive was a Wellington of No. 103 Squadron (of No. 1 Group), whose
pilot, a giant New Zealander, Clive Saxelby, brought
it in along the Rhine and without opposition re-

leased the bombs into the marked area. Saxelby
then pulled away and headed for England. It had
been an easy drop and the engines of the Wellington sang beautifully as it cruised over Holland. Out
of the dark came strange flashes which punctured
the fuselage, shattered bits of equipment, and
erupted into a fire in the plane's midsection. The
oxygen system went out immediately, controls went
out of order, and the fire spread.

Saxelby pulled off his oxygen mask, opened the
side window of the cockpit, and for a fleeting moment saw a Messerschmitt 110 in the gloom. They
had been found by a night fighter. With the hydraulic system shot up, the wheels of the Wellington
had come down and the bomb bay doors had
opened, making control of the plane difficult in
addition to slowing it up. Saxelby dived away from
the German fighter while the navigator attempted
to beat out the midsection fire with his bare hands.
Fabric shriveled and pulled away; the tail too caught
fire and lost much of its fabric. The radio operator joined the navigator in fighting the fire, which
in time was extinguished, leaving wide patches of
exposed framework showing. But the controls were
almost too much for Saxelby (his copilot, a man unknown to him before that night, had been killed in

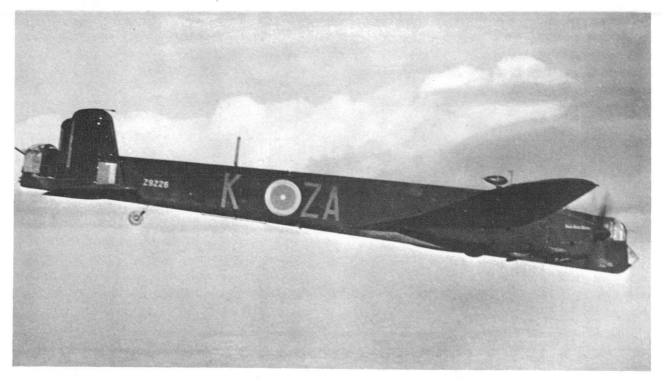

Night Mission VII: A Whitley of No. 10 Squadron airborne. Employing the obsolescent Whitley was an op- *erational barrel scraping; only twenty-three bombed the target during Millennium.* (U. S. AIR FORCE)

the attack by the Me-110). By lashing the control column with rope, Saxelby managed to maintain a near-level flight across the rest of Holland and the North Sea and to the first base they found in England—Honington.

Leslie Manser's Manchester was one of the main force bombers. Like so many of the heavily loaded two-engined bombers, the Manchester could not climb to a safer altitude without dangerously overheating the engines. Manser was forced to bring the plane in under the other bombers at around seven thousand feet. Although he could take some comfort in assuming that the flak would be concentrating on the greater number of aircraft, in truth the overladen radar operators found it simpler to select strays.

On the approach to the drop point the Manchester seemed poised upon the fingers of several searchlights. Just as flak accuracy decreased with altitude, it inversely improved the lower a plane dropped. With the main force up at least twice the height of Manser's Manchester, the stray was quickly boxed in by flak bursts. Manser, the pilot

so many had regarded as "too pretty" to be a pilot, selected an area within the target zone still untouched by fire. Bang On Barnes peered through the bombsight and centered on the area as Manser guided the Manchester across Cologne in even flight.

"Bombs gone," Barnes announced. The Manchester elevated upon losing its burden and, almost instantaneously, recoiled under a direct flak hit. The controls threatened to tear out of Manser's hands as he fought to keep the tumbling and rocking plane under control. But he realized, too, that they must get away from the searchlights—for the flak had plotted their range. Manser heaved forward on the control column and dived away from the lights. When they entered blackness he eased the plane out of the dive. It responded beautifully and came out at less than a thousand feet. They could not remain at that height either, for even ground machine-gun fire could reach them. Pulling back on the controls Manser guided the plane up to two thousand feet; should they have to jump it was a safer altitude also. The plane had taken a hit in the bomb bay, luckily after the bombs had been dropped. The fire had gone out, but that proved only a temporary blessing. The strain on the left engine had been too much. The instruments flickered strangely and then a flash of fire shot out of the engine.

Manser coolly ordered copilot Baveystock to feather the left engine and to activate the fire extinguisher. The rest of the crew, including rear gunner Naylor, who had been wounded by the flak, began to make ready to jump. As Manser and Baveystock watched, the flames from the engine swept back along the wing. The question was: How long before the fire reached the fuel tank in the wing and blew them all over the sky?

But Manser only said, "Let's wait." And they did, for like their skipper the men in the aircraft wanted most of all to get back to England. The eerie flames consumed the fabric of the wing, burned the engine mount, and then, after about ten minutes, the fire went out. Manser had been right. He turned the Manchester toward home as the crew attended to other important details. Naylor lay in a rest bed in the rear of the plane, attended to by radio operator Norman Horsley. But the plane continued to lose altitude and it seemed unlikely that they could ever reach England. All possible equipment which could be spared and torn loose was flung from the plane to lighten it—even guns. The Manchester, despite this, continued to lose air speed. The engine must soon give up—or blow up. Manser found it more and more difficult to keep the plane under control.

Reluctantly he ordered the crew to jump. Mills, the nose gunner, left through the front exit, followed by Barnes, the navigator. Horsley helped the wounded Naylor through a side exit and followed soon after. The plane by this time shuddered and wheezed and was dangerously near stalling point.

Baveystock returned to the cockpit to make certain that Manser had his parachute. He attempted to clip it on the pilot. But he was stopped by Manser, who ordered him to jump immediately. Baveystock went forward to the forward hatch and jumped. But the plane at this time was scarcely a hundred feet above the hedgerow- and dike-crossed countryside of Belgium. In remaining behind to check Manser's parachute Baveystock had all but canceled his chances of survival. He leaped into the darkness, pulled his chute ring—and plunged into the water of a drainage ditch. Although the parachute had not opened completely, it had decelerated Baveystock's falling speed and the water in the dike did the rest.

The Manchester continued on for only a few hundred feet before striking the ground with a terrific explosion. When he climbed out of the dike Baveystock tried to get to the burning wreck, but the heat of the flames—and the ammunition still aboard detonating—made it impossible. Manser had died in the aircraft; he had kept it aloft long enough to save his entire crew. Baveystock, Horsley, Naylor, and Mills, with the aid of the Belgian underground, finally returned to England. Navigator Barnes, injured in his parachute jump, was captured by the Germans. When the others eventually returned to England and told their story, Manser was posthumously awarded the Victoria Cross—the only participant in the Thousand Plane raid to receive it.

The final fifteen minutes of the raid involved the heavies, the Halifaxes and Lancasters of Nos. 4 and 5 Groups, which followed the main force to which Manser's Manchester belonged. Their function was to drop the 1000- and 4000-pound bombs into the furious chaos. These last two hundred planes would deliver the finishing touches to the destruction besides hindering whatever fire fighting was still possible in Cologne. By 2:25 A.M., Sunday morning, May 31, 1942, Cologne was a man-made hell. To the mystical Leonard Cheshire, who had completed a tour of duty and was then commanding a conversion unit (i.e., a training unit which prepared pilots accustomed to two-engined planes to operate four-engined craft), the hundreds of aircraft pointing toward the crimson glow which was Cologne was "the most monstrous sight in all the history of bombing." As he brought his Halifax in on the bomb run and the city came into view "there was a sudden silence in the aeroplane. If what we saw below was true,

---

Night Mission VIII: A typical German flak and search-light concentration over a German city (not Cologne). Flak was responsible for most losses over the target. Of the twenty-two British bombers lost over Cologne, sixteen fell to antiaircraft fire, four to night fighters, and two to a collision.
(ALIEN PROPERTY CUSTODIAN, NATIONAL ARCHIVES)

Cologne was destroyed. We looked hastily at the Rhine, but there was no mistake; what we saw below was true."

The orders had been that all bombing was to cease·at two twenty-five precisely; all planes which had not bombed were to turn back. This was to ensure the returning planes as much darkness as possible. The German night fighters were problem enough without having to contend with the day fighters also.

When he took off at 1:15 A.M., Flight Lieutenant George Gilpin had scant hopes of reaching Cologne by two twenty-five. The other aircraft of No. 61 Squadron had left an hour ago. His Lancaster, of the squadron's conversion flight, had been ignored while the rest of the squadron's Lancasters—sixteen altogether—were made ready. Though he

pleaded, Gilpin had little luck until the regular planes had been bombed-up and armed. Then all joined in, including himself and his crew, to get the plane ready. The bombing had been progressing for nearly an hour before Gilpin trundled the Lancaster to the runway, half expecting not to get the takeoff light. But it came and he gunned the engines and got away before anyone changed his mind.

Gilpin put the Lancaster into a climb and pulled away over England. They should have little trouble finding Cologne, for there were two navigators aboard the Lancaster. When Gilpin had been granted permission to go on the raid it was with the proviso he could scratch together a crew, for most of the men at his station were assigned to the regular squadron bombers. Gilpin had all positions

filled, having assigned the role of navigator-bombardier to an old school friend, John Beach. But there was still need of a nose gunner. It was while he was out seeking a gunner that Gilpin found Flight Officer D. H. Brewer, who, having never flown in a Lancaster, jumped at the chance to go. But Brewer was not a gunner in fact, but a navigator.

They crossed the North Sea at about seventeen thousand feet and below them saw streams of returning bombers of the first wave. Their Lancaster was the only plane flying toward Germany. Gilpin consulted with Beach, asking for an estimated time of arrival over the target.

"0305."

"Forty minutes late?"

This would be counter to orders and Gilpin was not anxious to break rules. Nor was he anxious to waste the effort. He asked Beach for a heading toward another target. But it never came; there was a curious silence on the intercom, an eloquent testimonial to the wishes of the crew. Gilpin let it go at that, for as they crossed over Holland the glow of Cologne lit up the eastern horizon like a premature sunrise.

The Lancaster, then, at three in the morning, was the only plane in the air over Cologne, shimmering below. A pillar of smoke reached up to fifteen thousand feet. It seemed ludicrous for a single bomber to drop its load into the carnage which hundreds of bombers had wreaked. But Beach, lying in the nose, guided Gilpin assiduously on the bomb run. Although there were no fighters now over Cologne, the searchlights stabbed into the air, holding the Lancaster in their blinding light. Then the flak came hurtling up, leaving drifting puffs in the sky. Carefully Beach centered on the aiming point in the center of the burning mass.

Since he was in the nose serving as a scratch "bomb aimer," Beach was not seated in his regular position in the navigator's seat behind Gilpin. On the bomb run a piece of flak tore through the cabin and ripped out the navigator's seat—luckily unoccupied. The impact shook up Gilpin a little but he continued with the run until he heard Beach's quiet "Bombs gone." Gilpin immediately dived the Lancaster out of the beams of light, and although the flak continued to track them, they left Cologne and made for the sea.

When they reached the Dutch coast for the flight over the North Sea and home, the Lancaster was flying on three engines, one having given up on the way. Day had come as they approached England —luckily there had been no fighters. Gilpin brought them all home safely. Millennium was over.

Perhaps with the landing of Gilpin's Lancaster, it could be said that the operation was concluded, but in fact it was not. Even before the great bomber, coming in on three engines and with one propeller feathered, touched down gently at the base at Syerston, a single twin-engined aircraft raced into the air before dawn from its base at Horsham Saint Faith in Norfolk. This was a de Havilland Mosquito of No. 105 Squadron, one of the units which had served with the Advance Air Striking Force in France during the early weeks of the war. Called the "Wooden Wonder" or the "Termite's Delight," the Mosquito was of practically all-wood construction, which eluded radar detection. It was also faster than the German fighters of the period.

On the mission to Cologne, the Mosquito was dispatched to drop bombs (for this highly versatile plane could be used as a bomber as well as fighter, among other functions) and to photograph the destruction of the Millennium bombing. The pilot brought the Mosquito over Cologne at twenty-three thousand feet during the early morning, but although his bombardier could release their bombs, the smoke made it impossible to photograph the damage. Three additional Mosquitos left Horsham Saint Faith at later intervals, and of the two which returned, it was with the same result: too much smoke—for a vast fire cloud rose up to fifteen thousand feet—to take photographs. Only the survivors in the city below realized the extent of the effect of Millennium.

III

German propaganda quickly sneered at British claims of a thousand bombers over Cologne, claiming that the figure was closer to seventy and that the defenses had accounted for nearly half that number. Early British estimates of the impact of the raid were naturally exaggerated. Upon viewing the devastation, however, five days after the attack when

Night Mission IX: de Havilland "Mosquito," which flew a reconnaissance mission to Cologne the morning after the thousand-plane raid and found smoke rising fifteen thousand feet into the air over the city.
(DE HAVILLAND PHOTOGRAPH)

Night Mission X: A Stirling coming in for a landing in England. (IMPERIAL WAR MUSEUM, LONDON)

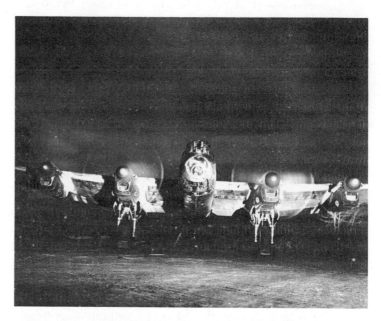

Night Mission XI: A Lancaster, engines warming up and wheels chocked, ready for the next mission.
(IMPERIAL WAR MUSEUM, LONDON)

reconnaissance photographs could be taken, it was clear that more than six hundred acres of the city had been eradicated.

Dismay was the mood in Cologne. Although the official Luftwaffe view was that a few English bombers had broken through the defenses, the city's police president reported that the "number of enemy aircraft over the city could not be estimated." Hitler's toady, Gauleiter Joseph Grohé, supplied his leader with his estimate of a "thousand or more," which Hitler used in a screaming attack upon the Luftwaffe.

The raid had killed 469 people and wounded 5027; more than 45,000 were bombed out of their homes. The incendiaries accounted for the most terrible aspects of the raid, spreading wildly and burning buildings and destroying life and property. This single attack caused the death of more people than all previous attacks upon Cologne combined.

Other than some spectacular figures, had the Thousand Plan accomplished what Harris had wished for? What had been the cost? And what would the future of this kind of warfare be?

The Millennium losses, considering the ambitiousness of the undertaking and the fact that so many inexperienced crews participated, were reasonably low. Forty-one aircraft were listed as missing on the morning after the raid; 3 planes of the intruder force were also missing. Thus it was officially noted that of the total aircraft involved in Millennium, 44 out of 1134 (combined bombing force and intruders) were missing.

And yet Churchill would have been prepared to defend the loss of a hundred aircraft and crews, if necessary, on the floor of the Parliament. Harris had predicted a loss of forty planes; he was a realistic professional. The casualty rate had been 3.8 per cent—a not unacceptable proportion. It was Harris's belief that "we should never have had a real bomber offensive if it had not been for the thousand-bomber attack on Cologne, an irrefutable demonstration of the power of what was to all intents and purposes a new and untried weapon." Another professional, Herr Goebbels, although no soldier, took his own realistic view of the raid when he noted in his diary that he could not "believe that the English have the power to continue such bombing attacks. . . ." Still he was nagged by the possibility of a number of such large-scale attacks, which

he admitted (to himself at least) "can damage us considerably." It was true that Harris would not be able to continue such attacks, risking his regular squadrons, his reserves, instructors, and trainees night after night. In fact, only one more raid of such scale took place in 1942 (June 25/26; the target was Bremen); an earlier attack upon Essen did not achieve the magical magnitude of a thousand. Not until the full weight of the U. S. Eighth and Fifteenth Air Forces came to operate over Europe could thousand-bomber raids become a daily and nightly procedure.

But Harris had made his point—the Thousand Plan had not failed. Cologne had suffered and, if not knocked out of the war, was thrown into confusion and industrial inaction for several weeks. The price of war, too, was brought home to the hapless civil population. The importance of morale under fire is always a questionable point—the human spirit endures under incredible adversity—but before the thousands of evacuees left Cologne they were compelled to sign a statement promising not to discuss the situation in Cologne. Though not readily measurable, the impact upon the German spirit was no less real. Harris had saved his command from the depletion it had suffered during the weeks before he was given its leadership. He had not "destroyed Cologne," as he had asserted, but he had saved Bomber Command and its continued existence and growth would have its effect upon the German war machine.

There were eventual changes in the Luftwaffe brought about by the Cologne attack; it was clear that aircraft would have to be siphoned away from the Russian front. There would be a greater need for more fighter protection over the cities of the Fatherland. Consequently, the German Army would lose some of its air cover. These were subtle yet far-reaching consequences.

There was an even more subtle, sublime might even be the word, sequel, the effect of which was pernicious to the Luftwaffe. This may have been the most important of all the "fruits" of Cologne. While the raid developed in all its fury, Hitler fumed at his headquarters at Rastenberg. His mind was saturated with the conquest of Russia and this sudden, full-scale onslaught from the west exasperated him. Göring was at that moment living the good life in his castle at Veldenstein. When the noon conferences took place on the Sunday following the attack, it devolved upon Jeschonnek and Bodenschatz (Göring's personal aide) to represent the Luftwaffe before the Führer.

Having heard reports from a representative of the Navy and the Army, Hitler turned to the young chief of staff. Jeschonnek did not begin immediately and was prodded by the Führer. "General Jeschonnek, I am waiting. . . ." Clearly Hitler was in a mood, although the devoted, naïve Jeschonnek appeared to be unaware of it.

"There was an RAF attack on Cologne," Jeschonnek began hesitantly, "a pretty heavy attack."

"How heavy?"

Jeschonnek shuffled some papers. "According to preliminary reports," he answered, "we estimate that two hundred aircraft penetrated our defenses. The damage is heavy . . . we are still waiting for final estimates."

"You are still waiting for final estimates . . ." Hitler mocked and shouted, "and the Luftwaffe thinks there were two hundred enemy aircraft!" His voice cracked and rose shrilly. "The Luftwaffe was probably asleep last night! But I was not asleep—not when one of my cities is under fire!"

The Luftwaffe, Hitler intimated, deceived him as usual. Thank God he could depend upon such reliable men as Gauleiter Grohé in Cologne.

"Let me tell you what Gauleiter Grohé has to say! Listen—I ask you to listen carefully—[shouting] there were a thousand or more English aircraft—you hear!—a thousand, twelve hundred, maybe more!" Hitler stopped, his face a livid, apoplectic study in wrath. Composed, but no less furious, Hitler then spoke in a cold tone. "Herr [not Reichsmarschall] Göring, of course, is not here; of course not. . . ."

Bodenschatz had slipped out of the room during the speech, upon assessing the situation. He reached Göring at Veldenstein by phone. "Chief," he said, "you had better come at once. There is trouble."

That he was *persona non grata* was obvious to Göring as soon as he entered the Führer's headquarters later that day. He had gone into the room briskly, but wearing an appropriate air of earnest sobriety. Göring was visibly shaken when Hitler disregarded his outstretched hand. The former corporal had never actually trusted flying men and he had been proved right. If he had failed to appreciate the potential of air power, from that moment on he would refuse even to attempt to understand it. The inner deterioration of the Luftwaffe was assured. Suspicion, vilification, abuse of function, and, even more damaging, the estrangement of Göring and Hitler, sealed the fate of the "Air Weapon."

Harris had not only won the battle; philosophically and morally at least, he had won the war.

6

X-SQUADRON

Lookouts in the small convoy of ships plying the night-shrouded North Sea quickened to the thick rumble of several aircraft engines bearing down from the direction of England. Immediately gunners brought their gun barrels around and waited; a challenge signal vaulted from the convoy commander's ship. Three dark, massive forms came hurtling toward the ships; the planes were barely fifty feet over the water and must have been doing better than two hundred miles an hour.

A Very pistol was fired from a side window in the lead plane and all the men in the convoy relaxed. The signal color was correct for the night, May 16, 1943; the aircraft were British. As was the custom, the convoy's skipper acknowledged recognition with the message "Good hunting" by Aldis lamp. From the lead plane another Aldis flashed as the plane grew smaller in the night. The seamen read the message as the light became a pin point:

We are going to get damn drunk tomorrow night.

As they pondered this curious intelligence two more groups of the same aircraft (Lancasters, they appeared to be) swept over the convoy toward Holland, probably on the way to Germany.

The pilot in the lead Lancaster was the young, stocky veteran of three tours of duty (bombers, night fighters, and bombers again) who was frequently referred to by his men as "the baby skipper," Guy Penrose Gibson. Not many weeks before

—in mid-March—he had returned from his 173rd sortie—a mission to Stuttgart—bringing his Lancaster back on three engines, expecting to take a much needed rest. Gibson hoped to have a few days' leave, the first in about a year, which he would spend with his wife in Cornwall relaxing. He would smoke a pipe, take walks with his dog, and forget about the war for a while. Instead he found himself leading a fantastic night mission.

At twenty-four, Gibson had served as squadron commander of No. 106 Squadron, had been awarded the Distinguished Service Order (with bar) and the Distinguished Flying Cross, and had acquired the reputation in Bomber Command as one of the finest minds in the service. Gibson had been born in 1918 in Simla, India, where his father had served as Conservator of Forests. He grew up in Kent, however, in the area which would serve as the setting for the Battle of Britain, and went to St. Edward's School, Oxford. Though powerfully built, Gibson never grew much taller than slightly over five feet. Whether or not this accounted for his physical drive is beside the point, for as recollected by the warden at St. Edward's, he "was one of the most thorough and determined boys I have ever known. . . ."

By the time he was well into his teens, Gibson had become air-minded and hoped to seek work as a test pilot. When he approached Vickers-Armstrong

Guy Gibson, who led one of the most daring bombing missions of the war during the Battle of the Ruhr. A born pilot and leader, Gibson earned a Victoria Cross for his part in the Dam Busters raid.

(IMPERIAL WAR MUSEUM, LONDON)

(who would later manufacture the Wellington), Gibson was told to join the RAF "to get all the flying time you can." However, upon applying Gibson was informed that his "legs were too short." But the determined Gibson had made up his mind and after exercising and stretching, he returned to the RAF and apparently, by sheer dint of will power, passed the physical requirements. In 1935 Guy Gibson began training with the RAF, hoping that when he had completed his courses, he might return to Vickers for a job as test pilot. The stocky youngster fell into the routine very well—he had a taste for pretty girls and drink and a love of animals. He also revealed a flair for flying and a mind which absorbed, classified, and retained details.

The political situation kept Gibson in the RAF after his enlistment expired and when war finally came he was a pilot of a Hampden in No. 83 Squadron based at Scampton in Lincolnshire. Gibson took part in the frustrating operations during the "Phony War," as well as more profitable strikes upon targets in the occupied countries and the Sealion barges during the Battle of Britain. Upon completing his tour with the bombers, Gibson was stationed—for "a rest"—with No. 29 Squadron, Fighter Command. While serving with this night fighter unit, Gibson succeeded in shooting down three enemy aircraft. Following his "rest" tour Gibson was sent to an Operational Training Unit, which did not please him at all. But it was a good post, for Gibson had married Evelyn Mary Moore, a young and pretty actress, and he spent much time at home. Even so, Gibson did not like the role of flying instructor and made it fairly obvious. Not long after Arthur Harris took over Bomber Command Gibson managed to get an interview with him and within days (two, in fact) was posted, in February 1942, to No. 106 Squadron as Wing Commander (Acting). Upon completing his tour with the squadron, its "baby skipper" looked forward with longing to the easy days with Eve at Cornwall.

But he had barely unwound from the Stuttgart mission when he was informed the following day that he would not go on leave; he was to be posted at Headquarters, No. 5 Group instead.

Air Officer Commanding of No. 5 Group was Air Vice-Marshal the Honorable Sir Ralph Cochrane, like Saundby an old prewar squadron mate of Harris. Cochrane, scion of a noble Scots family, was a lean, no-nonsense, crisply decisive man whose aviation experience dated back to the First World War. When Gibson reported to him at group headquarters at Grantham, it was with the gloomy expectation of being assigned to write a textbook on bombing. Having barely finished congratulating Gibson on the bar to his DSO, Cochrane immediately came to the point.

"How would you like the idea of doing one more trip?"

Visions of fighters and flak came into Gibson's mind. He had hoped all of that was over, at least for a while. But all he could do was ask, "What kind of trip, sir?"

"A pretty important one, perhaps one of the most

devastating of all time," Cochrane replied. "I can't tell you any more now. Do you want to do it?"

The urgency seemed so pressing that Gibson had begun trying to remember where he had left his flying kit. Certainly the trip of which the AOC spoke was scheduled for that very night. His answer reflected the state of his mind: "I think so, sir." Gibson was then sent away mystified.

But the trip was not scheduled for that night, or the next. On the third day after the first interview Gibson was once again ordered to Grantham's main office. Seated in Cochrane's office was a man Gibson knew, stocky, thirtyish, experienced Group Captain Charles Whitworth. Cochrane was cordial, even offered Gibson a cigarette before he broached the subject of "the trip." He began by warning Gibson that it would not be an "ordinary sortie. In fact, it can't be done for at least two months."

"Hell," Gibson thought, "it's the *Tirpitz*. What on earth did I say yes for?" The great 45,000-ton battleship, launched just six months before the war began, was a major source of anxiety to the British at this time (the *Tirpitz* did not prove as formidable in action as it promised, but this was not apparent in 1943). The battleship was then lying in Trondheim Fiord in Norway, all but impossible to reach by air and a threat to convoys to Russia.

Cochrane went on, without slipping Gibson the least hint of the nature of the target or of the mission itself beyond telling him that Harris regarded the training for the raid so important "that a special squadron is to be formed for the job. I want you to form that squadron. . . ."

Stressing the importance of the training and the little time in which it must be done, Cochrane suggested that Gibson go immediately to the personnel section to begin assembling his crews and arranging for aircraft and other equipment as well as ground crews. All Gibson knew actually was that he was to undertake some important mission or other and that his special squadron was to be based at Scampton, where Group Captain Whitworth was commander and where Gibson had begun his active career with No. 83 Squadron less than four years before.

When he left Cochrane's office for the personnel section Gibson's head swam and his ears rang with the order, "I want to see your aircraft flying in four days' time."

What aircraft, with what crews? Gibson wondered as he climbed the stairs to begin selecting pilots and crews and to start all the other gears meshing for the mysterious trip. Whatever it all ultimately would lead to, the trip was obviously of highest priority, for within two days a squadron of seven hundred men was formed and ordered to report to Scampton. In fact, its formation had come so quickly that the Air Ministry was itself not prepared for it and called it temporarily X-Squadron. Finally it was assigned the number 617.

II

That it was an elite unit was patent in the beribboned crews that began arriving at Scampton on March 21, 1942. "These were the aces of Bomber Command," Gibson noted. He had selected pilots he knew personally or by reputation; the rest were suggested by Bomber Command. It was a standing order, another tribute to X-Squadron's uniqueness, that the other squadrons must surrender requested crews on demand. This did not always work out to perfection. "Some of the squadrons which had been told by the SASO [Senior Air Staff Officer] to supply us with tip-top men had taken the opportunity to get rid of some of their duds. . . . Then another squadron supplied me, rather unkindly, with two pregnant WAAFs [Women's Auxiliary Air Force]. They were married, of course, but they weren't any use to me because they had to leave the service, anyway. There were other little games played on us which I won't mention." Gibson, however, managed to assemble twenty-one crews, some of them from his own No. 106 Squadron—all of them veterans with thousands of sorties to their credit.

When he called the 147 men of the aircrews together for their first official meeting, Gibson was still at a disadvantage. There was little of a solid nature which he could tell these 147 knowledgeable men. "You're here," he told them, "to do a special job, you're here as a crack squadron, you're here to carry out a raid on Germany which, I am told, will have startling results. Some say it may even cut short the duration of the war. What the target is I can't tell you. Nor can I tell you where it is. All I can tell you is that you will have to practice low flying all day and all night until you know how to do it with your eyes shut. . . ."

It would be some days before Gibson was to meet the gentle, white-haired man—a civilian—who had initiated all of this inexplicable activity. He was Dr. Barnes N. Wallis, an outstanding designer and aeronautical engineer employed by Vickers-Armstrong. Wallis, who had designed the structure of the airship R-100, had contributed also to the design of the Wellington bomber (in which work he had teamed up with Vickers' chief designer, Rex K. Pierson). Wallis's major conception was the geodetic system of construction, which made the Wimpy a rugged though comparatively lightweight aircraft.

A brilliant mathematician, the fifty-year-old engineer began to consider the problem of bombs as

Dr. Barnes Wallis, inventor-engineer-designer, who made many contributions to Britain's war effort as well as to aviation. (VICKERS LIMITED)

soon as the war started. Wallis, in his own way, was a proponent of strategic bombardment. When war came he believed that the standard bombs then available to Bomber Command lacked the power to destroy important industrial targets: the five-hundred-pounders then in use would not do. Also, unless targets were selected with care, what bombs were dropped would accomplish little more than temporary damage. Wallis, in short, began to visualize a superbomb to be dropped upon a super target. It followed that his mind would consider the Ruhr, the great center of Germany's heavy industry. Within this highly defended area lay a complex of great dams, targets which could not be dispersed like a factory, nor even very easily camouflaged.

Wallis studied the situation closely and selected three of the dams as primary targets: the Möhne, the Sorpe, and the Eder. The first two, as Wallis later explained to Gibson when finally the young wing commander was permitted to know what he was about to attempt, held back "about 76 per cent of the total water available in the Ruhr Valley. If they were to be breached, the consequent shortage of water for both drinking and industrial purposes might be disastrous. Of course, the damage done by floods if they were breached quickly would result in more damage to everything than has ever happened in this war." The Möhne Dam alone, holding back a lake about twelve miles in length, would release about 140 million tons of water, if breached, into the Möhne Valley.

The Eder Dam was not a water supply dam as were the other two, but a source of hydroelectric power. It was somewhat larger than the Möhne, with a capacity of about 200 million tons of water.

Such were the targets, but there were no bombs then existing that could burst them. An object which could hold back 200 million tons of water would not breach under the impact of a mere five-hundred-pound high-explosive bomb. It was to this problem that Wallis applied himself next, studying the structure of dams and of the nature of explosion: shock, tension, and dozens of other variables. When he felt he had the answers to all of the problems, Wallis took his idea to the Air Ministry. He was not greeted with open arms and cries of recognition. Although Wallis's idea had been conceived early in the war, it was not until Harris took over Bomber

Command that it trickled down to him. Nor did the astute Harris seize upon the Wallis plan with joy and expectation.

The various ministries had come to be all but besieged by hundreds of inventors, idea men, armchair generals, and just plain screwballs with thousands of schemes and gadgets for winning the war. Wallis's device for a big bomb (an "earthquake bomb," he sometimes called it) would require a large aircraft to carry it (he called that a "victory bomber"). Neither bomb nor aircraft existed when he submitted his plan. Because of his reputation in the industry, Wallis's idea was not completely dismissed, as were so many others at the time. But, depite that, it took a long time before anyone in the Ministry of Aircraft Production read his paper with any understanding. This was Sir Henry Tizard, who had championed Watson-Watt's radar. A committee was formed to study Wallis's formulations (among which the dams project was but one) and soon after, another committee was formed known as "The Air Attack on Dams Committee." It took months before the idea took on any definite form, depending not only upon the accuracy and validity of Wallis's computations, but also upon the advent of a bomber which could lift and deliver a bomb of tremendous weight. Meanwhile, new very high explosives were being developed. So it was that when the high-capacity bombs became feasible—according to Wallis's figures it would have to be about ten thousand pounds in weight, explosive as well as casing—the Lancaster was on hand to carry it.

Months of experimentation followed, with Wallis practicing on small models of dams and bombs and filling pages with computations. Quite simply, it was Wallis's idea that in order to breach so sturdy an object as the Möhne Dam, the special bomb would have to be released at low altitude, with the aircraft traveling at a specific speed. Before the bomb—which was shaped like an oil drum—was dropped, it must be made to revolve. Upon release it was supposed to skip and jump along the water's surface until it struck the dam. Then it would, because of the spin, roll down the face of the dam to the proper depth and only then explode. The tremendous forces, magnified by water pressure, would have the force of an earthquake and would, theoretically, burst the dam. That is what Wallis's figures said and that is what he believed.

Eventually, with models and with test bombs Wallis proved that it could be done. However, when he finally took his idea to Harris, the latter was skeptical. He had heard of the little man with the dams idea. Another crackpot with what Harris termed a "panacea target," single targets that everyone—except the Germans—would assume might end the war in a single blow. These targets, often as not, were difficult to hit, well defended, and, even if hit, might very well prove not so conclusive after all. They were costly in terms of crew losses, spectacular, even dramatic—but wasteful. Harris had his own plan for ending the war—a city by city erasure of German industries with large forces of heavy bombers. Wars were not decided with single panacea blows. Harris regarded Wallis with misgiving and doubt.

He told Wallis he found the idea a bit beyond belief and, further, he was not ready to risk a squadron of Lancasters on it. One of Wallis's champions was Joseph "Mutt" Summers, chief test pilot at Vickers, who had been assisting Wallis in testing the dummy bombs in a converted Wellington off the coast of England. At the point where the two stubborn men, Wallis and Harris, were about to clash, Summers interceded and promised Harris that they could prove that the bomb worked.

"Prove it," Harris snapped, "and you'll get your squadron."

The two men brought out the film that Wallis had been shooting over the past half year and with Saundby operating the projector, the four men observed the results of Wallis's experiments.

When the film ended all Harris would say was, "Very interesting. I'll think it over."

This was not very encouraging. Wallis found that others also were less than enthused and he had even been asked to stop "making a nuisance of yourself at the Ministry." Exhausted, depressed, and fed up, Wallis offered to resign from all war work. This only aroused an outcry of "Mutiny!" Wallis seemed to have come to a dead end. But other forces had been at work, for approval of the idea had come down from the Chief of the Air Staff, Sir Charles Portal; Churchill had voiced his approval and others had chimed in. The date was February 26, 1943; the operation must take place sometime in May, when the water level of the dams was at maximum. That left three months in which to select and train

The objective: the Ruhr dams, in this instance the Möhne, holding back more than a million tons of water. (IMPERIAL WAR MUSEUM, LONDON)

crews, make and test the bomb, and modify the Lancasters to carry it.

It was Mutt Summers who brought Gibson finally to meet Wallis after No. 617 Squadron had begun training at Scampton. By coincidence, it had been Summers who had advised Gibson, so many years before, to enlist in the RAF. The trip from Scampton had been exceedingly cloak and dagger. Gibson was driven south, past London, and left at a small country railway station. He took a train for Weybridge, where he was supposed to meet someone. The someone turned out to be Summers, who then drove Gibson to Wallis's home in the peaceful southern countryside. Gibson found Wallis "neither young nor old, but just a quiet, earnest man who worked very hard. He was one of the real back-room boys of whom little can be told until after the war. . . ."

An awkward situation arose immediately, for Gibson admitted that to date he had not been informed of the target or of the "Wallis bomb." Wallis checked a list of names of persons with whom he could discuss the project and did not find Gibson's there.

"This is damned silly," Summers said. But Wallis would not discuss the plan except in general terms. He did run a film he and Summers had made which revealed something to Gibson. He saw a Wimpy come in within two hundred feet of the sea and drop a strange cylindrical object. Gibson was certain that if that were a bomb, the detonation would blow the plane sky-high, but instead the cylinder bounced along as the Wellington pulled out of the way of danger.

Clearly, they were to come in low over a target situated on or near the water. Was it the *Tirpitz*, Gibson wondered, or was it the U-boat pens?

Wallis explained that the cylinder was, indeed, his special bomb, the placement of which would require exceptional skill. However, the test bomb was but a quarter of the size of the real thing, so that further testing would be necessary. Gibson asked if any full-scale bombs existed.

"No, not yet," Wallis admitted, "the first will be ready in about a week's time with a modified Lancaster to carry it. Avro's is doing a great rush job to get the special fittings put on; I believe they're working twenty-four hours a day. Now what I want to know from you is this. Can you fly to the limits

I want? These are roughly a speed of two hundred and forty miles an hour at a hundred and fifty feet above smooth water, having pulled out of a dive from two thousand feet, and then be able to drop a bomb accurately within a few yards."

Although still mystified, Gibson left Wallis knowing just a bit more about their proposed mission. He promised to see if it would be possible to meet the requirements for the bomb drop, but that was all. So it was that the two men worked, in their separate spheres, concurrently toward a date in the middle of May, the younger man without concrete information and the older one still uncertain that the weapon he had invented would actually work.

Gibson assigned his crews the unpleasant task of flying low over lakes, rivers, and reservoirs. Within days the complaints began coming in—reports of low-flying aircraft. Even Gibson's own maintenance crews complained of leaves and branches jammed into the radiators.

"This means you are flying too low," Gibson told his flight leaders "You've got to stop this or else someone will kill himself. And I might also tell you that the provost marshals have already been up to see me about reported dangerous low flying. We all know we've got to fly low, and we've got to get some practice in, but for God's sake, tell your boys to try and avoid going over towns and aerodromes and not to beat up policemen or lovers in a field, because they'll get the rocket if they do."

The following day Gibson was summoned to Cochrane's office. On the floor stood three large packing cases. Cochrane handed Gibson a screwdriver and promised he would show him the targets —although he would not tell him either what they were or where they were located. Gibson removed the lids and peered into the boxes—there perfectly scaled were models of three dams, obviously very large and sturdy. But Gibson's first reaction upon seeing them was a fleeting thought: "Thank God, it's not the *Tirpitz*."

Without revealing much more, Cochrane told him to take a plane and fly down to see Wallis in Weybridge. At least now the men could discuss the problem intelligently. It was Wallis who informed Gibson that the three dams lay in the Ruhr Valley— "Happy Valley" to the bomber crews because of the deadly flak barrages they never failed to encounter there.

Gibson wondered why the special bombs, and why the stringent conditions—altitude, speed—for the attack. Wouldn't any large bomb hitting the dams knock them out?

Wallis explained the difference between a vault dam—the curved type which held back water by its configuration "much the same as the arch of a bridge"—and the dams they were after, which were called gravity dams and which retained water by their own weight. "As these are a hundred and forty feet thick, of solid concrete and masonry, a hundred and fifty feet high, you can see that there is a colossal amount of masonry to shift." Wallis further explained that the attack would have to take place when the water level was at its highest. At that moment it was twelve feet from the top of each dam; they would attack when the level reached four. This would give them the proper water capacity and also leave the four-foot space against which the bomb would strike after its last bounce carrying it over the floating torpedo nets which protected the dam, and then permitting it to roll down the dam toward the base before detonating. This was precision at its most precise. Gibson looked doubtful. They were to do this at night in addition to all the other contingencies.

"I have calculated," Wallis continued, "that the water level will be suitable during the week May 13–19, that is, in about six weeks' time. This, as it happens, is a moon period—I think you will have to do it at night or dawn—you couldn't get into the Ruhr by day, could you?"

"God, no!"

That was settled. There was another point. In order that the bomb could make the correct number of skips before striking the lip of the dam, it must be released at just the right point. Otherwise it might bounce over the dam (which might prove fatal to the Lancaster which had dropped it) or might fall short of the dam and merely sink into the water and detonate without effect. It was just one more detail which needed attention. There was a sense of urgency about the entire project which Gibson found unsettling, but he returned to Scampton to continue the training. He promised to see Wallis in two weeks, on April 16, to observe the test drops of the first two full-scale prototypes of the Wallis bombs.

Early in April Wing Commander C. L. Dann from the Ministry of Aircraft Production casually dropped in on Gibson at Scampton. With breath-taking abruptness Dann broached the subject of getting the correct sighting of the Möhne and Eder dams. Considering the few people in on the project —Gibson was the only man in the squadron who knew of the targets—it came as a shock that a man could walk in off the street, so to speak, and begin talking about a most ticklish subject.

"How the hell do you know all this?" Gibson demanded. Dann explained that he was a bombsight expert and had been asked to help solve the problem in connection with the dams. A mathematician, Dann had studied the aerial photos of the Möhne and Eder dams and found that each dam had towers at either end two hundred yards apart. Using these as the base of a triangle, Dann very quickly devised a simple bombsight which could be made of a few pieces of wood. The bombardier simply lined up two nails with the towers through a peephole. When all came in line, it was—provided the speed of the plane was correct—the drop point. Within hours the device was tested and found to be remarkably accurate.

Dann's little gadget solved that problem, a skilled pilot could manage the problem of air speed, but neither man nor instrument could make certain that the plane was flying at the correct height. Flying over water was especially deceiving. Also, they would be down low in a darkened valley, surrounded by hills. It was a serious problem indeed.

III

While Wallis worried over the casing of his bomb, which did not stand up to the strain of the test drops, Gibson continued with the training of No. 617 Squadron. They had progressed beautifully in all areas but the sticky one of height—how to find 150 feet and how to stay there? One solution seemed to be trailing a weight from a wire. The weight would be placed at the 150-foot mark. When it struck the surface of the water they would be at the proper height. Upon testing it was found that the wire and weight trailed almost directly behind the plane. Judging by eye was completely useless. There seemed to be no solution to the problem.

One day another "back-room boy" appeared out of the depths of the Ministry of Aircraft Production.

He was Sir Ben Lockspeiser, KCB, FRS, and he had a suggestion—an old one really, which had been employed in the Great War. Altimeters then were even more primitive than those of 1943, so it might be possible to employ classic trigonometry instead. Place spotlights in either wingtip so angled that when they converged on the surface of the water the distance from the aircraft to the water would be exactly 150 feet. This made sense and was almost as simple as the little wooden bombsight that Dann had conceived.

Gibson dispatched a Lancaster to Farnborough (Royal Aircraft Establishment), where Aldis lamps were fitted into the nose and near the tail (this was Gibson's slight variation on the idea). This task Gibson had assigned to Squadron Leader Henry Maudslay, who commanded B Flight of the special unit. Upon his return the following day, Maudslay took the Lancaster up at dusk and demonstrated the device for Gibson. When the beams of light merged beneath the low-flying plane Maudslay found that he could maintain the correct height with a little help from the navigator. Within days all the Lancasters were fitted with fore and aft Aldis lamps and practiced using the "spotlight altimeter calibrator" under observation of ground instruments. It was found to work with amazing accuracy. As Gibson watched the demonstrations he could not help but wonder about how much flying around with Aldis lamps on would aid the German gunners.

Late in April Gibson had an urgent summons to meet with Wallis. The little man's face was lined and he was visibly tired when he told Gibson, "The whole thing is going to be a failure unless we jiggle around with our heights and speed."

What could this possibly mean?

Wallis explained that he had continued experimenting with the bombs, shattering most of them. Upon studying the films and graphing the results Wallis had come up with one more set of conditions: Could they approach the dams at 60 feet and at a speed of 232 miles an hour? "If you can't," Wallis added, "the whole thing will have to be called off."

Dire thoughts raced through Gibson's mind. If 150 feet was low, 60 feet was very low. At that height you would only have to hiccup and you would be in the drink.

He promised, however, to try that night. The deflection of the Aldis lamps was changed and although the big aircraft seemed to be moving along awfully close to the ground, accuracy was excellent. It could be done and on May 1 Gibson called Wallis to reassure him. When another test was run at the new height and speed the bomb worked. But the time drew nigh, for from April 17 through May 1 the water level in the Möhne had risen five feet, within ten feet of the lip. The high-level period would soon be upon them; all the modified aircraft would be required and the bombs were yet to be manufactured.

The first special Lancaster had been flown into Scampton on April 18, another nineteen following at intervals—the last arrived on May 13. Around the same time lorries delivered the Wallis bombs to Scampton; the bombs were factory-fresh and still warm. The odd devices, weighing 9250 pounds, carried a charge of RDX, a very high explosive, weighing 6600 pounds. The cylinder itself was five feet long and fifty inches in diameter. The bombs were not cranked into the aircraft as was normal, but the Lancasters were lifted at the tail by a crane and lowered onto the bombs. These were fitted into the special cutout in the fuselage with the axis of the bomb at right angles to the centerline of the Lancaster's fuselage. The effect, since the bomb bay doors had been removed, was as if a garden roller had been installed into the aircraft. When the bomb was about ready to be dropped a hydraulically operated motor attached to pulley by a belt drive was activated and the bomb would begin to spin (backward toward the tail). At the point of release the spin would reach five hundred revolutions per minute. It was this rotation which carried the bomb skipping over the surface of the water and then, with the remaining momentum, rolled it down the face of the dam to explode at the correct depth. At least, that was the plan.

Gibson delegated the job of checking the modified aircraft to his engineering officer, the "plumber," Flight Lieutenant C. C. "Capable" Caple, and the handling of the bombs to his armament officer, Flight Lieutenant "Doc" Watson. There were still the routes to plot—coming and going to the dams—which would best avoid flak concentrations and night fighter fields; there was the question of communications. This last problem was solved when it was decided that in addition to the standard radios, all of the Lancasters were to be equipped with Very High Frequency Radio Telephones. This enabled the men to communicate with each other directly and would make it possible for Gibson to direct the operation in the target area. Such intercommunications had never been used before on bombers.

As the middle of May approached the pressures increased and Gibson himself showed the strain. He was irritable, impatient, and quickly lost his temper. A large carbuncle blossomed on his face; when he saw the base doctor (who knew nothing of the impending mission), Gibson was informed that he was "overworked. You will have to take two weeks off." Gibson burst out laughing and left. In two weeks it would all be over.

On May 15 Cochrane dropped by and told Gibson that, weather permitting, the squadron would take off the next night. After two and a half months, it seemed almost like good news.

During this period of training Gibson had divided the squadron into two flights, but for the raid itself there were to be three waves. The first, led by Gibson, consisted of nine Lancasters, which were to attack the Möhne Dam first; if successful, and if any bombs remained, they would continue on to the Eder Dam. These two dams were to be attacked from 60 feet and at 232 miles an hour, as had been calculated by Wallis. A second wave—which in fact would take off first—was made up of five bombers and would attack the Sorpe Dam (which was of a different construction from the other two) from the lowest possible height and at 180 miles an hour. The third wave, five Lancasters, was to be a mobile reserve and under control of No. 5 Group headquarters (Cochrane) and not Gibson. Since all reports of the success or failure would come into Group HQ, the mobile reserve aircraft could be sent by Cochrane to any unbreached dam or to other dams in the area. It was hoped that, in addition to the Möhne, Eder, and Sorpe dams, Gibson's crews might also deal with such smaller dams as the Lister, Schwelm, and Ennepe.

Of the original twenty-one crews, nineteen therefore would carry out the raid. One of the special Lancasters had been damaged five days before the raid during a training mission (spray had shot up against the low-flying aircraft and damaged the underside badly enough to put the plane out of action).

The other eliminated plane was forced to stand down because of an illness among the crew. In all, the nineteen Lancasters carried 133 men.

IV

The first Lancaster to take off from Scampton was piloted by Flight Lieutenant R. N. G. Barlow of the second wave (which took off first because of the greater distance to its target); it was nine twenty-eight in the evening of May 16, 1943. Within two minutes the second plane took off, Sergeant V. A. Byers, pilot; then, one minute after him, Pilot Officer G. Rice in the third aircraft; within eight minutes Flight Lieutenant K. L. Munro lifted his heavy Lancaster off the runway and vanished into the east. (At this moment—9:39 P.M.—Gibson's first wave (Möhne) began taking off.) The fifth and last plane of the second-wave force (Sorpe), piloted by a blond giant from Brooklyn, Flight Lieutenant Joseph C. McCarthy, did not get away on schedule. In fact, there was a delay, infuriating to McCarthy, of more than a half hour.

"Our favourite Yank, F. L. McCarthy, caused quite a disturbance," the squadron diary [written by squadron adjutant Flight Lieutenant H. R. Humphries] noted. "He arrived at his aircraft and after finding she had hydraulic trouble came dashing back to our only reserve aircraft. When inside he noticed he had no compass card and came rushing back to Flights frantically screaming for one. He had also pulled his parachute by mistake and the white silk was streaming all over the ground, trailing behind him. With perspiration dropping off his face, good old Mac ran back to his aircraft with everyone behind him trying to fix him up with what he wanted."

Of the five aircraft of the second wave only McCarthy's actually dropped its bomb on the target. The first two planes, Barlow and Byers, were lost. The latter was hit by flak at Texel as he crossed over the Dutch coast, and Barlow fell (whether by accident or by flak is unknown) into the Zuider Zee. Rice too had trouble at the Zuider Zee, for the Lancaster was down too low and the plane struck the water; two engines fluttered out and the Wallis bomb ripped off the plane. Rice could do nothing else but return to Scampton on the remaining two engines. The fourth plane, Munro, was hit by flak also, just as it crossed into Holland at Vlieland,

knocking out the intercommunications systems. It was pointless to continue on the mission, so Munro also returned to Scampton.

By the time McCarthy finally took off, so "browned off" (as the current expression went) that he was ready to leave without a parachute, all of Gibson's first wave had already left. McCarthy continued on alone, unaware of the fate of Byers and Barlow and that Munro and Rice had been forced to return to base. His navigator, Flight Sergeant D. A. McLean, plotted a dog-leg course, across the North Sea almost due east to Vlieland, then south across the Zuider Zee, an eastward turn where the course intercepted the Rhine. Slightly north of the Möhne, McLean set them on a southerly leg; the Sorpe lay just a few miles southwest of the Möhne.

McCarthy eased the Lancaster into the misty valley, hoping to get as low as possible. He had to be especially wary of the hills at each end of their run; it would mean dive in, slow up to the prescribed 180 miles an hour, drop bomb, and pull out before piling up against the farther hill. Warily, McCarthy circled the target—which looked just like the model they had studied during the final briefings. There was no flak at least. Coming down low through the mist, however, almost put them in the water. They were low enough. The bombardier, Sergeant G. L. Johnson, zeroed in on the aiming points as McCarthy held the Lancaster in a steady run.

"Bomb gone," he called out; almost at the same instant, McCarthy pulled back on the throttles and the control column to get away from the target and to avoid the looming black hills. He was leveling out over the hills when the bomb shattered against the dam wall. Circling back, the crew saw that the bomb had hit the parapet and had caused damage. But the dam had not burst. They wired the message back to No. 5 Group—where Wallis, Harris, and Cochrane awaited all scraps of information about the raid. McCarthy then turned "T for Tommy" for home.

Gibson took off at nine thirty-nine (the same time as the hapless Munro) in company with the aircraft of pilots Flight Lieutenants John V. Hopgood and H. B. Martin. Just as they were about to leave Gibson had said to Hopgood, "Hoppy, tonight's the night; tomorrow we will get drunk." It had been a long-standing tradition to say this just before a mis-

142

THE BIG LEAGUE

Crew of G George, special Lancaster ED 932/G (the G suffix denoting that the aircraft carried special equipment and must be constantly under guard): Flight Lieutenant R. D. Trevor-Roper, the squadron gunnery leader and mid-upper gunner of G George; Sergeant J. Pulford, flight engineer; Flight Sergeant G. A. Deering, *rear gunner; Pilot Officer F. M. Spafford, bombardier —"bomb aimer" in RAF terminology; Flight Lieutenant R. G. Hutchinson, the squadron's signals leader and radio operator of George; Wing Commander Guy Gibson; and Pilot Officer H. T. Taerum, navigator.*

(IMPERIAL WAR MUSEUM, LONDON)

sion, dating to their days together in No. 106 Squadron. Earlier Squadron Leader Melvyn Young (known as "Dinghy" because he had been twice saved from the sea) had also contributed another standing "joke." As they enjoyed the traditional luxury before takeoff (repeated after a mission) of bacon and eggs, Young asked Gibson, "Can I have your egg if you don't come back?"

"Sugar off," Gibson replied banteringly and then "told him to do something very difficult to himself."

Young led the second three-plane element (the other pilots: William Astell and David Maltby) and Squadron Leader Henry E. Maudslay led the third, consisting of his plane and those flown by David Shannon and L. G. Knight. The latter's plane was air-borne by ten o'clock.

The first-wave aircraft took a different course from that of the second wave; it was a more southerly route crossing over the Dutch coast south of Rotterdam, almost skirting the northern boundary of Belgium. They had crossed over the North Sea without incident, except for a brief meeting and an exchange of messages with a small British convoy. As they approached the coast, all gunners took their positions and Gibson, still holding the Lancaster to an altitude of less than a hundred feet, zigzagged around the known flak positions. He was assisted in this delicate operation with directions from the navigator, Canadian H. T. "Terry" Taerum. Gibson's plane, *G George,* followed by the eight others in the first wave, thus threaded its way across Holland and Germany. The route twisted and turned at irregular intervals to confuse the German defenses, which were having a difficult time of it also because the bombers flew too low to be picked up by radar.

The frequent shifts in route were complex and required concentration. Over Holland an airfield not on their maps suddenly sprang out of the night. It was heavily defended, although no fighters rose to challenge them. Near it was a check point for another turn in the route. Gibson radioed the two formations following closely behind him to look out for the nest of guns near Gilze-Rijen. The others made their turns, but Flight Lieutenant William B. Astell's Lancaster, in the second element, came within flak range of the airfield. The Lancaster lifted away for a moment, then flew into the ground, burned for a few seconds, and shattered when the Wallis bomb detonated.

After crossing the Rhine the eight remaining planes of Gibson's force passed into the Ruhr—Happy Valley. Flak barges along the river opened up with gunfire and followed the aircraft with searchlights, but lost the British planes among the trees. Gunners in the planes exchanged fire with the German gunners, disrupting their aim and at times even putting out the blinding lights. But all eight Lancasters flew past Dortmund, Hamm, Soest—all known flak centers. Just beyond Soest were the Ruhr hills over which lay Möhne Lake, at the end of which squatted their first target. Gibson studied it and found that the dam "looked grey and solid in the moonlight as though it were part of the country-side itself and just as immovable. A structure like a battle-ship was showering out flak all along its length, but some came from the powerhouse below it and nearby. There were no searchlights."

The effect of the flak over the water was curious, for the varicolored reflections on the smooth black surface doubled the actual number of shells spurting out at them. Gibson estimated the number of guns as twelve firing from five different positions on and around the dam. The shells were either 20 or 37 millimeter—"nasty little things."

Pulling away from "those bloody-minded flak gunners" Gibson circled the area, orienting himself and planning the next move. Over the intercom he heard the crew chattering.

"Bit aggressive, aren't they?"

"Too right they are."

"God, this flak gives me the creeps," Gibson interjected.

"Me too."

Gibson called in the other planes and found all answered but Astell. *Had Bill got the hammer?* "Well, boys," Gibson said with no enthusiasm whatsoever, "we had better start the ball rolling. Hello, all Cooler aircraft. I am going to attack. Stand by to come in to attack in your order when I tell you."

As the others dispersed out of range of the flak, Gibson circled to get into position for a run on the dam. He called John Hopgood: "Hello, *M Mother.* Stand by to take over if anything happens."

"OK, Leader. Good luck."

Gibson, now two miles from the dam, put the plane into a flat dive. The features of the Möhne stood out clearly in the light of the moon. In sharp relief stood the two towers on which the bombardier would set his little wooden sight. He was an Australian, Pilot Officer F. M. "Spam" Spafford, who reacted to the setting with professional interest. "Good show," he said. "This is wizard!"

But as they came down toward the surface of the lake, Spafford, in the "bomb-aimer" position in the nose, said excitedly, "You're going to hit them. You're going to hit those trees!"

"That's all right, Spam," Gibson told him, "I'm just getting my height."

Then to navigator Taerum, "Check height, Terry."

Flight Engineer Sergeant J. Pulford managed the throttles and flaps to maintain the precise air speed. Spafford lined up the sight with the two towers at either end of the dam and flicked on the fusing switches. The Wallis bomb began to revolve. Taerum gave directions for height, the searchlights in the fuselage having been turned on. When the two beams met he called out "Steady," and they were

The Wallis bomb as it was released from the specially converted Lancaster. The cradle that held the bomb actuated the bomb's backward revolution, which caused the bomb to skip over the surface of the water. The cut-out fuselage to accommodate the bomb and the gear may also be seen. The Lancasters thus equipped were called the "Steamrollers of Scampton."

(IMPERIAL WAR MUSEUM, LONDON)

at sixty feet. The gunners at the dam opened up on the illuminated target. The flak came twisting through the darkness as Gibson raced for the dam. The two gunners in the plane returned the fire as Gibson, almost certain they were flying into oblivion, bore down upon the target taking directions from both Taerum (height) and Spafford (distance and line).

The air reeked with cordite and the plane shuddered under the vibration of the guns firing. The sky was crisscrossed with spent tracers. A Very light popped out of the Lancaster in the hope of blinding the flak gunners. Suddenly Spafford's voice came over the intercom: "Mine gone."

Someone said, "Good show, Leader. Nice work." Gibson gunned the Lancaster up and away from the flak and from the explosion. There was a thunderous booming behind them and when Gibson turned the Lancaster, a thousand-foot water column hung in the air. Spafford had placed the bomb exactly right, but except for churning water, there seemed to be no real damage. Gibson studied the effect and waited until the surface calmed down before ordering the next attack. The spotlights would not work unless the surface was smooth. The eight planes circled as far from the guns as they could,

waiting. Gibson spoke to Hopgood. "Hello, *M Mother*. You may attack now. Good luck."

Hopgood brought his plane in from the same direction as had Gibson. The gunners were now alert to the direction of the attack and concentrated heavily on the approaching plane. Hopgood speared into the flak. About a hundred yards from the dam a flash of fire shot behind an inboard engine. The bomb did not drop until too late (possibly because the bombardier had been hit), so it fell onto the powerhouse, overshooting the dam. Hopgood's Lancaster staggered on as if the pilot were attempting to gain altitude. At around five hundred feet *M Mother* flared and crashed into the ground.

"Poor old Hoppy," a voice said over the intercom. Although the plane burned furiously, two men actually escaped, the bombardier, Flight Sergeant J. W. Fraser, and the rear gunner, Pilot Officer A. F. Burcher. The other five men, including Gibson's old friend Hopgood, died in the crash.

Still the Möhne Dam stood intact. Gibson ordered the third attack, by Squadron Leader H. B. "Mickey" Martin in *P Popsie*. The run was repeated, again with heavy flak fire. Gibson had drawn off some of the flak by bringing *G George* into range and shooting at the German gun positions. Martin's bomb fell a few yards short and had little effect upon the dam. The Lancaster itself was rather badly shot up; a fuel tank in the right wing—luckily empty—was punctured and the aileron shredded. But Martin brought the Lancaster away without further damage.

He added his plane to Gibson's as a decoy when the fourth plane, Squadron Leader Melvyn Young's *A Apple*, attacked. The bomb seemed to fall exactly right but the dam continued to stand. The next plane was piloted by Flight Lieutenant D. J. H. Maltby; this was number five. Again the area lit up with flak and machine-gun fire as the great bomber, seemingly held to the surface of the lake by two streams of light, bore down on the dam. The bombardier, Pilot Officer J. Fort, placed the bomb with uncanny accuracy. The squat barrel-like object bounced along the surface of the water, struck the wall, and then rolled down. A great geyser of water shot up and again the water roiled and churned.

Waiting for the disturbance to subside, Gibson swung around to get another view. He alerted the next pilot, Flight Lieutenant David Shannon, to prepare for his run. As Gibson came down he saw unusual eddies in the water and it appeared that the dam had moved. He heard someone shouting, "I think she has gone!" when the dam gave way. It was a massive rent of a hundred yards through which a mountain of water spilled into the valley below. Gibson's radio operator wired the news to Group headquarters at Grantham that the Möhne Dam had been successfully breached. The time was just four minutes before one o'clock in the morning of May 17, 1943.

Wallis had listened to the report of each released bomb with increasing misgiving. He had hoped one good strike would do the job, but on and on the raid went: *G George, M Mother, P Popsie, A Apple,* and then *J Johnny*—Maltby's plane—and the signal that the Möhne had burst. Wallis stood still for but a moment before throwing his arms over his head and literally danced around the room. Harris and Cochrane stopped him long enough to shake his hand in congratulations. At the same time the men in the seven Lancasters orbiting the Möhne burst into cheers, "to shout and scream and act like madmen. . . ."

From where he circled the frightful scene, Gibson saw not only the wall of water ramming through the valley, destroying everything in its path and overtaking fleeing automobiles, but also the still burning wreckage of Hopgood's plane just beyond the dam. *Hoppy has been avenged,* Gibson thought and then, after ordering Mickey Martin and Dave Maltby to return to base, led the way south- and eastward to the Eder. Only three aircraft still carried bombs—Henry Maudslay's, David Shannon's and L. G. Knight's. Melvyn Young as deputy leader made up the fifth plane, though his bomb had been expended on the Möhne.

The five aircraft encountered much fog as they flew through the valley leading to the Eder Dam. Although there were no antiaircraft defenses at the Eder, the hills surrounding it, plus the fog, made it an exceptionally difficult target to find. Gibson had arrived first and succeeded in locating the fog-enshrouded target, but until he had fired a Very light over the dam, the others had not been able to pick it out.

Shannon began moving in for the attack, which would be the same as those upon the Möhne. But there were complications. The Eder was more inaccessible than the Möhne. A castle stood in the bomb run. The plane would have to dive in over the castle, from about a thousand feet to the required sixty, zero in on the target, drop the bomb, and pull up before crashing against the cliffs of a mountain just about a mile beyond the dam. Shannon made at least five attempts but always something happened and he zoomed away without dropping the bomb. Finally, giving up for the moment, Shannon decided to circle the area to become better acquainted with it.

While Shannon studied the terrain, Gibson sent in *Z Zebra,* Henry Maudslay's Lancaster. Maudslay too found it a difficult run and made two attempts without dropping the bomb. On the third all eyes watched as the big Lancaster slipped down over the castle, leveled out on the lake. The spotlights converged under the plane on the water and soon a red Very light arced out above *Z Zebra*. The bomb had been dropped. But something had gone wrong; the bomb had been released too late. It fell, struck the parapet, and caught Maudslay's plane in the blast. The whole valley erupted in a glaring flash. Gibson was stunned. *Henry had disappeared.* There was no burning wreck on the ground. Desperately Gibson called, "Henry—*Z Zebra*—are you OK?"

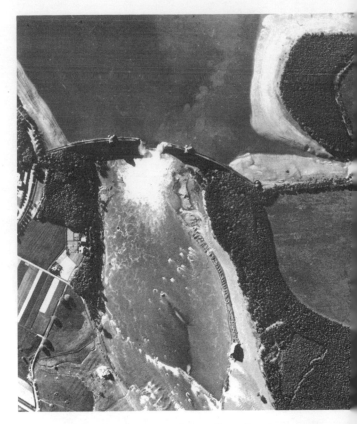

The Möhne Dam before and after: an aerial reconnaissance photograph taken before the mission (left) shows the dam wall and, faintly, the protective torpedo nets. The bombs had to be dropped at the correct speed and altitude to be able to bounce over the net,

strike the wall, roll down the wall under the water, and burst against the face of the wall. The effects of the blast may be seen in a photograph taken the day after the raid—the Möhne breached; lower water level exposes sand of the banks.

(IMPERIAL WAR MUSEUM, LONDON)

Although no plane was in sight, all were certain they heard Maudslay's voice faintly: "I think so, stand by." And then there was nothing.

Shannon returned again and, after a test run, came in for the second time (on his second round of attempts). The plane dropped the bomb perfectly as Flight Sergeant L. J. Sumpter, the bombardier, brought the towers into line and pressed the release. The bomb detonated against the face of the dam, but it continued to stand.

There was only one more left; unless it worked Gibson would have to ask for aid from the mobile reserve planes. Lester Knight, an Australian, brought his Lancaster in for a practice run. It went wrong and he pulled away and circled, with Gibson giving him advice over the radio telephone, and came in for another try. Carefully Knight brought the Lancaster in, down to sixty feet and straight for the dam; bombardier Flying Officer E. C. Johnson guided Knight toward the drop point and the bomb

fell when all imaginary lines of the mathematical problem converged. The bomb struck the wall, rolled down, and then from out of the depths a terrific boom erupted, shooting water a thousand feet into the air. As if shaken by a great earthquake the Eder Dam cracked, spouting tons of water into the sleeping valley below. To Gibson the rushing waters seemed more destructive than those of the Möhne, ripping through the countryside, uprooting everything in their path, and even as he watched he "saw them extinguish all the lights in the neighborhood as though a great black shadow had been drawn across the earth."

With no bombs remaining, Gibson ordered the four surviving Lancasters to return to base. The Eder had been breached at one fifty-four in the morning. Dawn was on the way and they would do well to get away before the fighters came out in droves. They had been air-borne for more than four hours, fuel would be low, and with the coming light, the fighters would be thick. On the homeward flight they again passed over the Möhne. The geography of the valley had been completely changed. They continued flying down low to confute fighter passes.

The Lancasters droned over Germany and Holland and strove for home. But over Holland, just as he passed over the coast, Young's plane was hit by flak. He could not nurse it all the way to Scampton, and for the third—and last—time Dinghy Young ditched. No one survived the crash into the sea. So it was, then, that of the nine planes which Gibson had led into Germany that night, he returned leading only Shannon and Knight—to join those of Martin and Maltby, which had come back earlier.

When Gibson had radioed that he had no additional bombs, the five aircraft of the mobile reserve, the third wave, were directed to their targets by Group headquarters. These Lancasters had taken off shortly after midnight and by the time Gibson had turned for home the bombers were being dispatched to their targets. The first plane off was *C Charlie,* guided by Pilot Officer W. H. T. Ottley, who was ordered to attack the Lister Dam; the radio operator, Sergeant J. Guterman, acknowledged the message. That was the last heard from Ottley's crew. It may have been his plane that Gibson, then on his flight home, saw flying at five hundred feet in the vicinity of Hamm. "He got the chop," Gibson noted, wondering who it had been. He and his crew believed that it might have been a German night fighter which had been tracking them, hit by its own antiaircraft fire. But it was probably Ottley's *C Charlie,* for the wreckage of his plane was found near Hamm the next day.

Three planes were dispatched to the Sorpe Dam to add to the destruction which McCarthy, of the ill-fated second wave, had accomplished. These were *S Sugar* (Pilot Officer L. J. Burpee), *F Freddie* (Flight Sergeant K. W. Brown), and *Y Yorker* (Flight Sergeant L. T. Anderson).

S Sugar never got beyond Bergen op Zoom, Holland, where it fell to flak or a fighter. *F Freddie* had trouble finding the Sorpe because of the thickening mist, but Brown dropped down low and released some incendiaries which illuminated the area. Bombardier Sergeant S. Oncia was then able to place the bomb precisely on the target, although

this second strike did not add to the damage—the Sorpe remained standing. When *Y Yorker,* which had taken off one minute behind *F Freddie,* came upon the target area pilot Anderson found the valley completely filled with mist. Neither Sergeant L. Nugent, the navigator, nor Sergeant S. Green, the bombardier, could find any landmark upon which to base a bomb run. *Y Yorker,* crewed with disappointed men, was forced to make the return trip to Scampton still carrying the Wallis bomb.

O Orange (Flight Sergeant W. C. Townsend) was sent to the Schwelm Dam, which was found despite the early morning mist. Townsend made three runs on the target before bombardier Sergeant C. E. Franklin released the bomb. It was a perfect drop, but the single bomb had little effect upon the dam. The time was then 3:37 A.M., and when *O Orange* crossed the Dutch coast for the final leg of the flight daylight was breaking over the North Sea. When Townsend set his plane down at Scampton his was the last of the Lancasters which would return from the dams mission. Eight would never return; of the fifty-six men aboard these aircraft only two survived. Nearly half of the superb crew which had made up No. 617 Squadron was lost. It was, in the phrase of historians Charles Webster and Noble Frankland, "a costly success."

v

The "Dam Busters," as the squadron was popularly called, had furnished bomber chief Arthur Harris with a demonstration of the fallacy of attacking panacea targets, but on the other hand proved him wrong when he insisted that the Wallis bomb (or any bomb then available) could actually breach a well-built dam. Wallis had been proved correct in his theoretical conceptions of bomb design and the effects of certain bombs upon dams—but his strategic thinking had been optimistic. The major catastrophe he had expected—which was also expected by those more militarily oriented than he—did not result. The havoc was serious enough and for many it was total tragedy, but despite the inundation, the rupture of the Möhne and Eder dams had no long-range or even long-lasting effects upon the German war effort.

Goebbels admitted that the "attacks of the British bombers on the dams in our valleys were very successful. The Führer is exceedingly impatient and angry about the lack of preparedness on the part of the Luftwaffe." It was true—a single blow by so few aircraft had had a decided impact. Nearly a thousand people drowned (many caught in air raid shelters) and more than two hundred were listed as missing. About half of the casualties, however, were slave laborers from the east—they were easily replaced from Germany's store of prisoners from Poland and Russia. Livestock too perished in the flood and thousands of acres of agricultural land were despoiled. Seventy per cent of the harvest in the Ruhr and Möhne valleys was ruined, as was all of the root crops, such as potatoes.

Industrial stoppages resulted with the washing out of railroads, the blacking out of electrical power, and, most of all—as a result of the Möhne breach —because of the shortage of water. A critical lack of water for drinking purposes afflicted about four and a half million people in the area; also industries requiring water, such as the coking plants in Dortmund, were forced to operate at a loss in production for two months.

The effects were extensive but not decisive. Within weeks, or at most within two or three months, the Germans had cleared away much of the dam-

Post-mission debriefing: Bomber Command Chief Harris and Air Officer Commanding, No. 5 Group, Air Vice-Marshal Sir Ralph Cochrane (standing) get a first-hand report of the dams raid while members of G George talk with a Bomber Command intelligence officer (left seated); bombardier Spafford speaks as navigator Taerum and gunnery officer Trevor-Roper listen. These three men of Gibson's crew, like their leader, were later killed in other missions.

(IMPERIAL WAR MUSEUM, LONDON)

age and the Ruhr remained the major industrial center of the Third Reich for the rest of the war. Had all dams been breached that night of the Dam Busters' raid (a physical impossibility, of course, in terms of men and bombs), the tale would have been different and much sadder for Germany. If the Sorpe (which was in fact immune to the Wallis bomb because of the dam's structure) had gone, the effects would have been more serious. Following the night of May 16/17, 1943, all important German dams were allotted heavier defenses. Further attempts upon them would have meant simple suicide—and none were made.

As he had promised the now dead Hopgood, Gibson and the survivors got drunk. Gibson, however, left early to begin writing to the next of kin of the fifty-six men who had not returned. Wallis, though elated by the success of his bomb, was depressed at the thought of the loss of the young men. He stood around with the survivors that early morning, an untouched drink in his hand and tears in his eyes, saying, "If I had known, I wouldn't have started this."

In wartime, however, the exchange of fifty-four young lives for victorious headlines, for a setback for the enemy, seemed worth it. No one would question the attack, its costs, or the result: not when the very spirit of the moment seemed permeated

The Queen and King visit No. 617 Squadron after the mission to award decorations. In the background the Queen speaks with an airman. In the foreground the King exchanges views with "Our favourite Yank,"

Flight Lieutenant Joseph C. McCarthy of Brooklyn. Gibson is to the King's left, back to camera.
(IMPERIAL WAR MUSEUM, LONDON)

with destruction, sacrifice, death, and "good show." It was as normal as being alive.

Eve Gibson, who had assumed that her husband had been, as she had been informed, having an easy time of it at a training school, learned from the newspapers that he was an international hero. Gibson joined her for a rest after he had completed writing his letters. When he joined Eve, Gibson was a very old young man.

No less than thirty-three decorations were awarded for the dams raid. This was unusual, for the British are parsimonious with their decorations. Gibson was given the Victoria Cross. Among those who received the Distinguished Service Order was the Brooklynite Joseph McCarthy. The squadron was the most celebrated in Britain by then. Harris, despite his distaste for special units, decided to keep No. 617 Squadron together as a unit, and to employ it upon highly specialized targets demanding high precision. Although it was all but impossible to replace the lost crews immediately, No. 617 Squadron did operate as a precision night unit during the rest of the war. In fact, among other amazing feats—such as blasting a railroad tunnel in northern France with another Wallis bomb, the "Tallboy"—it was No. 617 Squadron which eventually finished the *Tirpitz,* which had so haunted Gibson.

But by this time the brilliant young commander was dead. After the raid he was sent to the United States, accompanying Churchill, on a kind of goodwill tour. When he returned in the spring of 1944 Gibson, who it was thought had already done his bit, was offered work as an executive with commercial firms—which he readily turned down. He was even asked to run for Parliament, an idea with which he toyed for a while, but he withdrew from that also. He grew restless, for he had been a year "off Ops." and he was unhappy. Finally he went directly to Harris and bullied his way back into active duty with No. 627 Squadron.

Gibson was base operations officer of the squadron, which like No. 617 was in No. 5 Group. The squadron began operations as a Pathfinder force (with No. 8 Group), marking targets with the Mosquito. Attached to No. 5 Group, the squadron took part in various special operations—bombing, target marking, dropping of "window"—the metallic ribbon which disrupted German radar—and minelaying.

On the night of September 19/20, 1944, Guy Gibson voluntarily assigned himself the task of master bomber on a raid to the Ruhr. He would fly around the target, a factory at Rheydt, directing the operations of the attacking Lancasters. When the attack was over, Gibson radioed the bombers. "OK, chaps. Now beat it for home." It was the last time his voice was heard, for over Holland something occurred and the Mosquito smashed into a hill. The men were buried by the Germans in a common unmarked grave near Bergen op Zoom. It was there that Burpee in *S Sugar* had "got the hammer" too a year before when Gibson and his X-Squadron had made history.

7

TIDAL WAVE

At Casablanca, French Morocco, Winston Churchill and Franklin Roosevelt met in January 1943 to outline the future Grand Strategy of the war. In this beautiful setting facing on the sea, following the successful launching of Operation Torch, the invasion of north Africa under Lieutenant General Dwight D. Eisenhower, the Allied leaders and their Combined Chiefs of Staff came to several key decisions. Uppermost in their minds, though they did not always agree upon details, were aid to Soviet Russia, sustained pressures on the Mediterranean flank, a future cross-Channel invasion of Europe, and the question of the Pacific war.

Among the objectives to be gained before the larger strategies could be achieved, at least in Europe, was control of the German submarines so effectively menacing Allied shipping. Another was the Luftwaffe, which stood in the way of strategic bombardment and any hopes for an invasion of Europe in 1944. Both these obstacles could be dealt with by air power. When he came to the Casblanca conference it had been Churchill's intention to persuade Roosevelt to get the American Air Force to give up its devotion to strategic bombardment by day and join the Bomber Command nighttime area assault. After five months of bombing, the U. S. Eighth Air Force had not yet dropped a single bomb on Germany proper. The first mission of the Eighth Air Force's Bomber Command was a modest—only a dozen B-17s participated—strike upon the marshaling yards at Rouen-Sotteville, France, on August 17, 1942. All twelve bombers returned safely and it was at least a sign that bombers in formation could bomb pin-point targets in daylight and make it back to their bases. Such high-altitude attacks, it was believed, would make it difficult for flak-gun accuracy, and the combined gun strength of the formation itself would make fighter opposition costly.

The British had found in their experience that daylight operations were deadly; and the Germans had learned this also. But the Americans persisted in clinging to the concept of precision daylight bombardment. This was not mere bullheadedness, although it was believed that a heavy bomber with its massive firepower (the Flying Fortress was armed with a dozen .50-caliber machine guns and the Consolidated B-24 Liberator with ten) and protective armor could withstand attack by fighters. The best argument in favor of American daylight precision bombardment was simply that the aircraft were designed for it and the Americans were trained for it. A change in operational technique would entail a prolonged retraining of crews, modifications in the aircraft, and a consequent delay. Even under "normal" wartime conditions, it had taken long enough to mount the Rouen-Sotteville attack, small as that was. Assembling men and equipment was a complex matter, considering the demand for both.

Casablanca: Franklin D. Roosevelt and Winston Churchill meet to plan the future strategy of the war with their chief military advisers. Standing behind them are (from left) Lieutenant General Henry H. Arnold, Admiral Ernest J. King, General George C. Marshall, Admiral Sir Dudley Pound, General Sir Alan Brooke, and Air Chief Marshal Sir Charles Portal.

(U. S. AIR FORCE)

Until the United States could contribute its full share to the offensive the operations of the Eighth Air Force from the United Kingdom were, of necessity, circumscribed. Up until the Casablanca conference, the heavy-bomber missions were, in a sense, experimental pinpricks, experimental because there was a good deal to learn under combat conditions and pinpricks because Major General Ira C. Eaker, who commanded Eighth AF Bomber Command, did not have sufficient numbers of planes and crews to do anything else. An effective attack force which could strike deep inside Germany and still be able to fight its way in, bomb, and return must contain about three hundred heavy bombers. The largest force Eaker had been able to muster in the half year from August 1942 to the January 1943 Casablanca meetings was but a third of that number.

In that half year one of the major lessons learned was that if German fighter pilots proved aggressive enough, there really was no such thing as a true "Flying Fortress." Although Eighth Air Force losses had not been excessive in the half year of operations, there had been losses and interferences with bombing runs. These were not spectacular, but planes and crews were lost and targets could not be eliminated because they had not been accurately bombed. What was needed, then, was an Allied fighter plane which could escort the bombers to and from target areas to engage the German fighters. At the time of Casablanca no such fighter with the range say to go to Berlin and back was in action. The P-40 could not do it, nor could the Hurricane or Spitfire. Thus the British preferred their major bombing raids to take place at night and the Americans went out during the day. The advent of the Thunderbolt (Republic P-47) and the Mustang (North American P-51) was yet almost a whole year away. In the interim the skies over Europe would be lacerated in the most monstrous air battles in history.

At Casablanca Eaker convinced Churchill of the efficacy of the American plan and the Prime Minis-

The Boeing B-17 "Flying Fortress," on which the U. S. Army Air Force based its "precision daylight bombardment" concept—and which British Bomber Command rejected as inviting the disastrous possibility of high casualties and aircraft losses. Because of the bristling heavy armament of the B-17 it was believed it could stand off German fighter attacks. This did not prove to be true in combat; Luftwaffe pilots developed a hazardous technique of head-on attack that was most effective. The B-17F (left), the first Lockheed-built B-17, though an improvement on the earlier models still lacked firepower in the nose. This was later resolved with the addition of twin guns in the "G" model. The other photo, a view from the port waist-gun position, shows one of the nine .50-caliber machine guns (plus one .30) carried by the Flying Fortress. (ERIK MILLER; LOCKHEED/U. S. AIR FORCE)

The Consolidated B-24 "Liberator," which came after the B-17 and which would join it in bombing Germany. The B-24 was not as easily flown as the B-17, nor could it achieve the altitude of the Boeing. It did, however, have a greater range and could carry a heavier bomb load. The prototype (left), the XB-24 was initially flown in 1939 (the first B-17 flew in 1935) and had no gun turrets. Top view of a B-24D clearly shows the high-aspect ratio wing designed around the low-drag Davis airfoil as well as the nose-gun position (before the nose turret was installed in the B-24G), top and tail turrets.

(CONVAIR/GENERAL DYNAMICS; U. S. AIR FORCE)

Standing in the way of the American daylight attacks upon German industry were the German fighters such as this Messerschmitt Bf-109G; engine-mounted 20-mm. cannon could rip a wing off an enemy bomber. Though formidable, the cannon had a tendency to jam; as did the wing-mounted cannon of the Bf-109F.
(ALIEN PROPERTY CUSTODIAN, NATIONAL ARCHIVES)

ter, though reluctantly, dismissed his own plan of suggesting to Roosevelt that the American daylight approach be abandoned. Out of this came what was called the Casablanca Directive, outlining in effect the joint future operations of British and American Bomber Commands. Operating as before, British by night and Americans by day—thus giving Churchill his cue for the phrase "bombing around the clock"—the bombing offensive was to be based upon a system of target priorities. These were agreed upon by the Combined Chiefs of Staff, advised by industrial analysts such as Britain's Ministry of Economic Warfare. The targets, in order of priority, were the German submarine construction yards, the aircraft industry, transportation, oil installations, and other targets in enemy war industry.

In effect, therefore, the Directive left the interpretation of how this was to be accomplished up to General Eaker and Air Chief Marshal Harris. Although the Directive implied precision attack, it did not deny the area attack. Harris, with his experience, had little respect for plans on paper and continued to go his way. "The subject of morale had been dropped," Harris noted, "and I was now required to proceed with the general 'disorganisation' of German industry, giving priority to certain aspects of it such as U-boat building, aircraft production, oil production, transportation and so forth, which gave me a very wide range of choice and allowed me to attack pretty well any German industrial city of 100,000 inhabitants and above. But the Ruhr remained a principal objective because it was the most important industrial area in the whole of Germany, which was why it had been originally chosen for morale-breaking attacks; the new instructions therefore made no difference."

Eaker by April 1943 had formulated what the British refer to as the Eaker Plan, but which was more officially known as "The Combined Bomber

The most potent adversary of the American daylight bomber streams, the Focke-Wulf 190 (in this instance the FW-190A of JG 26). Nicknamed the Würger ("Butcher-bird"), the 190 was heavily armed—two machine guns on upper cowling, two cannons in the wing roots, and two more machine guns farther out on the wings. The major weakness of the FW-190 was that its performance fell off above twenty thousand feet (the B-17s operated above this altitude). It was still a tough fighter when dealing with enemy escort planes as well as bombers. Although superior to the Me-109, the Focke-Wulf was not built in the quantities the Messerschmitt was.

(IMPERIAL WAR MUSEUM, LONDON)

Offensive from the United Kingdom" (April 12, 1943). A month later a modified version of the plan, code word "Pointblank," was approved by the Combined Chiefs of Staff. This defined the mission of the U. S.-British Air offensive, which, in general terms, was aimed at weakening German resistance so "as to permit initiation of final combined operations on the Continent." It called for an expansion of the American bombing forces in Europe, pointing out that "at least 800 airplanes must be in the theater to dispatch 300 bombers on operations." Until such a force existed, there would be little point in attempting precision attacks upon the German aircraft industry, which remained second on the priorities list.

Lest there be misunderstandings and consequent resistance from certain strong-minded air marshals, it was emphasized that "This plan does not attempt to prescribe the major effort of the R.A.F. Bomber Command. It simply recognizes the fact that when precision targets are bombed by the Eighth Air Force in daylight, the effort should be complemented and completed by R.A.F. bombing attacks against the surrounding industrial area at night."

Under the section entitled "Intermediate Objective" another important point was made: "The Germans, recognizing the vulnerability of their vital industries, are rapidly increasing the strength of their fighter defenses. The German fighter strength in western Europe is being augmented. *If the growth of the German fighter strength is not arrested quickly, it may become literally impossible to carry out the destruction planned and thus to create the conditions necessary for ultimate decisive action by our combined forces on the continent.*" In other words, the invasion of Europe would be stalled unless the Luftwaffe could be "neutralized."

Eaker, however, almost immediately had to give up some of his planes to the Mediterranean when the Northwest African Air Force was formed to assist Eisenhower's ground troops in the invasion of north Africa; more would go when "Husky," the invasion of Sicily which had been decided upon during the Casablanca meetings, went into effect. It would be extremely difficult for the Eighth Air Force to mount the Pointblank operations if its forces continued to be drained off to other theaters. At the moment when Eaker hoped for "at least 800 airplanes" in order to mount raids of three-hundred-bomber

strength, he was aware of the fact that in the three months since Casablanca the average American bomber attack force consisted of a mere eighty-six planes.

II

Sometime between the end of June and the Fourth of July, Eaker lost his two veteran B-24 groups, the 44th and the 93rd. These were soon joined by the newly formed, inexperienced 389 Bombardment Group—also equipped with Liberators. They combined with two units already in the Mediterranean's Ninth Air Force: the 98th and 376th Bombardment Groups (B-24s). All units began operations against various Husky targets, including, on July 19, Rome. On the following day all were ordered off operations to begin intensive training near Benghazi in Libya.

The curious feature of this training, besides the heavy security precautions, was the fact that the airmen were being trained to fly the Liberator at an extremely low level. This was a worrisome feature considering the flying characteristics of the Liberator and the danger of passing through prop wash near the ground. Also mystifying was that very few knew what the assignment was all about. The answer lay in that parenthetical phrase (referring to "attacks upon Ploesti") which had appeared following "Oil" in the Combined Bomber Offensive paper.

This Rumanian city was situated in the south central section of the country known as the Wallachian plain, in the heart of the oil-producing regions. Ploesti lay in the center of vast fields, refineries, cracking plants, great complexes which supplied Nazi Germany—thanks to dictator Ion Antonescu—with more than half of its crude oil supply. A full third of Germany's petroleum needs came from Ploesti; the other two thirds came from other sources including its own synthetic plants, which extracted petroleum products from coal. Without oil Germany could not function militarily, a fact of which Hitler was acutely aware even before Pearl Harbor. There were pitiable outcries from the Navy, the Luftwaffe, and the panzer-dependent Wehrmacht. Even with Germany's synthetic plants increasingly productive, Ploesti remained the major source of oil. And oil, if the Combined Chiefs and their Committee of Operations analysts had been aware of the critical situation

Liberators practicing for a low-level mission over the Libyan Desert near Benghazi, north Africa.
(U. S. AIR FORCE)

in Germany, would have been placed first on the priorities list, not fourth.

To Harris Ploesti represented another despised panacea target. Besides, it was not within reach of Bomber Command in England. He continued to concentrate upon the Ruhr. Eaker complied with the spirit of the Combined Bomber Offensive whenever he could muster enough planes to strike at the sub pens or other high-priority targets within reach of the Eighth Air Force. But his resources had dwindled so much because of the diversion of several of his heavy-bomber groups to Africa.

These purloined groups came into the province of Major General Lewis H. Brereton, a cocky bantam of a man who commanded the Ninth Air Force. Brereton, who had been in command of the Far East Air Force in the Philippines when the Japanese struck, had moved out of the Philippines into Java. When Java fell Brereton worked his way across Burma and India until he arrived in Egypt late in June 1942. His nine battered Flying Fortresses became the United States Army Middle East Air Force. In close co-operation with the RAF, the Middle East Air Force assisted in the war upon Rommel by bombing Mediterranean supply ports and convoys at sea. Prior to the breakthrough at El Alamein, the force attacked the harbors of Tobruk and Benghazi, among others, and when Rommel was driven out of Africa, it set up bases around Benghazi—although by this time the unit was called the Ninth Air Force. Brereton's forces by then had been joined by the Northwest African Air Forces

Lewis H. Brereton (here a lieutenant general), commander of the Ninth Air Force at the time it made its attack on Ploesti. (U. S. AIR FORCE)

(Major General Carl Spaatz) to work with RAF, Middle East. The missions of all these air forces were co-ordinated by Mediterranean Air Command under Air Chief Marshal Sir Arthur W. Tedder. It was a complex international co-operative effort which, despite differences, worked very well.

This was because ultimate command of all units actually continued under normal national division. Americans served under American leaders and British under British; no attempt was made to intermix the units. At the high levels of command there was a good deal of give-and-take, a willingness to co-operate, and mutual respect, so that despite the command complexities—a concession to political needs—operations came off remarkably well.

So it was that on June 11, 1943, Brereton received a message from Tedder "concerning Operation SOAPSUDS. It will be mounted from the Middle East, and three more heavy groups are en route to join the Ninth Air Force." Soapsuds was the initial code name for the Ploesti bombing, later changed to "Tidal Wave." Coincidentally, exactly one year before to the day of Brereton's diary entry American bombers had taken off to bomb Ploesti. This was done by the "Halverson Detachment," led by Colonel Harry A. Halverson. Originally equipped with twenty-three B-24Ds, the Halverson Detachment was to have been sent to Chinese bases for bombing missions against Japan. However, delays en route found Halverson in north Africa at a critical moment, and his Liberators were pressed into service there. Taking off on June 11, 1942, Halverson led thirteen Liberators toward the oil fields of Ploesti. One plane was forced to turn back and a dozen succeeded in reaching the target after a long over-water flight, crossing over neutral Turkey. Although accomplishing little damage, the Halverson Detachment planes had struck the first American blow against the Axis. No American life was lost, although one aircraft crash-landed and four, short of fuel, landed in Turkey, where their crews were interned. But the implications of the remarkable mission were lost in the excitement of the news from Midway, which still dominated newspaper space. Those planes which returned from Ploesti remained in the Middle East and were absorbed into Brereton's Ninth Air Force.

Colonel Jacob E. Smart, of Arnold's staff, had conceived the idea of a low-level mission against Ploesti. Surprise, it was hoped, would thus be achieved despite the fact that the Liberator was not designed for low-level performance. A large force, it was assumed, coming in low could deal much damage to the oil complexes. There was another assumption: that except for sporadic Russian attacks upon Ploesti, no large-scale attempt had been made since the Halverson mission, and therefore the German defenders might be caught off guard and unprepared.

Although it was soon proved by aircrews that the Liberator could indeed operate at zero altitude, the assumption that the Luftwaffe was unprepared at Ploesti was ill founded. It was, in fact, one of the best defended targets in all of Europe. The heavy antiaircraft concentrations ringing the city were under the efficient control of Oberst Alfred Gerstenberg, a former faculty member of the Russian-based Luftwaffe air center at Lipesk. In addition to Gerstenberg's guns, several Luftwaffe units were within calling distance of the oil fields—three fighter groups equipped with the Me-109 and a night fighter group with the Me-110. The Rumanians too could supply fighters, but the Germans did not count upon them. Although some were given Messerschmitts, most Rumanian pilots were saddled with inferior Rumanian and Bulgarian fighters.

As commander of 9th Bomber Command, Brigadier General Uzal G. Ent was entrusted with the detailed planning of the mission. Like Brereton, Ent had his serious reservations about a low-level attack; likewise, so did the group commanders leading the mission. But when a conference was held by Brereton in Benghazi on July 6, he "invited no discussion whatsoever among the commanders" and "stressed the necessity for absolute ruthlessness in the immediate relief of any Commander who at any time during the training period showed lack of

Colonel Jacob E. Smart, who believed that Ploesti could be hit by a surprise low-level bombing to throw off what was also believed to be weak defenses.

(U. S. AIR FORCE)

Brigadier General Uzal G. Ent, chief of 9th Bomber Command, and upon whom the planning of the Ploesti mission devolved. Ent did not care for Smart's concept of the low-level mission. (U. S. AIR FORCE)

caught up in the grandeur of the conception. Perhaps he was conscious of the historic impact of such an undertaking when he told the crews, "You should consider yourself lucky to be on this mission." More than three hundred of his auditors would not have agreed; they were dead the following day.

III

The cast for this historical drama included a number of iron men. The leading one was undoubtedly the unpopular, but tough, Colonel John R. Kane, leading the 98th Bomb Group ("Pyramiders"). A hard-driving professional warrior out of Texas, Kane carried the nickname of "Killer." Whether this applied to his attitude toward the Germans or his own men—or himself—is disputable. That he was obsessed with making war upon the Germans could not be denied. When the mission to Ploesti was activated Kane rescinded the orders which would have enabled men in the 98th who had completed their tour of duty to return to the United States. This did not endear him further to his men, who had

leadership, of aggressiveness, or of complete confidence."

It had been Brereton's decision, selected from two suggested plans, a high-level attack launched from Syria or the low-level attack from Benghazi, to attempt the low attack. Once he had decided he adhered to the decision whatever his personal feelings and those of the men actually given the job of carrying it out. Even a petition signed by the group commanders and by Ent made no difference. Late in July Tedder had suggested postponing the attack or canceling it in favor of attacks upon aircraft factories at Wiener Neustadt near Vienna. But now Brereton opposed Tedder on the grounds that "the Ploesti refineries are more important to the Axis war effort than the Messerschmitt factory and because training had almost been completed for Tidal Wave and to call it off now would seriously impair the morale of the entire Bomber Command." Would a cancellation have been as bad for morale as much as knowing your commander (Ent) believed the mission would be a success "even if none returned"?

Despite his misgivings Brereton was certainly

John R. "Killer" Kane (here seen as an air cadet), who would lead his "Pyramiders" (98th Bomb Group) to Ploesti despite a number of hitches. (U. S. AIR FORCE)

never loved him. Kane was as courageous as he was coldly ruthless. He was one commander Brereton would have never replaced. It was also unlikely that Kane would have fulfilled the requirements of "officer and gentleman," but he was an amazing war leader.

Another fine leader was Colonel Leon Johnson, leading the 44th Bomb Group (nicknamed the "Eight Balls"), a businesslike, quietly efficient veteran; Lieutenant Colonel Addison Baker led the 93rd Bomb Group, known as the "Traveling Circus," originally "Ted's Traveling Circus." This was in honor of the commander, Colonel Edward J. Timberlake, who had preceded Baker as group leader. Timberlake was involved with the Ploesti raid as an operational planner because of his experience with B-24 operations, most of it earned in the north African campaign. In turning over his Traveling Circus to Baker, Timberlake was acknowledging Baker's capabilities as a superb leader.

Colonel Keith K. Compton ("K.K."), a Missourian, led the 376th Bomb Group ("Liberandos"). Described by a former squadron mate as "a real gung ho type," Compton had served with Timber-

Keith K. Compton, "a real gung ho type," commander of the "Liberandos" (376th Bomb Group); mission leader Ent would fly in Compton's aircraft to Ploesti—and back. (U. S. AIR FORCE)

lake and was placed by the latter in command of the Liberandos. This group would lead the mission and General Ent would fly in Compton's plane.

The fifth group, the recently activated 389th Bomb Group, was led by Colonel Jack Wood. These unseasoned men had taken the name of "Sky Scorpions." Although a detachment of the 389th had arrived in Libya as early as July, most men participating in the raid would not have had any combat experience.

Major Ramsay D. Potts, Jr., a Tennessean, who "wanted to fly and wanted to fight Hitler," was a twenty-six-year-old deputy commander in Addison Baker's 93rd. A brilliant young leader, Potts had guessed long before he was told that the target for which they trained would be Ploesti. During this period, Potts recalls that the weather at Benghazi "was absolutely frightful." The air was so filled with fine sand (which ruined engines and other parts of aircraft) that at times it was impossible to see five feet ahead. Aircraft became so hot that touching them resulted in serious burns. Dysentery afflicted one and all, from colonel to sergeant.

Leon Johnson, commanding officer of the "Eight Balls" (44th Bomb Group), a superb battle leader.

(U. S. AIR FORCE)

Scale map (1:5000) of Ploesti built for the Air Force by RAF technicians in England in a week and flown to Africa. It was transported from group to group for study in a truck. Top (just left of center line) is Concordia Vega, largest production unit at Ploesti; counterclockwise, in wedge-shaped area, is Xenia, one of the smaller installations; almost directly below, near bottom, Columbia Aquila; to immediate right below is Astra Romana; to far right near center (i.e., directly east of Ploesti) is Romana Americana, owned by American Standard Oil; although a target, it would not be hit during the mission. (U. S. AIR FORCE)

But training continued despite the hardships. A dummy target area, duplicating in full scale the dispersed installations at Ploesti, was built by engineers. Practice missions at zero altitude were made upon the target. One mission, on July 28, wiped out the desert Ploesti in two minutes. The RAF provided a beautifully made table-top, three-dimen-

sional map of Ploesti which was studied by pilots, navigators, and bombardiers. Special films were made based upon the most recent, though outdated, intelligence. The smooth, confident voice of John "Tex" McCrary, an ex-newspaperman turned Air Force public relations expert, assured the crews of the weaknesses of Ploesti's defenses. "The fighter defenses are not strong and the majority of the fighters will be flown by Rumanian pilots who are thoroughly bored with the war." As for antiaircraft, it was estimated that there were a mere "eighty heavy AA guns and 160 light AA guns," but these were "largely disposed for a night attack" and the "heavy ack-ack should not trouble you at low altitude." Besides, all "the antiaircraft guns are manned by Rumanians, so there is a pretty good chance there might be incidents like there were in Italy at the beginning of the war—when civilians could not get into shelters because they were filled with antiaircraft gunners."

But there were forty batteries of the wicked 88s (88-mm. rifles which were employed against tanks and ships as well as aircraft)—240 guns in all, besides the smaller 37-mm. and 20-mm. guns: hun-

Edward Timberlake, former commander of the "Traveling Circus" (93rd Bomb Group), assisted in the planning of the Ploesti mission. The photograph was taken while the group was still stationed in England.

(U. S. AIR FORCE)

dreds of guns ringing Ploesti and many of them manned by Luftwaffe gun crews, not Rumanians. It was not deception, merely wishful thinking based on the best and latest intelligence reports. But it was the basis for one of the more horrible realizations to be met in the target area by the men in the five groups of Liberators.

At dawn on Sunday, August 1, the first of 178 Liberators, *Wingo-Wango,* piloted by First Lieutenant Brian Flavelle and carrying the mission navigator Lieutenant Robert Wilson, lifted out of the Libyan dust and pointed for the island of Corfu, a three-hour flight across the Mediterranean. At this point the mission would bear northeast across the mountains of Albania and Yugoslavia and eventually the Danube River. This led into the Wallachian plain and Ploesti. The trip would cover, for those who made it both ways, a distance of roughly twenty-seven hundred miles.

The cumbrous, slab-sided "pregnant cows," swollen with fuel for the long trip (additional tanks were installed in the bomb bay of each plane), seemed to struggle to rise off the ground. Although the extra fuel meant sacrificing pay load—1000-

Aircrew: men who would fly the mission to Ploesti; 93rd Bomb Group. (RAYMOND C. WIER)

pound and 500-pound bombs as well as incendiaries —each Liberator carried more than 4000 pounds of explosives: a total of 311 tons of destruction in the entire striking force. All planes were overloaded, some of them made heavier by extra nose guns (in formation lead planes which were to attack flak-gun installations on their bomb runs) and armored crew stations protecting the men from ground fire.

The bombs carried delayed fuzes; the first two waves would thus drop bombs timed to detonate after a period of from one to six hours. This would make it safe for the planes which followed to drop their bombs, theoretically, without flying into the bursts of the preceding aircraft or through the fires the early bombs might have set. There were seven major target areas. Five were situated at Ploesti; another was at Brazi, which was almost adjacent to Ploesti and just to the south; the seventh target was at Campina, about eight miles northwest of Ploesti.

Aboard the 178 Liberators were 1725 Americans and one stowaway, an Englishman. RAF Flight Lieutenant George C. Barwell, a gunnery expert, had been given unofficial permission to fly as topturret gunner in the plane of Major Norman C. Appold, leading B Section of the leading group, the Liberandos (376th). Led by Compton, the

Pre-mission pep talk: General Brereton addresses the 376th Bomb Group before its men boarded their Liberators for Ploesti. Curious portent: as he spoke a sudden wind came up and Brereton was blown off the platform. (U. S. AIR FORCE)

376th Bomb Group put up twenty-nine B-24s; at the head of the formation flew Flavelle's *Wingo-Wango,* leading the bombers to Ploestl. Tucked into the 376th formation was Compton's plane, *Teggie Ann,* carrying the mission command pilot, General Ent.

Following the Liberandos came Baker's Traveling Circus (93rd) with thirty-nine aircraft and Killer Kane's Pyramiders (98th) with forty-seven tawny (almost moth-eaten in appearance) B-24s; the Eight Balls, Johnson's 44th Bomb Group, came up with thirty-seven bombers; behind Johnson were the Sky Scorpions (389th), led by Wood, with twenty-six Liberators. Each group, some divided into two forces, had its assigned targets; all were scheduled to approach their targets in the order in which they had taken off. A strict radio silence was maintained in order not to alert German detection stations. Unknown to the men aboard the Liberators, the Germans were aware of a large force taking off from Libya, although the destination was not known.

"The very first news of the Ploesti operation was bad," Brereton noted in his diary. *Kickapoo,* which had taken off with Kane's Pyramiders, developed trouble shortly after pilot First Lieutenant Robert Nespor had it air-borne. With flame shooting out of an engine, Nespor turned around and headed back for the field. In coming in he was forced to attempt a landing upon a runway still obscured by clouds of red desert dust. *Kickapoo* came in, settled onto the runway, roughly bounced along, and rammed into a concrete telephone pole. Only two men survived the burning wreck.

But the armada, led by *Wingo-Wango,* continued on its way. From time to time over the Mediterranean a Liberator here and there feathered a propeller—a sign of engine malfunction—wheeled out of the formation, jettisoned bombs and fuel into the sea, and headed back for Africa. Before they came within sight of Corfu, ten Liberators had gone; six of these came from Kane's Pyramiders.

The remaining 167 planes were bearing down on Corfu when the lead plane began to behave peculiarly. As the other craft in A Section scattered out of harm's way, *Wingo-Wango* swooped and dived, climbed and dived directly into the sea. Even during these shocking moments radio silence was not violated and no one could know what had oc-

Wingo-Wango, Brian Flavelle's Liberator, has silently fallen into the Mediterranean, taking "Tidal Wave's" lead navigator Robert Wilson with it.

(RAYMOND C. WIER)

rurred in the lost plane. Only a tall column of smoke rose from the Mediterranean marking the spot where the aircraft had plunged. The formation was supposed to continue on its way—and it did, except for Flavelle's wingman, First Lieutenant Guy Iovine. Unable to leave the stricken ship, he dipped his B-24 down and circled over the spot hoping to find survivors to whom he might drop rafts. But there was no one, and then to his dismay Iovine found that he was unable to get the heavy plane back up to formation altitude. There was nothing to do but head back to Benghazi.

The mission navigator was lost in Flavelle's plane; the deputy navigator was in Iovine's. John Palm, in *Brewery Wagon,* moved into the lead spot; his navigator, young William Wright, was now chief navigator of the mission to Ploesti.

Now 165 of the original 178 planes turned northeast over Corfu. Spotters, still uncertain of the formation's destination, kept close watch on the B-24s and telephoned various Luftwaffe stations in the area. But there was some suspicion in Bucharest that the target might be Ploesti.

The formation had hugged the sea for the first leg, but as it approached Albania the Pindus Mountains would necessitate a climb. The mountains peaked to nine thousand feet, but a build-up of cloud massed up to seventeen thousand feet. Compton led the 376th through at sixteen thousand feet, followed by Baker's 93rd. Kane elected to go through at twelve thousand feet leading his 98th, which had spread out according to procedure for passing through cloud, and was followed by Johnson's 44th and Wood's 389th Groups. At sixteen thousand feet a tail wind hurried the two lead groups toward Ploesti while at twelve thousand the three other groups bucked winds through the soup. Thus when the five groups finally emerged from the cumulus, Compton's and Baker's formations were out of sight of Kane, Johnson, and Wood's Liberators. Radio silence made it impossible for the force to reassemble for the final attack. By this time also men in the American bombers had seen enemy planes hovering below them, unable to climb to the height at which the bombers flew without proper oxygen equipment. These were Bulgarian pilots in antiquated fighters. Leon Johnson then realized that all hopes for surprise had come to nothing. And with the three groups trailing the two lead groups, all chances of making a concerted attack upon the seven target areas were likewise lost.

About sixty-five miles west of Ploesti lay the first IP (Initial Point), the city of Pitesti. It was here that the formations were to assume attack altitude, about five hundred feet, and the 389th would leave the other groups to attack the Campina targets. The final IP was the town of Floresti, about thirteen miles northwest of Ploesti. Turning southeast at Floresti would bring the four remaining groups in over Ploesti for their low-level bombing runs.

Brewery Wagon, the lead plane of the 376th Group, carrying William Wright, the new mission navigator, continued on past Pitesti. Slightly behind was Teggie Ann, flown by Captain Ralph Thompson, as copilot to Compton and carrying mission leader Ent as a passenger. Brewery Wagon passed over Targoviste on the way to the final IP, Floresti; here the most fatal incident of the mission occurred. Mistaking Targoviste for Floresti, Compton ordered Thompson to make the southeast turn for the final run on the target. Palm's Brewery Wagon continued on the correct flight path, but all planes following saw the command ship turn and turned in train. Brewery Wagon wavered, seemed about to join in the wrong turn, but convinced that Wright was correct, Palm continued directly on to the target alone. But Teggie Ann, meanwhile, pointed both the 376th and 93rd at Bucharest instead of Ploesti.

Ramsay Potts, among the first to realize that the lead plane with Compton and Ent had made a wrong turn, broke radio silence to warn of the error. But too late; Potts was forced to turn also because of being boxed in by the formation. (U. S. AIR FORCE)

Major Ramsay Potts, leading B Section of the 93rd, realized instantly that the turn had come too soon. So did Major Norman Appold of the 376th. It was too much for both men and they broke radio silence—it no longer mattered—shouting, "Not here!" (Appold) and "Mistake!" (Potts). The latter hoped to break away from the formation, but was "boxed in and had no choice but to turn."

The two lead groups were now heading into Gerstenberg's most potent flak-gun concentration—and for the capital city of Rumania, a city of no military consequence. Within minutes the spires and steeples of Bucharest came into view. To the men in the racing Liberators, now around fifty feet above the ground, it did not at all look like the target for which they had been briefed. Alerted gun crews ran to their 88s and alarms rang in fighter bases for miles around. Why the Americans should attack Bucharest was a total mystery, but Rumanian and German alike ran to his gun station or to waiting fighter aircraft. The Battle of Ploesti had been prematurely ignited.

Addison Baker, leading the 93rd, which had followed the 376th on the wrong course, was aware also of the wrong turn. So was, by then, Ent and Compton in *Teggie Ann.* But it was Baker who reacted first. Seeing the church spires of Bucharest ahead instead of the stacks of Ploesti, which stood to his left, without breaking radio silence Baker executed an almost right-angle turn toward the target. With near miraculous skill and remarkable discipline the rest of the Traveling Circus followed: Lieutenant Colonel George S. Brown leading A Section swinging to Baker's right, and Ramsay Potts, with B Section, wheeling to Brown's right. Now in a broad frontal formation the 93rd approached Ploesti from the south instead of from the west as it had been briefed. Ploesti looked strange to the navigators and bombardiers as its stacks loomed up out of the ground.

IV

The one plane on the correct course, John Palm's *Brewery Wagon,* all but embraced the earth as it charged for the target. Almost on Ploesti *Brewery Wagon* took a direct .88 hit in the nose, killing young William Wright, who had led the formations

The payment for Ploesti begins: the antiaircraft guns, having been forewarned by the wrong turn, are ready for Brewery Wagon, *which had not made the error—thanks to the navigation of William Wright, whom Ent overruled—and which continued "as briefed" for Ploesti until struck in the nose by a German .88 shell.* (RAYMOND C. WIER)

The 93rd, having swung back on course because of Potts's realization of the navigational error of Teggie Ann, *passes by a burning Liberator.*

(RAYMOND C. WIER)

A view from the cockpit of Kenneth O. Dessert's Liberator; flame billows up from an oil tank. To the right, in the lower left-hand corner of the windscreen may be seen Hell's Wench, *carrying Group Commander Addison Baker and mission planning assistant John J. Jerstad. Struck by an .88 shell and burning, the plane continued on its run over the target and crashed; no one survived, not even the two men who parachuted from the burning plane.* (RAYMOND C. WIER)

Lieutenant Colonel Addison Baker, commander of the 93rd Group, here photographed in his office using the public address system, while the group was still stationed in England. Baker died in the crash of Hell's Wench *and was awarded a Medal of Honor for his role in the mission to Ploesti.* (U. S. AIR FORCE)

so brilliantly, and bombardier Second Lieutenant Robert W. Merrell. Palm too had been hit; his right leg was all but blown away. With three engines gone—two of them gushing flame—there was nothing to do but salvo the bombs and try to land. Half in shock upon learning that his leg remained attached to him by the merest shred, Palm had been unaware of the attack of a Messerschmitt on *Brewery Wagon* as it came crunching into the ground. Copilot William F. Love foamed the engines and the distressed plane came in without further burning. Palm, who later had his right leg amputated below the knee, and the seven other survivors were taken prisoner by the Rumanians and Germans.

Having turned for Ploesti, leaving the 376th still on the wrong course to Bucharest, Baker's 93rd ran into the muzzles of flak guns awaiting them. The alarms which had alerted the capital's defenses also quickened the rings of guns around the true target area. Baker flew directly into an inferno: the planes were so low that gun crews simply boresighted and used instantaneous fuzes. So it was that *Hell's Wench,* Baker's plane, with young Major John J. Jerstad, one of the important assistants to Timberlake in the planning of the mission, as copilot, bore down upon the target area. One of the first obstacles was the balloon barrage. *Hell's Wench* flew into a cable, which luckily snapped, freeing the balloon. But then an .88 shell smashed into the nose of the Liberator and more hits followed, into the wings and the cockpit. Aflame, *Hell's Wench* proceeded toward the target; but Baker knew it would not remain aloft with the bomb load and he jettisoned the explosives. The plane continued leading the rest of the 93rd toward the target. A chute or two blossomed out of *Hell's Wench,* and it appeared that Baker had attempted to bring it up high enough to enable the men to have sufficient altitude from which to drop.

Hell's Wench, still burning, continued to lead the force into the target area, attempting to clear the stacks which spiked up into its path. To observers it appeared to be completely afire in the cockpit area although still seemingly under control. About three hundred feet above the ground *Hell's Wench* suddenly veered into the earth with a splashing flame. Baker had succeeded in bringing his group over the target, but everyone—including the few men who had been able to leave the doomed plane —died.

Those who followed placed the first bombs into the Ploesti target area. The first bomb fell from Walter Stewart's *Utah Man,* only survivor of Baker's three-plane wave. However, the bombs rained down upon targets assigned not to the 93rd, but to the 44th (still coming up, though late, but, as briefed, in company with Kane's 98th). Liberators had begun dropping out of the force before Ploesti was reached as point-blank antiaircraft fire smashed into the low-flying aircraft. Black funeral pyres dotted the route to the target. Gunners in the aircraft engaged in duels with the enemy machine gunners and antiaircraft crews. Some of the machine-gun fire from the planes ignited the unimportant tank farms, smudging the area with leaping flames and dense, black smoke, introducing just one more hazard into the affrighted air.

It was an unimaginable scene as the thirty-four (of the original thirty-nine) 93rd Bomb Group planes swept through at more than two hundred miles an hour and barely off the ground. Their attack could only have taken minutes, but lifetimes ended and complex actions occurred in those few minutes. More than half of the attacking planes did not come out of the fiery target area. Some struck balloon cables; some were hit by flak or other gunfire; some, flying through the turbulence of earlier planes, simply slammed into the ground. Hidden guns popped out of fake haystacks or special mobile flak nests on railway cars with drop sides. Liberators trailed sheets of flame and crashed into fields of wheat or corn even before arriving at the target.

Ramsay Potts, in *Duchess,* led the final 93rd element, Target Force 3, into fumid Ploesti. Deeply fearful that the wrong turn had "wiped out our chance for a successful mission," Potts knew his small force would not be able to hit its target. Having weathered a murderous sequence of flak guns, it would be difficult enough to find an alternate target. Potts and his wingmen turned to find their assigned target but with Astro Romana directly in their line of flight began dropping bombs; this target in the original planning had been assigned to Kane's 98th. The planes behind and around *Duchess* began shredding parts of fuselage or wing,

some continuing on but others smashing to earth in fiery, gashing crashes. One of Potts's wingmen, *Jersey Bounce,* with nose shot away, engine trailing flame, painfully rose over various obstacles until pilot Worthy Long managed to skid it into a clearing, where it burst into flame. Half the crew managed to get out of the plane.

Rumanian fighters, which had vaulted into the air from near Bucharest, initiated attacks on the harassed 93rd Liberators. As one of Potts's B-24s emerged out of the target area, a low-winged monoplane clung to the big aircraft. Apparently in distress, the Liberator roared above the streets of Ploesti with the little Rumanian fighter underneath (all but scraping the street) firing into its belly. With a massive boom the American bomber crashed into the women's prison, in which not only the crew of the plane but around sixty prisoners died trapped in the flames.

As Potts led the remnants of the 93rd away from Ploesti, he was on a near-collision course with planes of the 376th, now coming in to bomb. Ent and Compton had faced the frightful truth: they had led the force into a wrong turn. During the run from Targoviste to the outskirts of Bucharest they had, indeed, "served their time in hell." And there was more to come. Ent spoke into the command channel and ordered the 376th away from Bucharest, turning north and following a railroad linking the capital with Ploesti. The question now was: Should they circle to come in from the briefed course or should they bomb from a completely unfamiliar approach?

This vexing question was answered when Ent, observing the savagery of the antiaircraft fire, ordered the men to hit "targets of opportunity." The B-24s had been flying north, directly into heavy flak, and most then swerved away to the east, to strike at whatever targets they could find. According to the original plan the target of Compton's planes was the Romana Americana refinery—deliberately selected because of its onetime (i.e., before the Germans took over) American ownership. There must be no favoritism displayed in the Ploesti attack. Because of the confusion, as well as the heavy flak reception, the Romana Americana complex was not hit at all that day.

Major Norman Appold led his five Liberators of

Norman C. Appold, who had like Ramsay Potts realized Teggie Ann *had made a wrong turn, but who pressed on toward Ploesti and saw a mass confusion over the target. Despite this, Appold bombed his target of opportunity, Concordia Vega.* (U. S. AIR FORCE)

the 376th directly into Ploesti instead of spreading out as did the other planes. Appold had selected what appeared to be an untouched target of importance (it was: Concordia Vega, which had been assigned to Baker's 93rd). But even as he approached on the bomb run, Appold was disconcerted to see other B-24s flying through the smoke directly toward him; these were the survivors of Potts's force leaving the target. But there was more for Appold to see: as he bore down on Concordia Vega more B-24s appeared to be converging upon him. These were Killer Kane's Pyramiders, somewhat late after joining up upon emerging from the cloud mass, and now on the proper target run.

If ever there was a demonstration of just how a carefully planned military operation could go awry thanks to the simple introduction of human error, Ploesti became a classic.

There is a classic Army axiom: when in doubt

do everything. Appold, however, was not in doubt. He had selected his target and went for it; blind good fortune would have to see to the rest. His five bombers groped through the hail of fire and smoke and dropped their bombs directly into the target area. Only then did he lead his planes up and over Potts's planes rushing away from Ploesti. Appold turned also and, while Barwell in the top turret engaged in duels with various low-lying gun positions, pulled away from the nightmare in noon-time Ploesti.

The other 376th aircraft, seeking targets of opportunity, scattered in sweeping turns to the west of Ploesti. Compton's *Teggie Ann* salvoed into a small complex of buildings, not one of the briefed targets. Other planes followed suit, dropping their loads to the north and west of Ploesti before veering south near Floresti—where they converged with Jack Wood's Sky Scorpions, which had bombed at Campina.

V

It was at Floresti, the third IP and correct turning point for the run into Ploesti, that Kane's 98th and Johnson's 44th began their massed approach. The dividing line between the two forces was a railroad track running from Floresti to Ploesti. A heavily armed flak train ran along this track, firing at Kane's Pyramiders to the north and Johnson's Eight Balls to the south as the two forces, flying abreast, came upon Ploesti.

While Kane's Pyramiders and sixteen of Johnson's Eight Balls bore down upon their Ploesti targets, Colonel James Posey, also of the 44th, led an additional twenty-one Eight Ball Liberators toward his target, Brazi, about five miles southwest of Ploesti. Here was located the Creditul Minier refinery, production center for high-octane aviation fuel.

Leading in *V for Victory,* piloted by veteran John H. Diehl, Posey swept into Brazi in the first wave. Diehl had to pull the plane up to avoid chimneys, but the bombs fell precisely into the target area. Brazi had not been struck by any of the earlier planes which had scattered over Ploesti seeking targets. This part of the mission occurred exactly as planned—and the Brazi refinery was totally destroyed at a cost of two Liberators.

Kane's Pyramiders come in over Ploesti to find that their targets have already been hit by Baker's Traveling Circus. (JERRY JOSWICK: U. S. AIR FORCE)

But the fate of the remaining Eight Balls and the Pyramiders was totally different. As they approached Ploesti, it seemed that they would be further hindered by murky rain clouds low over the target area. Several Liberators in both Kane's and Johnson's forces had been damaged by the flak train, and the dark cloud was but one more unforeseen hitch. But as they charged down upon Ploesti it became clear that the "rain" was in fact smoke, the effusion of the bombings by the 93rd Group. This smoke, now rising above bombing height, not only added turbulence, but also secreted chimneys, barrage balloon cables, and bracing wires of the chimneys. Intense flame, too, shot into the air intermittently throughout the entire target area.

It was at this point that both Johnson and Kane could have swerved off course and fled. Their targets, obscured by smoke and livid with flame, had already been struck. They could turn back and no one would question their decision. It is unlikely that the thought so much as flickered through the minds of these two quite opposite men. Johnson expressed their attitudes when he said that "we had all agreed ahead of time that we weren't going

that far without trying to get our targets. . . ." Kane had come to bomb Ploesti and he would not leave until he had. So he led his decimated Pyramiders into the inferno. One of his crew, Raymond B. Hubbard, recalled that the "fire wrapped us up. I looked out of the side windows and saw the others flying through smoke and flame. It was [like] flying through hell. I guess we'll go straight to heaven when we die. We've had our purgatory."

"It was more like an artist's conception of an air battle than anything I have ever experienced," Johnson later told Brereton. "We flew through sheets of flame, and airplanes were everywhere, some of them on fire and others exploding. It's indescribable to anyone who wasn't there."

Kane, at the controls of *Hail Columbia,* churned up the target area with his fixed front guns and led the way into Ploesti. The heat was so intense at his attack altitude that his left arm was singed; *Hail Columbia* also received a hit in an engine and when the smoke- and flame-blacked B-24 escaped from the inferno it was flying on three engines. Of the forty-one planes which had begun the target run at Floresti, only nineteen followed Kane out of the smoke. But their bombs lay in the assigned target zone, compounding the destruc-

The 98th Bomb Group flies over an already burning Astra Romana. Stacks in the heavy smoke were as much a danger as German flak.

(JERRY JOSWICK: U. S. AIR FORCE)

tion laid on by the distracted 93rd. There had been, however, just one more hazard—the explosions of the delayed-action bombs.

Johnson's "White Five" target force of sixteen Liberators flew directly into a curtain of black smoke, evidence of the earlier visit of Baker's Traveling Circus. The great B-24s, twisting and turning to avoid balloon cables and chimneys, wallowed like so many winged whales in a fiery sea. With shocking regularity the leviathans foundered to the bottom of the murky ocean, spurting red, bloodlike flame. Of the sixteen planes which entered the "White Five" (Colombia Aquila refinery) target area only seven, with Johnson's *Suzy-Q* in the lead, came out.

But leaving the area of the target did not conclude the nightmare, for both Kane's and Johnson's survivors came under severe fighter attack—mainly Luftwaffe men in Me-109s. As he raced away with all the power his three straining engines could muster, Kane's *Hail Columbia* was laced by fighter fire, with punctures in the wing (with a resultant buckled wing spar), the tip of a propeller shot away, and a holed blade on another. Knowing he could never make it back over the planned with-

Leon Johnson's 44th approaches Columbia Aquila, only to find it burning; of the sixteen planes that flew in, only seven came out.

(JERRY JOSWICK: U. S. AIR FORCE)

One of the targets hit "as briefed," Steaua Romana, the objective of the green "Sky Scorpions" (389th Group) led by Jack Wood.

(JERRY JOSWICK: U. S. AIR FORCE)

drawal route to Benghazi, Kane set course for Cyprus, throwing out all excess weight on the way.

The Sky Scorpions (389th) were led with only the slightest hitch by Jack Wood to their target at Campina ("Red Target"). Wood too had inadvertently led his formation into a wrong turn; he corrected it by a smoothly executed turnabout and a vault over a small ridge. The Scorpions came in in two forces, Wood leading a dozen B-24s and Major John A. Brooks, his deputy, leading seventeen. With forward firing guns chattering, Wood led the forces into the until then untouched Steaua Romana complex. Like Posey's attack upon Brazi, Jack Wood's attack upon Campina was "as briefed." His group had the least losses of all involved. Of the twenty-nine attacking planes, six were lost, one of them flown by Second Lieutenant Lloyd Hughes, the only man of the Ploesti mission below the rank of major to receive the Medal of Honor.

Hughes's Liberator had been struck by flak as it approached the drop point. A wide stream of fuel poured out of a ruptured bomb bay tank, twist-

Lieutenant Lloyd Hughes (as an air cadet), one of the Sky Scorpions who did not leave the target area; Hughes was awarded the Medal of Honor for the mission. (U. S. AIR FORCE)

dos (376th), they came under fighter attack. From the dropping of the first bomb by *Utah Man* just before noon, until the last—placed by the 389th's *Vagabond King,* piloted by John B. McCormick— less than a half hour had elapsed. But for the survivors, most of them spread across the skies of Rumania with damaged planes, wounded, dying, and dead aboard, there were still the fighters to contend with until the German and Rumanian planes ran out of fuel. Keeping the tattered, scorched Liberators air-borne was an epic in itself.

The plan, having gone so completely astray, no longer held. On paper it had been intended that all targets would be hit simultaneously and that all survivors of the attack should return to the Libyan bases together. Thus would they be able to defend each other in formation with massed guns. The withdrawal from Ploesti was not orderly as different groups in various stages of distress left the target areas. Some planes were badly damaged and could not keep up with a formation, others came away under fighter attack.

An attempt was made to form ragged groupings

ing and flashing under the big plane like a liquid ribbon of fuze. Now on his bomb run, Hughes did not attempt to land or to evade the wall of flame which stood in the path. In an instant Hughes's Liberator was set afire. The bombs fell into the target, but the stricken plane, a white sheet of pure fire streaming from the left wing, had no chance. Obviously still under control, Hughes seemed headed for a stream bed for an emergency landing. A bridge loomed in the path of the burning plane, but the plane rose above the obstruction, lowered again—and then a wing tip brushed the riverbank. The blazing Liberator whirled across the earth, spattering molten wreckage and scarring the meadow in its scorching death throes; all but two men in the plane died in the crash.

The Sky Scorpions were the last to bomb in the Ploesti area, and in addition to dodging the target-of-opportunity seekers of Compton's Liberan-

"Getting the hell out": a Liberator at treetop level rushes away from burning Ploesti. Some bombers nearly scraped the earth and returned with cornstalks in their bomb bays.

(JERRY JOSWICK: U. S. AIR FORCE)

for the sake of survival. Some aircraft, not badly damaged, throttled down to remain with others which could not keep up and thus became easy targets for fighters. A trail of ammunition belts, radios, guns, seats—anything no longer required and which added weight to a struggling plane—followed the Liberators from Ploesti to the sea. The least hurt groups, the 376th (Liberandos) and the 389th (Sky Scorpions), managed to form up and head for home over the planned route, although not as a single unit. Some of the 44th and 98th (the worst hit Eight Balls and Pyramiders) joined together for the flight back, but the Pyramiders' leader, John Kane, with other planes in tow, made for Cyprus. It was a shorter flight than to Africa, although not without its Bulgarian mountain barrier. Planes which could not make it even that far landed in neutral Turkey, where crews were interned. In all, seven Liberators came down in Turkey, and one ditched into the sea off the Turkish coast; twenty-three came down at Allied bases in Malta, Sicily, or Cyprus.

It was nighttime before Kane brought *Hail Columbia* into the RAF base at Nicosia, Cyprus. Although the flare path was lighted, the exhausted

In the wake of "Tidal Wave," Rumanians fighting the fires at Ploesti. Although smoke and flame were impressive, the attack did not knock out the target. (U. S. AIR FORCE)

Journey's end: a Liberator sets down in north Africa after the Ploesti mission. (U. S. AIR FORCE)

iron man brought the wheezing Liberator in a little short, snagging the landing gear in a ditch which the British, with characteristic perversity, placed at either end of runways. The main wheels snapped and the Liberator came in on its nose and with tail threatening to rise and upend them. Kane and copilot John S. Young pulled on the controls to prevent flipping onto their back. The tail came down as the battered aircraft bellied screechingly along the runway. Bumping along, Kane was surprised to see two wheels and a propeller racing ahead. The plane twisted to a halt, and for the first time in more than twelve hours, Killer Kane left his seat.

On the return flight to Benghazi more planes were lost to the last fighter attacks and fell into the sea; two aircraft flying in formation entered a cloud and never came out—they had collided. Finally, after nearly twelve hours of waiting, the men at Benghazi heard the first of the survivors approaching. Brereton awaited the arrival of Compton and Ent, from whom he had had no word since around noon, when the simple message "Mission Successful" had been radioed from Ploesti.

In the deepening African twilight the giant bombers fluttered back, their engines whining from strain, the planes themselves whistling because of bullet- and flak-riddled surfaces. Planes came in without brakes, without proper control, some crash-landed with dead and wounded aboard. When the dispirited Ent revealed to Brereton the story of the mission, the latter realized that he had no triumph on his hands. The extent of damage to Ploesti would not be known until reconnaissance photographs were taken. From eyewitnesses it was clear that Ploesti had been hard hit, so that Ent's curiously premature and wildly optimistic "Mission Successful" message seemed less ironic.

But the ravages of the toll began to come in, intimated by the condition of men and aircraft as they landed at Benghazi. Ramsay Potts brought *Duchess* down and his feet had barely touched the ground before he was telling Timberlake of a military nightmare.

Of the 164 Liberators which had gained the target area, 41 had been lost to enemy action. An additional 14 (including the 8 interned in Turkey) were lost through other causes, such as the takeoff accident of *Kickapoo,* the inexplicable dive into the sea of Flavelle's plane near Corfu and the collision in the clouds over Bulgaria. Thus the total plane loss added up to 54. (And of those which had returned to Benghazi, barely 30 were still flyable.) This would mean too the loss of 540 men.

The final death toll of the Ploesti raid, according to Air Force files, came to 310. The number of wounded was initially given as 54 (3 of whom were in Turkey), but that number plus 20 lay in hospitals in Rumania. More than 100 prisoners, also, spent the rest of the war in Rumania.

The cost to the Ninth Air Force for less than a half hour's work was, indeed, high. This was implicit in the awarding of no less than five Medals of Honor (the highest number for any single air action) to Ploesti raiders, to the quick—Leon Johnson and John Kane—and the dead—Addison Baker, John Jerstad, and Lloyd Hughes.

On August 4, 1943, following the preliminary estimates, Brereton noted in his diary, "While the TIDAL WAVE operation was extremely successful, I was somewhat disappointed because we failed to hit White No. 1 and 2 at all." White No. 1 was Romana Americana, the American-leased section of Ploesti; No. 2 was Concordia Vega, which had, in fact, been hit by the determined Appold with his five planes that had not swerved away, as had the others of the 376th, to seek targets of opportunity. Brereton assigned his discomfiture to the fact that the 65 to 75 per cent destruction he had hoped for had not been achieved. Still, he believed that a 60 per cent figure had been reached and had "put a serious dent in Germany's oil supply." As reported centuries before by Plutarch, it had been another victorious warrior, Pyrrhus, who had said, "Another such victory . . . and we are finished."

In truth, the extent of damage was closer to 40 per cent, and while bombs and fire (as well as crashing aircraft) did knock out some facilities for four to six months, no "serious dent" was put in Germany's oil supply. In fact, Ploesti had never produced to full capacity, so that other units could be activated to make up the loss. With slave labor in plentiful supply, the Germans very quickly restored the damaged facilities, and Ploesti, instead of being knocked out of the war, was as potent as ever. It was not until late in the spring of 1944 that any more attempts could be made upon the heavily defended target. When the U. S. Fifteenth Air Force, based at Foggia, Italy, was formed and powerfully armed with B-17s and B-24s, Ploesti could be struck en masse from high level. By that time, too, long-range American fighter planes could escort the bombers to and from the target.

But Ploesti was never to be an easy target, with its heavy flak concentration, and many men died attempting to put a stopper to Hitler's oil supply. By the end of August 1944, a little over a year after Tidal Wave, the oil fields did stop functioning. In September the Russians moved in and occupied the ruin. It had taken thousands of bombers (and a further expenditure of more than 350 bombers lost). In short, the men who undertook and carried through Tidal Wave had attempted the impossible. Their true achievement could be measured only in courage and not decisive results. For the tragedy of Ploesti is that there were no decisive results.

8

SCHWEINFURT

OVER another panacea target, ball bearings," Air Chief Marshal Sir Arthur Harris exclaimed with undisguised scorn, "the target experts went completely mad." The outspoken Briton, it is true, was speaking from the vantage point of hindsight, but he was no less critical and skeptical at the time. He resisted all pleas, suggestions, and even demands which had initiated with the "panacea mongers" despite their quite accurate information that about half of Germany's supply of ball bearings, so essential to the machines and instruments of war, was produced in the Bavarian city of Schweinfurt.

Harris rejected the claims for Schweinfurt's importance (in which rejection he was not correct), stating that even if Schweinfurt were entirely destroyed the effect upon German war production would not be as disastrous as was "so confidently prophesied." The fiery Bomber Command leader, standing firm against his own chiefs of the Air Staff, argued that Schweinfurt was a relatively small city and would therefore be difficult to find at night, that it was heavily defended, and that even several full-scale attacks would achieve, in his firm but considered opinion, only dubious results.

For months the doughty Harris endured the pressures of his chiefs, who in general agreed with the American policy of concentration upon selected targets. They argued that massive destruction in a few key industries would naturally be more effective than

widespread small destruction in many. Harris preferred the larger population centers, for such cities were easier to locate—and they housed many, many Germans. These were the cities to destroy, not little Schweinfurt with its population of sixty thousand. While the crisis boiled in Bomber Command, the American Eighth Air Force, committed to the spirit and letter of the Combined Bomber Offensive, a major objective of which was the crippling of the German aircraft industry, prepared to spring upon Schweinfurt.

Eighth Air Force Bomber Command (more correctly VIII Bomber Command) had, since its initial modest mission to the Rouen-Sotteville marshaling yards (August 17, 1942), concentrated its slowly expanding forces upon such ungrateful targets as submarine pens, besides various industrial targets in the occupied countries and Germany and Luftwaffe airfields. By the beginning of 1943 it was grievously clear that the German Air Force was indeed a formidable enemy. As German pilots gained experience against the American bomber formations, composed mainly of the Flying Fortress and the more recent Liberators, tactics were devised to interfere seriously with bombing missions. The early Fortresses and Liberators were weak on frontal armament, so German pilots learned eventually to attack in small formations, ranging from single aircraft to a half dozen, from the front. The head-on

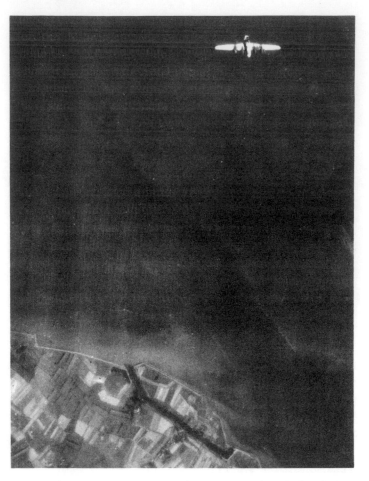

Aircraft of British Bomber Command and the American Eighth Air Force, by night and by day, shared the menace of German flak guns in occupied Holland. Flying Fortress Lady Liberty *falls toward Flushing after being cut in half by a direct hit.* (U. S. AIR FORCE)

attack, considering the double closing speed of the two aircraft, the always present danger of collision, and the sight of twinkling wing guns and cannon, was unnerving, to say the least. Although aggressive Luftwaffe fighter attacks did not succeed in turning back any of the American bomber forces, they did succeed in knocking aircraft down and, with the head-on attack, in interfering with the accuracy of bombing. Flak was another problem, but a more impersonal one, and one which depended to some extent upon chance. A German pilot in an Me-109 or an FW-190 was out to get you, specifically, and this was rattling.

It was true, then, as noted in the Combined Bomber Offensive document, that before the major target systems could be dealt with, the Luftwaffe

must be eliminated. This did not preclude attention to other targets. Weather, the number of operational aircraft, the range limit of escort planes also played a part in the planning.

The force that Eaker was capable of dispatching in the year which separated Mission No. 1, when a dozen B-17s flew to Rouen-Sotteville, and Mission No. 83, when 237 bombers struck various German operated airfields in France, had grown. But postholing runways, wrecking operations buildings and barracks, and destroying parked aircraft could only be defined as tactical—warmaking with an immediate, short-range objective. The more strategic aspect was notable in missions toward the end of July 1943—Missions 78, 79, 80, for example—when the Fiesler aircraft components factory at Kassel, the Focke-Wulf plant at Oschersleben, and the Heinkel works at Warnemünde (all of which

Colonel Curtis E. LeMay, commander of the 3rd Air Division (right), who led the first shuttle bombing mission from England to Regensburg to north Africa. To LeMay's right: Brigadier General Haywood S. Hansell, commander of the 1st Bombardment Wing (units of which later comprised the 1st Air Division). When this photograph was taken LeMay was commander of the 305th Bomb Group. Later in the war both Hansell and LeMay were to play important roles in the development of the B-29 as an air weapon.

(U. S. AIR FORCE)

belonged to the complex which turned out the formidable FW-190) were heavily hit. They were also zealously defended; the three days' missions cost forty-four heavy bombers. And, if the Eighth had not succeeded in erasing the factories from Germany's war economy, it did initiate serious thought among the German High Command about dispersing such factory complexes, which dispersal promised to disrupt production as critically as damage.

The first anniversary of the Eighth's first mission from Britain was to be celebrated with Mission No. 84, the most impressive up to that moment. It sparkled with superlatives: more aircraft than ever before, more bomb tonnage than ever before; the deepest penetration into Germany ever attempted and a strike against the then two most critical targets: the Messerschmitt factories at Regensburg and the ball-bearing plant at Schweinfurt.

"It was a bold strategic concept," Lieutenant General Ira C. Eaker has written of the Regensburg-Schweinfurt mission. "It was the first shuttle bombing mission of the war. The 3rd Air Division, the

Aircrew quarters, Grafton-Underwood, England. Men of the 384th Bomb Group hug the stove between missions. Galoshes are a concession to England's muddy airfields. The steel helmet was not an affectation; it was worn by aircrews in combat. (ROBERT CHAPIN)

force attacking the Messerschmitt fighter factory at Regensburg, took off from English bases and landed in fields in North Africa. The decisions by the VIII Bomber Commander, Major General Frederick L. Anderson [who replaced Eaker, now head of the Eighth Air Force], and the 3rd Air Division Commander, Colonel Curtis E. LeMay, to proceed to Regensburg with but part of the force, when the 1st Air Division [led by Brigadier General Robert Williams] was delayed in take-off due to weather, were *two* of the most dramatic and courageous command decisions of the air war in Europe. This battlefield was a thousand miles long and five miles above the earth. It was fought in sub-zero temperatures and the gladiators, friend and foe, wore oxygen masks."

Brereton's Ninth had bled at Ploesti; now, less than a month later, it would be the turn of Eaker's Eighth.

Major General Frederick L. Anderson, commander of the Eighth Air Force's Bomber Command during the Schweinfurt missions. (U. S. AIR FORCE)

II

By June of 1943 about ten heavy bombardment groups had arrived in England, taking over ex-RAF

With a jack raising the wing, 384th Group ground crew men prepare to remove a wheel from a B-17.
(ROBERT CHAPIN)

stations in East Anglia and the Midlands. One of the most recent arrivals was the 384th Bombardment Group (H) based at Grafton-Underwood, from which the first heavy bomber strike had been made the previous August. In time the 384th adopted the slogan "Keep the Show on the Road," the contribution of Major S. L. McMillan, deputy group commander, who went down on the group's second mission—a strike upon the docks at Hamburg. Writing from a German prisoner of war camp, McMillan provided the heartening phrase, the philosophy of which the men in the group might have found ironic. In its first four days in combat the 384th lost ten aircraft on the wrong side of the Channel.

These losses, as well as the others decimating 8th Bomber Command, were more a tribute to the Luftwaffe's assertiveness than a reproach to the capabilities of the 384th Group. Even if bomber formations had grown larger during the critical first year of 8th Bomber Command's operations (thus massing defensive firepower), numerous German

fighter bases dotted the routes to and from the targets. Allied fighter planes could not venture beyond a certain point because of limited range. From that point on, it was a running battle of unexampled destructiveness and terror.

Obviously one solution, until the advent of the fighter capable of escorting the bombers round-trip, was to rid the sky of the Luftwaffe. So it was that the Regensburg-Schweinfurt mission was visualized as a double blow: directly upon the Messerschmitt factory itself and indirectly by striking at Schweinfurt's anti-friction-bearing complex which supplied ball bearings for several war industries.

"The plan of attack," Eaker has written, "called for the 3rd Air Division with 150 Flying Fortresses to cross the Channel at 8 A.M., fly to Regensburg, more than three hours away from English bases, attack the fighter factory there, and proceed to landing fields in Africa, fuel being insufficient for return to England.

"The 1st Air Division with 150 heavy bombers would follow 30 minutes later and bomb the ball-bearing complex at Schweinfurt, returning to English bases. It was visualized the 3rd Air Division would bear the brunt of German fighter reaction on the way in, and the 1st Air Division would have to fight its way out. Such long-range U.S. fighters as were then available would escort the 3rd Division in and the 1st Division out."

The 384th was one of the groups belonging to

B-17F of 384th Bomb Group; triangle on tail signifies that the group belonged to the 1st Air Division; "P" was the group's code letter. (ROBERT CHAPIN)

The airman's English enemy: the weather. Sudden changes made takeoff and assembly difficult and frequently led to collision over bomber bases. After a mission bad weather added to the toll when distressed aircraft attempted to land. (U. S. AIR FORCE)

the 1st Air Division and was alerted by a field order the evening before the mission was scheduled. Speculations about the nature and location of the target for what was rumored to be a "big one" had begun six weeks before. Would it be Berlin, or Hitler's private fortress in Berchtesgaden? Berlin seemed likely, for the Eighth had not yet struck at the capital of the Third Reich. Each group was ordered to pick their best navigator-bombardier team and to detach them to headquarters for special training. "We didn't know where the target was," Malvern Sweet, navigator of *The Ex-Virgin,* admitted, "but we could draw pictures of what it looked like."

During this same period of waiting, partly to recuperate from previous mission losses and partly to await a good turn in the weather, LeMay, commander of the 4th Combat Bombardment Wing (later the 3rd Air Division) placed his crews on bad-weather practice. The foresighted commander's reasoning was characteristically clear-cut: it was unlikely that they would have clear weather over both the bases and the target. Practicing blind takeoffs would take care of the poor visibility over England, LeMay calculated. Once above the clouds—and provided target visibility was good—all would be

as well as could be. LeMay planned to lead the force to Regensburg and then to Africa. But his foresightedness, as it eventuated, led to an ominous twist in the outcome of the mission.

The 1st Bombardment Wing (later the 1st Air Division) was preparing for the mission in its special training of navigator-bombardier teams. It was not, however, unlike LeMay, giving due consideration to the weather contingencies.

After several scrubbings, the mission was finally "laid on" for August 17, 1943. As was its capricious wont, English weather contributed its set of unknown factors. "It was so foggy," Curtis LeMay recalls, "that we had to lead the airplanes out with flashlights and lanterns, in order to get them onto the runway." The weeks of instrument takeoff paid off; LeMay managed to get all 146 B-17s of the 3rd Division off the ground and above the clouds. As division leader, LeMay flew in the lead aircraft of the 96th Bombardment Group and found to his consternation that there were no escort fighters to be found in the sky. Then there was a further hitch: the 1st Division too was socked in by fog but could not get off the ground as scheduled (this was timed for ten minutes after LeMay's force had crossed the enemy coast). With the approach of the Schweinfurt force, some of the German fighter attack, it had been hoped, would be drawn off the Regensburg force; and friendly fighters—eighteen squadrons of American P-47s and sixteen squadrons of Spitfires—could take on the Luftwaffe as planned.

Because he had to arrive at the African bases before dark, LeMay could not wait for the fog-bound 1st Division, nor could he spend time hoping for the arrival of the fighters. So he proceeded on to Regensburg. "Our fighter escort," LeMay has written, "had black crosses on their wings." In truth, American and British fighters did arrive to protect some of the other groups, although not the 96th with which LeMay flew—for the bombers stretched across miles of air—but had to turn back when fuel ran low. They returned to their bases to refuel and rearm in order to take off again to escort the Schweinfurt bombers.

LeMay meanwhile hurtled through a ferocious air battle. Flak had begun coming up at Woensdrecht, within minutes after the B-17s had crossed the North Sea. Eight minutes later German fighters ripped through the formations and the battle was on. For almost two hours, until Regensburg was reached, the violent battle ensued and both German and American aircraft fell. LeMay and his surviving men placed the bombs neatly into the Messerschmitt factories, hitting every important building besides destroying a number of finished aircraft awaiting delivery to the Luftwaffe.

"I lost twenty-four out of my hundred and twenty-seven planes which attacked the target at Regensburg," LeMay has noted. His battered formations, however, pushed onward from Regensburg for North Africa. This confused the German fighters, who expected the B-17s to return over the same route flown on the way in. It was on this final leg of the mission that six of the Regensburg force's twenty-four losses occurred, some falling over Italy and others splashing into the Mediterranean. LeMay landed at the base at Telergma in Africa and found facilities more than primitive. His losses had been the second highest (the first: the June 13 attack on Bremen, which cost twenty-six planes) sustained by the Eighth Air Force in its year of operations. There had not been any fighter protection, so far as he could see, and upon arriving at Telergma he found that no arrangements has been made to house his men or to service the B-17s. Though he had gone to Africa himself a month before to arrange for the shuttle mission, the war had moved on in North Africa, taking LeMay's arrangements with it. LeMay was not in a good mood when he reported on the first, historic shuttle mission from England to Africa: and he was not shy about letting this be known.

LeMay's Regensburg groups had gotten away around 9:35 A.M. But the Schweinfurt force, unable to take off in the heavy fog, was "stood down." This was a hopeful development for the waiting men; perhaps, like all the others, this mission too would be scrubbed.

During the early morning briefing, when the cover was removed from the large wall map and the men had a chance to see their route and target, there was an audible reaction. That it would be a long mission had already been gleaned by many from the bomb load and the fuel they carried. Berlin remained the favorite of the rumor mongers. Whistles, indrawn sighs, and several "Wows!" greeted the map unveiling in the briefing room of the 546th Squadron of the 384th Bombardment Group. There was a seemingly interminable ribbon

running from the base at Grafton-Underwood across the North Sea, over occupied Holland, and deep into Germany. There had never been so long a ribbon. before.

Considering the probabilities which the crews must face, a special effort was made by the briefing officers to stress the importance of Schweinfurt as a target; why they carried a mixed bomb load of five-hundred-pound general-purpose bombs and incendiaries: the ball-bearing factories at Schweinfurt were floored with wood. This was, they were informed, so that if a bearing dropped to the floor it would not be damaged. No detail was too minute, apparently. The GPs would open up the factories and the incendiaries would set them ablaze. A thorough job must be done, for "we don't want to have to go back there."

Lieutenant Frank A. Celentano, ex-Cornell law student, and a navigator in the 546th Squadron, sat through the briefing in a state of unease. He had been assigned to a strange ship, *Lucky Thirteen,* because his regular plane, *Battle Wagon,* was under repair. But that was not the worst of it. The squadron had been assigned the low position in the 384th Group's formation—low and at the rear: "Coffin Corner." In this most vulnerable position in the formation, German fighters generally struck with most telling effect.

And then the waiting followed. "If you didn't get off right away," Celentano recalls laconically, "you lost enthusiasm." The longer the wait, the more apprehensive the crews became; tension set in. The longer they waited, the more likely the Germans would guess the target. "Word had gone out that the mission was bound to be called off. We were hoping it would be, particularly because of the weather. The danger of collision was ever-present. There was nothing quite so chilling as pulling up above the clouds into the clear air and seeing a column of black smoke rising up from the clouds. It was always a sign that two planes had come together in the overcast."

For more than three hours Celentano and the other crews of 230 Flying Fortresses had a good deal to think about: from the soupy English weather to the long ribbon on the map. And then, unexpectedly, about one in the afternoon, a green flare shot up from the control tower and it was time to crank engines. Celentano settled in his position in

Lieutenant Frank Celentano, navigator of the 546th Squadron, 384th Group, who went to Schweinfurt for the first time in Lucky Thirteen *in the low rear position in the bomber stream—"Coffin Corner" to airmen.*
(FRANK CELENTANO)

the nose of *Lucky Thirteen* as pilot Lieutenant Philip M. Algar gracefully lifted the heavy B-17 off the runway and climbed, without incident, through the clouds. He tucked the plane into Coffin Corner at the end of the 384th's bomber stream, the eighteenth plane in the formation. Major Thomas P. Beckett, leading the group that day, brought them into the wing formation, which then joined the division, led by Brigadier General Robert Williams.

Even before they arrived over Germany, *Lucky Thirteen*'s luck had gone bad. Over Holland the formation had come under 20-mm. attack and *Lucky Thirteen* rocked to the blast of a hit in the plane's center section. Both waist gunners, Loring C. Miller and John Schimenek, were hit. Miller, unaware of his own injury—a sliver of shell had punctured his lung—called in to inform Algar that Schimenek had been hit. He said nothing about himself. But soon Miller was too busy to think about the pain in his chest.

"There were at least 200 enemy fighters attacking us," Celentano was later quoted in the London *Daily Herald.* "F.W. 190's, some with the old yellow noses, some painted black and some half black and white. Some were painted just like our P.47s and maneuvered like them but they did not fool us.

"It's a lot of ballyhoo to say that Germany's first-line fighters have all been shot down. They came at us four abreast and fought like hell."

"When we got over the enemy coast we had to lose altitude because of the lowering overcast," Beckett in the lead plane related later. "That's where the fighters got to us. Although we had fighter support, enemy fighters kept hitting us anyhow."

During the fighter attack, mainly by FW-190s, Miller manned his waist gun, but the seriousness of his wound began to show. He remained, however, at his gun, firing at the countless attackers. Algar ordered radio operator Francis Gerow to take over Miller's gun and Miller was forced to lie down. Even then he indicated to Schimenek that he was all right and need no attention and that Schimenek must remain at his own gun.

"After the fighters left," Beckett continued, "we climbed back to altitude. When we got to the target there were no fighters there." But by this time there were a number of 384th planes gone too. Celentano found that *Lucky Thirteen* had graduated from Coffin Corner during the battle to squadron lead—and that there remained only two or three planes to lead.

Lead navigator of the 384th was Lieutenant Edward J. Knowling, who brought the survivors of the

A Flying Fortress neatly tucked into formation—in "Coffin Corner."

(ERIK MILLER/LOCKHEED-CALIFORNIA)

The 384th encounters flak over the target; bombs have begun to descend through the overcast and the flak comes up. German fighters generally pulled away at this point to let the radar-directed antiaircraft guns do their work. (ROBERT CHAPIN)

A B-17 falls over Schweinfurt after a fighter attack.
(U. S. AIR FORCE)

hour-long fighter assault over Schweinfurt. A squadron commander of one of the other groups, the 305th, formerly commanded by LeMay, observed bitterly, "Our navigator has an easy job today. All he has to do is follow the trail of burning Fortresses and parachutes from the task forces ahead of us."

The 384th's lead bombardier was Second Lieutenant Joseph W. Baggs, who found the target area partially obscured by a smoke screen. As he came in, eye peering through the bombsight, he picked what appeared to be the target. "At that time it was about the only thing I could see that resembled the target as described," he said at the debriefing later. "But as we got closer I could see our target at the right. I saw the race track and knew where I was. . . ." Correcting and adjusting his sight, Baggs led the 384th to the target. "As we got over the target we noticed that the first building on the target was on fire," Baggs said.

In *Lucky Thirteen* it was obvious that if Loring Miller was to have any chance for life, the plane would have to get below an altitude at which an oxygen mask was required. As soon as the bombs were dropped into the ball-bearing factory area, Celentano plotted the shortest course for Grafton-Underwood. Algar then began an immediate but gradual descent to a lower altitude; he also throttled to maximum speed. From time to time, until normal breathing could be resumed, the now unconscious Miller had to have his oxygen mask removed to empty it of blood. Otherwise he might have drowned in his own blood.

Celentano had plotted their route so skillfully that *Lucky Thirteen* skirted most of the heavy flak areas, and, as luck would have it, there were no further fighter attacks. By this time, perhaps, the German fighter pilots were exhausted, after fighting LeMay's Regensburg force earlier and the Schweinfurt aircraft coming and going. *Lucky Thirteen* thundered in over Grafton-Underwood shooting red flares from the side windows, indicating wounded aboard, and as Algar touched the runway an ambulance trailed the bomber until it stopped. Schimenek and the grievously wounded Miller were rushed to the hospital. The shell fragment was removed from Miller's lung and he recovered. For his "gallantry and devotion to duty," Sergeant Loring Corwin Miller of Stockton, California, was awarded the Silver Star.

The Focke-Wulfs and flak were not the only weapons employed by the Germans that day over Schweinfurt. Teutonic genius for destruction seemed unlimited to the point of creativity. Some of the fighter bombers, Ju-88s and Me-110s, were equipped with rocket launchers and spread terror through the bomber formations when their smoking missiles pierced them. A direct rocket hit snapped a B-17 in half and trapped the entire crew in the gyrating pieces of the falling aircraft.

The sky was transformed into swiftly moving, soaring debris- and smoke-glutted battleground: tracers interlaced in beautifully intricate but mad patterns, smoke of various shadings floated among the clouds, pieces of exploded or collision-shredded aircraft fell to earth, and the sky was dotted with white (American) and yellow (German) parachutes.

Observing the battle from his perch in the nose of *Lucky Thirteen,* Frank Celentano had found it difficult to fathom; as he watched in fascinated helplessness a crewman leaped from a badly burning Fortress. The figure fell away from the distressed plane toward the safety of the earth; but when the chute opened it too was aflame. In an instant the airman's brief refuge had ended and he had a 25,000-foot fall in which to consider the fortunes of war.

Other German aircraft introduced another innovation. They actually flew over the American bombers and dropped bombs upon them timed to detonate within the bomber formations. While neither accurate nor effective, the tactic was unnerving to the American crews, and now and then a B-17 actually fell to the air-to-air bombing.

There was yet another curiously fiendish device. German fighters, FW-190s, trailing cables from which bombs dangled, approached the American bombers from above—which incidentally brought the fighter under attack from the top-turret guns of the Fortresses. When the German pilot brought his plane with the bomb dangling in the proper position, he electrically detonated it. This method was not very effective either, but during the fighting some

Back at Grafton-Underwood, ground crews anxiously search the sky for returning aircraft.

(ROBERT CHAPIN)

actually worked. As one tail gunner, Sergeant Thomas Murphy of the 381st Bombardment Group, watched, an FW blew the wing off a B-17 with the cable device.

If the German High Command did not understand its own air weapon and if the Luftwaffe High Command was remarkably ineffectual in its strategy, there was no denying the courage of the Luftwaffe's pilots or the imaginativeness of their tactics.

Despite the unrelenting ferocity of that German opposition, however, the bomber formations fought through to Schweinfurt, dropped their bombs, and then fought as tenaciously to get back to England. It was a monotony of terror. But then the German fighters began to withdraw as fuel and ammunition depleted, and the Fortresses, some of them hardly more than a pile of flying wreckage, struggled to get back home.

At Grafton-Underwood the last of the 384th's strays had begun to straggle in. Five of the eighteen planes which had taken off would never return: *Deuces Wild, Snuffy, M'Honey, Vertical Shaft,* and *Powerhouse II.* Fifty men: of these forty were taken prisoner, four escaped and made their way back to England eventually, and six were killed. One plane which circled Grafton-Underwood was *El Rauncho,* piloted by colorful Randolph Jacobs. Like *Lucky Thirteen, El Rauncho* had trouble almost from the start of the mission. Over the enemy coast a 20-mm. shell holed the left wing; that was followed by a flak burst in the wing which interfered with aileron control. The fuselage was struck, the top-turret gun simply stopped operating, and the oxygen supply of the ball turret gunner leaked. There was a gash in the tail. But no one, luckily, was hit, and Jacobs completed the mission and brought the plane home. When he lowered the landing gear and the air spun the wheels, Jacobs saw that a piece of flak had lodged in one of the tires. Suddenly, too, the two port engines sputtered out and the plane fell thousands of feet before Jacobs brought it under control about eight hundred feet over the field. The landing gear came up but there was no time to feather the windmilling propellers as he brought *El Rauncho* in for a wheels-up, belly-scraping landing.

"The *El Rauncho* pointed steeply down, then levelled off at the tree-tops and began feeling for the runway," Walter E. Owens, historian of the 384th, has written. "She must have been going a

hundred and fifty miles an hour when the friction of aluminum on concrete began throwing off sparks. The plane slid at a terrific pace the full length of the runway, screeching all the way and leaving a shower of sparks behind. At the far end she whirled abruptly about and careened over an anti-aircraft emplacement, finally coming to a stop only twenty-five yards from a parked aircraft."

With studied calm Jacobs climbed out of the wreckage. After begging a light for his cigar, he turned to look at the pile of junk which had once been a Flying Fortress and said, "I guess they didn't want us to get at their nut and bolt factory."

There were thirty-six 1st Air Division B-17s missing testifying to that fact. The day's total losses, then, added up to a total of sixty Flying Fortresses lost on the Schweinfurt-Regensburg mission, more than twice the toll of any previous mission. And this does not count those planes like *El Rauncho* which, although they had returned to England, would never fly again. Six hundred men too were lost— dead, wounded, and missing—in Germany, France, and Holland. To these could be added the wounded, like Loring Miller, who would be out of action for a long time. Other planes carried severely wounded men who died days or weeks after the battle; some men were dead on arrival. In short, mere numbers of aircraft lost do not fully reveal the full extent of losses.

The bombing at Regensburg had been excellent, but that at Schweinfurt not quite so good. The Germans reported that eighty high-explosive bombs had fallen into the two major bearing plants; in one more than six hundred machines were destroyed or damaged. A drop in production followed, which gave the Germans pause. They must seek out other sources of high-quality bearings, of Swiss or Swedish manufacture if need be, and consideration would have to be given to the dispersal of ball-bearing facilities. While this would make the industry a less neat panacea target, it also produced a loss in production which was almost equally effective.

But two facts were underscored by the hard-fought missions. One was expressed bluntly by the 384th's Frank Celentano, in direct contradiction to popular newspaper reportage, when he said, "It's a lot of ballyhoo to say that Germany's first-line fighters have all been shot down." The other, hanging like a gloomy cloud over the Eighth Air

A wounded airman of the 384th Bomb Group is lifted into an ambulance after returning from a mission in a shot-up B-17. (ROBERT CHAPIN)

Force, was that they had not not wiped out Schweinfurt.

They would have to go back.

III

Meanwhile, however, small missions were "laid on" to relatively nearby targets in France and the Low Countries to which the bombers could be escorted by the P-47s. It was not until September 6 that the Eighth had recovered enough to attempt another large-scale mission—this time to bomb aircraft and friction-bearing factories in Stuttgart. The three B-24 groups which had been detached to North Africa for the Ploesti mission had returned to England and what operational strength remained of these groups was added to the B-17 divisions. Replacements made it possible finally on September 6 to dispatch no less than 407 bombers, of which 69 were B-24s. The Liberators were employed in a diversionary sweep over the North Sea while the Fortresses aimed at Stuttgart. Weather once again interfered with the operations and only 262 bombers succeeded in bombing—and most of these targets were targets of opportunity. The day's losses, however, were high: 45 Flying Fortresses.

Most of September 1943 was notable for its poor bombing weather, so experiments were made with blind-bombing equipment in certain lead aircraft. At first there were only twelve radar (H2X) sets available, which were scattered through the bombing divisions. With these few sets in lead planes, the divisions could be led directly, more or less, over a target obscured by cloud. Specially trained operators manned the equipment, and reasonably good, if not excellent, results were obtained in the early attempts. These missions marked the initiation of what would eventually be called "Pathfinder" bombings. The lead plane of each group equipped with H2X found the target, and when this plane dropped its bombs, all other planes in the group did the same. Eventually exceedingly accurate blind bombing by radar became a common practice.

However, if the Allies could find targets electronically through the overcast, so likewise could the Germans find enemy aircraft. In order to confuse gun-directing radar, various devices were used, such as "window," strips of metal-coated paper which when dropped from aircraft made it difficult for antiaircraft radar to distinguish, so to speak, the wheat from the chaff. Another device was called "carpet," a transmitter carried in aircraft for jamming radar receivers.

But in September 1943 these were experimental attempts and did not always contribute much to the Combined Bomber Operation plan. Early in October it was possible, with new planes and crews, to concentrate on industrial targets inside Germany. On October 4 more than 360 heavy bombers took off for assorted targets in the vicinity of Frankfurt, as well as French airfields and marshaling yards in western Germany.

The second week of October 1943 proved to be one of the most critical in the history of the Eighth Air Force. On the eighth a large force (more than 350) bombed Bremen and Vegesack (with a loss of thirty planes). The next day another sizable force (a total of 352) bombed various targets, ranging from naval targets in Poland to the Focke-Wulf factories at Marienburg. This last was a superb demonstration of the efficacy of Eaker's confidence in daylight precision bombardment. The factory area was blanketed by five-hundred-pound general-purpose (GP) bombs plus incendiaries and all but wiped out. The damage was so severe that

THE FLIGHT IS DROPPING "WINDOW," WHICH CREATES THE SO CALLED "WINDOW CLOUD".
THE SCOPE OF THE RADAR ON THE RIGHT SHOWS THE RESULT.

THE PLANES MUST REMAIN IN THE "CLOUD". OTHERWISE THEY WILL REGISTER ON THE RADAR SCOPE.

PLANES A AND B ARE EQUIPPED WITH CARPET. PLANE C WILL ALSO BE "HIDDEN" AS IT IS IN
THE SAME AREA. THE SCOPE AT THE RIGHT SHOWS THE RESULT.

THE PLANES HAVE MOVED CLOSER TO THE RADAR SET. PLANES B & C ARE STILL "HIDDEN"
BUT PLANE A IS TOO CLOSE AND STICKS OUT ALTHOUGH IT IS STILL JAMMING.

The workings of "window" and "carpet" as explained to airmen of the Eighth Air Force. Both devices con- fused German detection and flak-gun-aiming devices. (ROBERT CHAPIN)

no attempt was made to repair the factory. Losses for the day amounted to twenty-eight planes. The next day, October 10, the bombers attacked rail and waterway targets at Münster. The Luftwaffe swarmed out in full fury that day, concentrating on a single group in the formation, decimating that before going on to another. Of the 236 planes bombing Münster, it was the thirteen of the 100th Bombardment Group, in the lead, which took the worst of the new tactic. Of the day's thirty losses, twelve belonged to the 100th (a turn of fate which gave rise to the legend of the "Bloody Hundredth"), the single exception being Robert Rosenthal's *Rosie's Riveters,* which alone returned to England.

The total losses of those three consecutive days in October were eighty-eight planes. At such a rate, 8th Bomber Command could be eliminated from the war in a week. The Münster mission was officially Number 114; following that a three-day pause permitted the bomber forces to recuperate for the next one.

IV

Colonel Budd Peaslee, who had served as a popular commander of the 384th during its first missions, had been made deputy wing commander of the 40th Wing (the 92nd, 305th, and 306th Bombardment Groups) of the 1st Air Division. When Mission 115 was "laid on" it was Peaslee's turn to act as 1st Division air commander for the mission.

"From the beginning," Peaslee has written, "Mission Number 115 was in doubt. A persistent low overcast had hung over the English bases for three days." To the mission-scarred men, the day broke propitiously. "There was considerable speculation that the mission would be scrubbed and they could return to their sacks till noon. This was a happy thought but it was not to be."

Briefings were held in the dank, bone-chilling darkness as crews assembled to learn of the day's target. A dull silence invariably descended when the map was uncovered showing the black ribbon stretching from England into Germany. *Yank* staff correspondent Walter Peters attended one of these briefings; he was detailed to fly that day in the first combat mission of a B-17 newly named *Yank.* Upon leaving the briefing room he overheard an

erudite though unsophisticated radio-gunner offer the intelligence that the city they were to attack that October 14 was "named afer a very special pig."

Apparently, to the unseasoned airman the name of Schweinfurt had little other significance.

To Budd Peaslee it had more than etymological portent. His old command, the 384th, had bled over Schweinfurt in August. It meant, too, that as air commander of the 40th Wing, he would lead them again along with the rest of the 1st Division deeply into Germany and, he hoped, back. The hope was that the "first" Schweinfurt had proved so rough a mission because of chance; the second might very well prove to be a "milk run" (an easy mission).

As air commander Peaslee was to fly as copilot in the lead aircraft, flown by Captain James K. McLaughlin of the 92nd Bombardment Group. At different points over England the 92nd would be joined by the 305th (Curtis LeMay's old command) and 306th Groups. These three groups constituted

Budd Peaslee, air commander of the 1st Division on Mission 115 (Schweinfurt), October 14, 1943.

(ROBERT CHAPIN)

A B-17 of the 303rd Bomb Group in an East Anglian wheat field near Molesworth before the Schweinfurt mission. (U. S. AIR FORCE)

the 40th Combat Bombardment Wing. Also participating would be the 91st and 381st Groups (under supervision of the 1st Combat Bombardment Wing) and the 41st Wing (303rd, 379th, and 384th Groups). These three wings made up the striking force of the 1st Air Division, which was to contribute 149 Flying Fortresses to the striking force.

The 2nd Air Division, B-24s of the 93rd and 392nd Groups, was also to bomb Schweinfurt. Their sixty Liberators, however, did not get to the target.

The 3rd Air Division was to contribute seven groups (also combined into wings for command purposes): the 94th, 95th, 96th, 100th, 385th, 388th, and 390th. This division would provide a total of 142 Flying Fortresses.

Theoretically, if all went as planned, a total of 291 Fortresses and 60 Liberators were to go to Schweinfurt. But it was not to be. The Liberator bases, for example, were so badly fogged in that only 29 even managed to get off the ground. Unable to form up in the dense, swirling fog, 8 returned to their bases and the remaining 21 made a diversionary sweep toward Emden, hoping thus to draw away some of the German fighters from the B-17s, if they ever got off.

Peaslee sat in the left-hand seat of McLaughlin's Fortress, eyes on the control tower. There was still a question of whether or not Mission 115 would actually take place. But a weather plane, having crossed over Schweinfurt, radioed back that the target area was clear. The green flare went up and

the mission was on. McLaughlin throttled up the great plane and with Peaslee keeping an eye on the runway (to assure that the plane remained on the fog-enshrouded concrete), McLaughlin took off on instruments; at intervals, eighteen other 92nd Group B-17s followed. Above the clouds, in the brilliant sunlight, the planes assembled into combat boxes, proceeded to the assembly point, where the 306th Group joined them.

But where was the 305th? On this mission the group had been assigned the low position in the wing. However, in the confusion of attempting to assemble above the clouds, the 305th was unable to find the planes in the 40th Wing. Rather than scrub the mission, and thus deny the formation its sixteen aircraft, Major G. G. Y. Normand, in the lead B-17 of the 305th, attached to the 1st Wing. This left Peaslee's 40th Wing short an entire group. According to SOP (Standard Operating Procedure), he would have been justified in aborting; instead Peaslee relinquished command of the mission to Colonel Archie J. Olds, Jr. (then commander of the 45th Combat Wing). Peaslee then ordered his two groups to join up with the three groups of the 41st Wing.

One of the components of the 41st Wing was his old group, the 384th. On this Thursday Frank Celentano was acting as lead navigator for the group; he was in his regular plane, *Battle Wagon,* also carrying the 384th's air commander, Major George W. Harris. They lifted carefully through the haze, formed up, and proceeded toward Schweinfurt. Above the clouds it was a welcome sight to see the other B-17s of the group as well as the P-47s of the 56th and 353rd Fighter Groups (about a hundred in all), assigned to escort the bombers part of the way. On the return, also, they were to be waiting to protect the bombers.

Not so welcome, however, was the loss of several B-17s, forced to turn back because of engine trouble or some other mechanical malfunction. Twenty-six Fortresses returned to their bases for such reasons. The combined forces of the two air task forces were reduced from 291 to 265 Flying Fortresses. Once the bombers crossed the enemy coast the German fighters began pouncing on them. The American Thunderbolts swept down to intercept, and although many succeeded, they did not prevent some of the Me-109s and FW-190s from sweeping through the bomber formations. And when the P-47s were forced to turn back near Aachen because of their limited fuel supply, the Luftwaffe smashed down upon the B-17s in the most savage aerial assault of the war.

It was the first Schweinfurt all over again, with deadly interest. The interceptions by German fighters were so finely co-ordinated and timed that a suspicion arose (never actually confirmed, however) that the Luftwaffe had been forewarned of the mission. Whether or not this was true, the Germans were very well prepared for the invaders. Every possible technique employed in the past —unnerving head-on fighter attacks, cannons, rockets lobbed into the formations from the rear, and air-to-air bombing, as well as flak—was unleashed that day. If Ploesti represented a burning, low-level inferno, the second Schweinfurt was a freezing, high-level (above twenty thousand feet) inferno.

Wave after wave of German fighters, their guns winking in the wings, tore at the formations again and again. As at Münster, there was an attempt to concentrate upon a definite portion of the bomber stream. The 1st Division received the brunt of the attacks, with special attention to the lead planes, for the Germans knew that the air commander, lead

Fortresses of the 91st Bomb Group over Schweinfurt.
(U. S. AIR FORCE)

navigator, and lead bombardier flew in this plane. Likewise, the group in Coffin Corner was attacked ferociously. In this spot in the 1st Division it was the 305th Group, which had missed the rendezvous with Peaslee over England and had attached itself to the 1st Combat Wing. The Thunderbolts had barely turned for England when the 305th planes took their first mauling—and it continued all the way to Schweinfurt. Curiously, the battle let up over Schweinfurt itself, partly because the German fighters had to return to their bases to refuel—and to give the flak a chance. About two-forty in the afternoon the first bombs of the 1st Division fell upon Schweinfurt and continued to fall for about six minutes. Six minutes after that, at 2:52 P.M., the first bombs of the 3rd Division began tumbling from the bomb bays. The sky filled with 1000-pound and 500-pound high-explosive as well as 100-pound incendiary bombs, a total of 395 tons of the HE and 88 tons of incendiaries. And despite the ordeal through which the survivors had passed, the bombing was remarkably accurate and, as was later learned, effective.

But of the 291 bombers which in the original plan were to have set out for Schweinfurt, only 228 actually succeeded in placing their bombs on the target. The rest, other than those planes which had aborted, lay burning along the penetration route of the two air divisions. On the return flight, too, German fighter attacks were relentlessly pressed. The fighting was swift, concentrated, and confused; Fortress gunners claimed 186 German planes that day (although the more accurate total may have been closer to 35). Even if the claims had been realistic, it would still have been a costly exchange.

Sixty Flying Fortresses were lost over the Continent and 5 others were abandoned over England, making a total of 65 B-17s totally destroyed. In addition, 140 planes had returned in various stages of damage, 17 beyond possibility of repair. The human toll was even more depressing: 600 men were missing, the fate of many never to be known. Many died in exploding planes, or were trapped in gyrating B-17s, or were killed in fighter attacks or by flak.

The orphan 305th Group lost twelve of its sixteen aircraft before reaching Schweinfurt; three B-17s of the 305th dropped bombs on Schweinfurt—and only two returned to their English base at Chelveston

Bomb run: 91st Bomb Group Flying Fortress Bomb Boogie *now under the control of the bombardier in* the nose *as he zeroes in on the target. The bomb bay doors are open awaiting the moment of "bombs away."*
(U. S. AIR FORCE)

Strike photo of the 100th Bomb Group, Schweinfurt, Thursday, October 14, 1943. (U. S. AIR FORCE)

(one had aborted earlier in the mission). The 306th Group lost ten planes, which made it the second in losses. The 92nd Group, the third component of the 40th Wing, lost six B-17s (plus another which crash-landed in England), so that Peaslee's 40th Wing lost twenty-nine planes over the Continent, about half of the total of the entire mission.

High losses in individual units had a despairing effect on the survivors in those units and rendered them less potent while replacement crews were trained.

Schweinfurt revealed the terrible workings of chance in aerial warfare (always present in the form of flak), for not all units came under strong fighter attack. In part, the fate of an individual aircraft depended on its position in the formation. Although every group in the 1st Air Division lost at least one plane, there were three in the 3rd Division which did not lose a single B-17 (the 100th, 385th, and 388th). Bruce R. Riley, pilot of *Riley and Crew,* flew to Schweinfurt with the 3rd Air Division and found that "from the standpoint of the 390th Bomb Group, [it] was a rather routine mission. . . . During the short times I was

"Now we have got Schweinfurt," General Arnold said after Mission 115, and so it had appeared to the crews that left it burning. Schweinfurt was hard hit, but it was *not finished. But so had the Eighth Air Force been hard hit, if not finished.* (U. S. AIR FORCE)

able to glance away from our formation, I saw at least three Forts blow up ahead over the target, probably due to direct hits by flak. Our one loss was due to a fighter attack that ruptured three out of four fuel tanks on the plane that went down."

If chance, luck, fortune, or whatever that unknown but ever present factor present in every air battle was operative, so was truth. Despite the frightful and wholesale onslaught and the withering sight of blasted, burning, and falling planes, the bomber crews thrust on through the opposing German fighters, despite their various gadgets of destruction. There were no aborts over Germany; aircraft continued over the targets on less than full

engine power, some made bomb runs (the average time was six minutes) while burning, during which time it was likely that a B-17 would explode. Some did.

That truth was the fact of American courage. A second truth was more difficult to face. The losses over Schweinfurt, added to those losses already accumulated during the early weeks of October, proved clearly that such deep penetrations into Germany without fighter escort were self-defeating. The cost in men and aircraft was not worth it, however strategically important the target.

The October 14, 1943, Schweinfurt attack was, in fact, the most effective upon that target made

during the entire course of the war. There were fifteen others, however, which would mean fourteen sequels to the mission which Martin Caidin so aptly called "Black Thursday." It would appear, therefore, that when General Arnold announced to the newspapers, "Now we have got Schweinfurt," he was being overoptimistic. He was also being honest, insofar as he knew. Secret reports from inside Germany via neutral Sweden hinted at great devastation at Schweinfurt. Reconnaissance photographs, as well as the strike photos, sustained this belief. The Air Force informed its crews, via the official publication *Impact,* that "All five plants—representing about 65 per cent of the ball- and roller-bearing capacity of Germany—were so heavily damaged that *our bombers may never have to go back.*"

And they did not go back to Schweinfurt, not for another four months. The truth is that they could *not* go back. Air superiority over Germany had reverted to the Luftwaffe. But when they did go back, in the spring of 1944, in conjunction with the RAF's Bomber Command—the British bombed Schweinfurt for the first time on February 24, 1944 —many wondered why it was necessary if such devastation had been wrought in October.

Schweinfurt had suffered heavy destruction, which had interfered with production. But not forever, as intimated in the optimistic reports, but for a month and a half. Since Schweinfurt was granted four months of grace, there was time to repair the damage and to reorganize the anti-friction-bearing industry, which, as reported in the *United States Strategic Bombing Survey* (September 30, 1945), "precipitated, also, the disperal of the industry from Schweinfurt, forced the expansion or construction of old and new plants, and accelerated the program of substitution and redesign in order to reduce the excessive and often luxurious use of bearings in many types of equipment."

Under the organizing genius of Hitler's armament czar Albert Speer and more directly under Speer's special commissioner for ball bearings, Philip Kessler, the co-ordination of the industry was undertaken to disperse the installations as well as to in-

Crew of Battle Wagon *of the 384th Bomb Group assemble for a debriefing after the "rugged" mission to Schweinfurt. The group lost a total of nine B-17s on the mission, six over enemy-held territory and three battle-damaged planes abandoned over Britain.*

(FRANK CELENTANO)

ventory stock. The latter contained surprises for all, including the Germans. It was discovered that large surpluses of anti-friction bearings were stored in Germany by the millions and that, however effective the raid upon Schweinfurt had been, many industries requiring ball bearings continued to operate normally; redistribution of surplus stock made up for any losses.

The RAF and Eighth Air Force bombers joined eventually to eliminate Schweinfurt from the war map, but by then, because of dispersal, Schweinfurt was no longer a vital military target. By October 9, 1944, when the Eighth Air Force dropped more than eight hundred tons of bombs upon Schweinfurt, it was "a city which was less than one-half as important industrially as in August 1943," according to the *United States Strategic Bombing Survey.*

"Now we [had] got Schweinfurt," but it no longer mattered. Bomber crews viewed the Schweinfurt mission with characteristic dark humor but with more realism when they spoke of Black Thursday as the day when "We took out 150% of the ball-bearing industry."

It would be inequitous to assert bluntly that the two Schweinfurt missions accomplished nothing— despite the failure of the second, for all its pre-

Post-mission reconnaissance photo showing the heavily damaged factory areas of Schweinfurt.

(U. S. AIR FORCE)

cision, to "take out" the ball-bearing industry. In purely objective terms, numbers, percentages, the missions were frightfully expensive in loss of life and aircraft, but they were not total failures. The second mission to Schweinfurt, especially, has become a symbol of both courage and failure. That the one was not enough to prevent the other lay in the nature of the target itself and in the fact that long daylight flights without escort were doomed to terrible opposition.

Schweinfurt was not the greatest loss suffered by the U. S. Air Force in the course of the war; later battles over Berlin claimed more bombers. It was the worst to date.

It was, in a word current at the time, "rugged." But any mission whatever the number or percentage of loss, was "rugged" if your plane did not return or did return badly chewed up by the Luftwaffe. Airmen who fought in the two major theaters of operations invariably referred to Europe as "the Big League" because of the potency of Luftwaffe fighters during the waning days of 1943 and the flak. Heavy bombardment during daylight, without massive formations and fighter protection, seemed to be at an impasse.

But inside Germany, unknown to Allied air leaders arguing about the cost of daylight missions and the foolishness of panacea targets, there was serious consternation. The bombing was taking on a serious pattern, no longer the derring-do of knocking out a dam, or a foolhardy low-level attack on an oil field. The bombing was beginning to look more business-like, less haphazard.

"The Luftwaffe leaders knew that they could not stop our bombers," Eaker has observed, "and save their weapons-making establishments." A subtle, almost sudden twist had come—at great cost perhaps, but it had come.

"For Germany," Eaker concluded, "it marked the beginning of the end."

Index

Note: References to illustrations are in *italics*